The Rise of American Influence
in Asia and the Pacific

LAWRENCE H. BATTISTINI

The Rise of American Influence in Asia and the Pacific

MICHIGAN STATE UNIVERSITY PRESS

1960

6 2 4 4 7

Table of Contents

CHAPTER ONE

The Lure of Asia and the Pacific

When the United States became an independent nation, political and economic power was centered in Europe and all of its principal states were under autocratic or semi-autocratic systems. With the exception of France, the ruling classes of these states in general looked with suspicion, disfavor and even fear upon the democratic and republican experiment that had been launched in America. At the same time, the powerful states of Europe were enmeshed in age-old rivalries and jealousies. France and Britain, who had been in conflict for centuries, were again at odds. Although separated by a great ocean from the Old World, the United States in its infancy was weak and powerless to oppose alone an armed attack launched with full force by either Britain or France.

Aware of the hostility and unfriendliness of many of the European powers, but more concerned that their rivalries and ambitions might directly or indirectly engulf the New World in flames that could conceivably consume the newly born American Republic, the leaders of the United States at the outset outlined basic principles that were to guide the nation in foreign affairs. These principles, which had their origins prior to the Declaration of Independence and which were outlined by Washington and reinforced by Jefferson, became venerated by succeeding generations of Americans as the immutable foundations of American foreign policy for a century and a half until the entry of the United States into World War II. These principles were: friendly relations and commercial intercourse with all nations, entangling alliances with none.

Shielded by its policy of "neutralism," its fortunate geographical isolation, and by the rivalries and jealousies of the great European powers, the United States was able to concentrate on internal development. It easily absorbed and conquered vast contiguous land areas. By 1848 the United States had practically completed its process of "Manifest Destiny" which brought under its sovereignty an immense territory of more than three million square miles, an area nearly as large as all of Europe, extending from the Atlantic to the Pacific and from the frontiers of Canada to the confines of present-day Mexico and the Caribbean. The economic development of the United States was steady and spectacular, until temporarily interrupted by the havoc and strain of a great civil war, but upon its termination the country entered upon an even greater economic development which by the end of the century had elevated it to one of the greatest industrial powers on earth. It was not until the latter part of the nineteenth century that the energies of the American nation burst out of the confinement of the Western Hemisphere and not until the end of that century that the nation took its place as a world power.

Although born of revolution and opposition to colonialism, the American Government did not seek to undermine existing non-democratic regimes or to aid and abet anti-imperialist movements. On the contrary, it sought to establish commercial relations with all states, regardless of their form of government or the extent of their imperialism. Nevertheless, the anti-imperialist tradition remained strong. Private Americans and even government officials never ceased denouncing autocracy, despotism, and colonialism. Hence, a legend developed throughout many areas of the world that the United States alone of all the Western nations did not seek to extinguish the sovereignty and independence of other nations for reasons of commercial plunder or power expansion.* In Asia especially, the leaders of industrially backward and defenseless countries came to look upon the United States as an avowed enemy

*The Latin-American countries, of course, were a notable exception in this regard. The revolt of Americans in Texas against the authority of the Mexican Government, followed by the Mexican War of 1846-48 that resulted in Mexico's loss of more than half her territory to the United States greatly embittered the Latin-Americans and filled them with distrust of their *Yanqui* neighbor. Subsequent American actions in the Caribbean area further alienated Latin Americans, who came to fully equate "Yankee imperialism" with that of the Old World powers.

2

of imperialism and a last hope of support against the encroachments of the European powers. As the full impact of the West began to be felt in Asia and domestic revolts broke out against the old order of things, democratic and republican elements likewise came to look to America for inspiration and support. In our early relations with Asian countries the leaders of the Republic laid down principles and patterns of policy and behavior that caused most Asians to hold a high opinion of America and to make a distinction between her and the other imperialist Western powers.

The United States took its place as one of the sovereign nations of the world with the conclusion of the Treaty of Paris in 1783 which terminated the Revolutionary War. By the terms of that treaty the territorial extent of the United States was limited on the west by the Mississippi River. Actually, most of the region west of the Appalachian Mountains was still largely unsettled territory, and nearly all of the population, less than four million in 1790, was concentrated along the Atlantic seaboard. Hence the United States at that time faced eastward, and the Atlantic was the broad highway which linked it commercially and culturally to Europe. Asia and the islands of the Pacific comprised a remote world, which could only be reached by circuitous and time-consuming voyages. To Americans of this period this world was almost as unknown as "Darkest Africa."

When the United States acquired its independence the economic system was largely an agrarian one which supplied nearly all of the people's agricultural wants and depended on Europe, principally England, for manufactured goods. Since the United States was then practically without industries that required imported raw materials and overseas markets for their finished products, its trading requirements were largely confined to the exchange of its own raw materials for manufactured items. During the early years of the Republic's development about 90 percent of all trade was with England.

Trade with the Far East arose primarily because of the enterprise of the seafaring New Englanders rather than because of any compelling need in America for the products of that area. In searching for new routes and ports of call, these hardy New Englanders were motivated by the hard reality that independence from England and dissociation from her Empire had closed to them the the old trade routes and markets on which they had formerly prospered, particularly the once lucrative trade with the British West Indies.[1] China was one of the first Asian lands to lure the American traders. In the very year that Washington was inaugurated as the first president of the Republic, fifteen American vessels called at Canton to take on cargoes of tea and silk.[2] The luxury cargoes of these vessels were typical of the early American trade with Asia. They were small in bulk and commanded high prices, but at the same time they were highly speculative and comprised only a small part of the total foreign trade of the United States at that time.

As Tyler Dennett has noted, Americans prior to the Revolutionary War had actually known Asia only through association with the tea which the British had shipped to Boston or which had been smuggled from Holland, the silks and cotton goods which had come from India, and the adventurous tales of pirates. In 1784 when the first American-owned vessel, the *Empress of China,* arrived at Canton the far Pacific was practically unknown to Americans and there probably were not more than a half dozen in the whole country who had ever personally been in any countries of that area.[3]

At the beginning of the nineteenth century, by which time a substantial and increasing number of American vessels began reaching the shores of Asia and its adjacent islands, even the knowledge which the Europeans possessed of far Asia and the Pacific was extremely limited. Large areas of the Pacific were still uncharted and knowledge of the Far East was more or less derived from the trade that was carried on with India, the East Indies, and the single port of Canton in China. Most of India was still unconquered by and unknown to the British. Except for Canton all of China was closed by imperial edict to the "barbarians," as the Chinese called the Westerners. Korea was locked in a rigid seclusion, and Japan permitted a very limited trade only with the Dutch, who were restricted to the use of a single port on the southern island of Kyūshū. Siberia was practically unknown, and only a small number of Russians had reached its Pacific shores.

As American and European trade increased substantially in

subsequent years, the rivalries of the great European maritime powers for privileged positions and special advantages sharpened. Slowly at first, and then with increasing momentum, the great European powers began appropriating lands and establishing their dominion over one country after the other. Fabled India had fallen to the British as a result of their victorious struggle against the French in the eighteenth century, and the trade of Americans and other nationals with that vast subcontinent had to comply with British regulations. The East Indies (now nearly all under the sovereignty of Indonesia) had been largely appropriated by the Dutch, and the Spaniards had established their dominion over the Philippines. Minor holdings had also been gained by the French and Portuguese in South and Southeast Asia. Far "down under," Australia and New Zealand had been made a part of the British Empire, but there were then only a few white inhabitants there. As the nineteenth century further unfolded, the rivalries of the Western powers in the Pacific area became enmeshed in the politics of Europe.

Early American interest in the trading possibilities of the Pacific area was stimulated by John Ledyard of Connecticut, who had accompanied Captain James Cook in 1776 on his last and most famous expedition to the Pacific. During the course of this voyage, Cook visited the Nootka Sound area, in 1778, and Ledyard thereby became acquainted with the fur resources of the Northwest Coast. Ledyard was probably the first American to visualize the possibility of a lucrative triangular trade involving New York, the Northwest Coast and China.[4] He envisaged the profitable exchange of cheap ironware and other inexpensive items for the valuable furs of the Northwest Coast, which in turn would be exchanged at a handsome profit for Chinese teas and silks. Upon his return to America in 1782, Ledyard attempted to interest entrepreneurs in outfitting trading expeditions to the Northwest Coast and China. Although he was unsuccessful in this undertaking, it was as a result of the interest he aroused that the *Empress of China* was outfitted and sailed from New York in February 1784 for Canton to initiate American trade with the distant Far East. The financial success of this venture encouraged entrepreneurs to outfit other vessels which began calling at Canton and ports in India, the

Indian Ocean area, and the islands of the southwestern Pacific. During the lifetime of the first generation of Americans after the close of the Revolutionary War, all this trade was known as the "East India Trade."

This early "East India Trade" provided a natural outlet for the bursting energies of the seafaring New Englanders for whom the most distant seas held no terrors. During this period New England was practically without industries, such as were to develop in the latter part of the century and transform it into the workshop of America. Even the rock-strewn soil was inhospitable to the plow, and offered the enterprising individual almost no opportunity to acquire wealth and improve his lot. Hence the lure of the sea, and especially the lure of trading in far-away lands where quick profits could be made on small investments.

The principal American ports engaged in this early trade were Boston and Salem, Providence, a few Connecticut towns, New York, Philadelphia and Baltimore. The men who initially financed the ventures were generally of modest means, but the substantial profits which could be made enabled many of them to accumulate small fortunes which were later channeled into the industrial development of America.

In this early trade cargoes were picked up and disposed of at various ports en route, with profits being made on each individual transaction. The trade had its risks, however, since shipwrecks were not infrequent and many voyages often failed to make a profit or even incurred a sizable loss. Piracy also took its toll. Moreover, the trade was highly speculative because of the fluctuating value of the luxury commodities involved. While many entrepreneurs made fortunes, there were those who occasionally went bankrupt.

The American seamen who participated in this early trade differed substantially from their British counterparts who were generally recruited from the slums of the cities and were in general a bad lot. The American seamen usually took to the sea as a means to an end, namely the accumulation of some capital to engage subsequently in some venture at home. Although the American seamen were poorly paid, many of them were able to increase their earnings by renting space in the holds of the vessels they manned and engaging in minor trading of their own. Later when entrepreneurs took to fur trading and sealing, the sailors generally shared in the profits. A considerable number of the sailors were able to amass small amounts of capital which enabled them to purchase farms or begin small businesses of their own, while others were able to become masters of vessels.

By the late 1830's, however, a different type of American was turning to the sea and in general he represented a lower type of person who did not differ very much from his British counterpart.[5] A main reason was the rigid discipline and hard conditions which seamen were required to accept. It consequently became impossible to obtain enough Americans of reasonably good character to man the ships, and captains were compelled to recruit ruffians and even men of foreign lands, including the islands of the Pacific. These later crewmen were not only rough and unruly, but carriers of alcohol, diseases, and many other evils to the ports and havens at which they touched. Commenting on the whaling service, for example, a Nantucket newspaper reported in 1836: "Too many ungovernable lads, turnaways from parental authority, or candidates for corrective treatment, too many vagabonds from the clutches of the police of European and American cities—too many convicts—are suffered to enlist in the service." The newspaper further lamented that "it is not surprising that revolts, mutinies, and murders, conflagrations and immense destruction of property so frequently arise."[6]

The early American traders took either of two routes in reaching the Far East. One route was eastward across the Atlantic Ocean, around the Cape of Good Hope, and then to the Indian Ocean and Canton. The other route was around the eastern coastline of South America, around Cape Horn, and then across the Pacific to intervening ports and Canton. Traders using the eastward route frequented the ports of the Indian Ocean, the East Indies and finally Canton.

American trade with Isle de France (Mauritius) began in April 1786 with the arrival of the *Grand Turk* of Salem, Massachusetts. Trade with India began in 1786 with the arrival of the *Chesapeake* of Baltimore. In the Anglo-American Treaty of 1794 (the Jay Treaty), the American traders were accorded special privileges in the India trade. This trade was of considerable extent, and prior to 1790 the total American tonnage in Indian ports was greater than that in Canton. With the War of 1812 the American trade in India declined sharply, but it picked up again in the 1840's.

Much more so than others, the American traders were constantly in search of new markets. In the early nineteenth century American trade with the East Coast of Africa, Arabia and Iran was probably greater than that of all other traders combined. American trading interests in Zanzibar were probably predominant until 1859. Trade with the pepper coast of Sumatra began shortly after 1790 and developed rapidly until by 1820 it probably equalled that of Canton in importance. Trade was also developed with Siam (Thailand), but it suffered from vexatious restrictions until the conclusion of a commercial treaty in 1833. Trade with Batavia (now Jakarta), in Java, was also of some importance and relations between Dutch and American merchants became very cordial. The Dutch Government was not sympathetic to American trading activities in Java, however, and it attempted to restrict them by means of high import and export duties. American trade with the port of Manila was only of slight importance, but after 1825 this port took on added importance as an "in-between" port of call for vessels sailing to Canton via the Cape Horn route.[7]

The fur trade with China sprang up partly because the early traders had overestimated the value of ginseng as an exchange item at Canton and were compelled to find a substitute product that would command a high price. Actually the *Empress of China* had been able to obtain an excellent price for the ginseng she carried, but within a few years the price the Chinese merchants were willing to pay for this herb fell sharply. Discovering that the Chinese were willing to pay handsome prices for sea otter and seal peltries, most of which were then supplied by Russians, the early American traders promptly turned to furs as their principal exchange item. Sea otter furs for the Canton trade were obtained on the Northwest Coast while the sealskins came to be obtained later at the Falkland Islands, the South Sea islands, and also the Northwest Coast. Although Americans enjoyed a favorable position in the fur trade, they encountered lively competition from Russians, Englishmen, Frenchmen, Portuguese and Austrians.[8] The fur trade at Canton was supplemented at an early date by pick-ups of sandalwood on the Hawaiian Islands and by *bêche-de-mer,* edible birds' nests, and sharks' fins, all of which were highly prized by the Chinese for making soups.

The fur resources of the Northwest Coast were exploited by Americans shortly after 1778, the year that Captain Cook visited Nootka Sound and obtained sea otter furs from the natives. It was actually as a result of the high prices obtained by Cook for these furs in Canton that American traders turned their attention to the Northwest Coast as a source of furs for the China trade. John Ledyard, a member of Cook's crew, on returning to the United States was probably the first to awaken the interest of American merchants in the lucrative possibilities of the Canton fur trade and the potentialities of the Northwest Coast as a source of supply.[9]

The first American vessels to obtain furs on the Northwest Coast were the *Columbia* and the *Lady Washington,* commanded by Captains John Kendrick and Robert Gray respectively. These vessels sailed from Boston in September 1787 and arrived at the Northwest Coast a year later, after having been separated by storms which they encountered in rounding Cape Horn.[10] With winter coming on, the two captains camped on the shore at Friendly Cove in Nootka Sound. The following spring, 1788, they bartered for sea otter furs. Captain Gray then took command of the *Columbia* and sailed her to Canton, where the furs were sold through an American firm. Although the profit made on this voyage fell below expectations, the venture demonstrated that the Northwest Coast offered excellent possibilities for traders engaged in the China trade. Within a little more than two decades, by 1811, fifteen American vessels carried some 18,000 sea otter skins to Canton which brought a return of more than half a million dollars. American vessels came to frequent the Northwest Coast regularly, and from 1790 to 1818 a total of 108 American vessels, most of which were from Boston, visited the area.[11]

It became the practice of the traders to spend one or two seasons on the Northwest Coast to gather enough furs to make a voyage to Canton profitable. It became customary to put in at some sheltered cove near an Indian village. The prices of the furs went up as the Indians learned that they were in high demand, and the traders were consequently compelled to exchange for them increasing quantities of such items as cutlery, blankets, clothing, firearms, nails, beads, sugar and rum. In 1811 John Jacob Astor, a New

York fur merchant, established a trading post at Astoria, near the mouth of the Columbia River, but with the outbreak of the War of 1812 the men at this post sold out to the British. The Treaty of Ghent provided for the restoration of Astoria to the United States, and in 1818 a U.S. naval officer was dispatched to repossess it.

Sealskins for the China trade were obtained from about 1790 to the outbreak of the War of 1812, a period roughly paralleling the prosperous period of the Northwest Coast fur trade. During the early part of this sealing period, seals abounded on the barren islands off the coasts of Patagonia, in the waters south of Cape Horn, and along the Chilean coast. They were slaughtered indiscriminately in such large numbers, however, that within two decades the herds that had originally numbered millions dwindled to a few hundred thousand and hunting for them ceased to be profitable. Before they were virtually extinguished, however, a large number of merchants and seamen of the Atlantic seaboard had amassed fortunes.[12]

The seal trade may be said to have been really initiated by Elijah Austin of New Haven, who in 1790 dispatched two vessels under the command of Captain Daniel Green to the Falklands and South Georgia. In that same year Captain Patten sailed the *Industry* to Tristan da Cunha and collected some 5,600 sealskins. The ease with which these expeditions acquired large quantities of sealskins and the high prices which were readily paid for them at Canton gave impetus to an extensive seal trade. During the next two decades American vessels in large numbers, especially from Connecticut towns, were to be seen off the coasts of the Falklands, Staten Island, South Georgia, and Masafuera of the Juan Fernandez group. By the time of the War of 1812, however, sealing had begun to decline, largely because of the depletion of the herds. In 1819 there was a conspicuous revival as a result of the discovery of new herds in unfrequented islands near Antarctica, but these herds were also depleted within a few years.

The little town of Stonington, Connecticut, played a noteworthy part in this new seal trade. It was from this town that the illustrious Captain Edmund Fanning sailed forth on so many of his historic voyages. It was from Stonington that Captain James P. Sheffield sailed in 1819 to roam far below Cape Horn to the remote South

Shetland Islands, where he discovered large herds of seals. As a result of his discovery, five vessels sailed out of Stonington in the following year under the command of Captain Benjamin Pendleton to these same islands, where they captured about 150,000 seals.[13]

Recent research has also disclosed that the real discoverer of Antarctica was a Stonington man, Captain Nathaniel Brown Palmer. In command of the sloop *Hero,* one of the five vessels in Pendleton's expedition, he sighted that bleak continent in November 1820. Of this historic event, Palmer's journal has the simple entry, "Land from South to ESE which I suppose to be a continent."* The peninsula of Antarctica that juts out toward Cape Horn today bears his name, Palmer Land. A Nantucket captain, Christopher Burdick, also reported sighting Antarctica in February 1821.[14]

The profits made from sealing, while it lasted, were enormous. It has been estimated that between 1793 and 1807 some 3,500,000 sealskins were taken from Masafuera alone and sold at Canton for high prices. Captain Fanning on one voyage made a net profit of $53,118 on an investment of $7,867. But it was not an easy business. The voyages were long, usually of two or three years duration, and the men were forced to endure great hardships. Gangs of seamen were customarily left on the bleak and cold islands for as long as a year to live in rude huts and gather seals until their vessels returned to pick them up.[15]

In constant search of products which might supplement, or even be substituted for the supplies of furs, the Yankee traders also developed an extensive commerce with the myriad islands of the Pacific. The entire South Seas were continuously scoured by American vessels in search for such items as sandalwood, tortoise shells, mother of pearl, edible birds' nests, sharks' fins, *bêche-de-mer* and other items which brought high prices at Canton.

Under favorable conditions the profits made from the trade in the South Seas might be considerable. Sandalwood obtained in the Fiji Islands for about one cent a pound, for example, sold at

*The discovery of Antarctica has been traditionally accredited to Lt. Charles Wilkes, an American, and Admiral Dumont D'Urville, a Frenchman. Each of these men in January 1840 came upon the ice barrier of the continent after having started out from different positions. (Edouard A. Stackpole, *The Sea-Hunters,* p. 355.)

Canton for as much as 34 cents a pound. The prices paid in Canton for items picked up in the South Seas fluctuated greatly, however, and many voyages were unable to realize a profit or incurred losses. The men in this trade were also subjected to unusual perils, as many of the islanders, especially in the Fijis, were cannibalistic, and many a shipwrecked American suffered a tragic ending at the hands of fierce natives.[16]

The search for profits lured the American traders to an ever-widening world. By 1832 they had called at most of the islands in the entire Pacific. Even settlements had been established, for varying periods of permanence, in widely scattered parts of the world: the Hawaiian Islands, in 1787; Nootka Sound, in 1788; the Marquesas, in 1791; Fanning Island, in 1797; the Fijis, perhaps in 1800; the Galápagos Islands, in 1832; and Peel Island of the Bonin group, in 1832.

The New England whalemen and their ships played a dramatic and intrepid part in carrying the American flag to uncharted regions of the Pacific and Antarctic oceans. These hunters of the sea discovered a number of islands and ventured into areas of the ocean seas that had never before been traversed by white men's ships. In the first half of the nineteenth century, and for some time afterward, the American whalemen often combined their quest of the whale with the search for seals and sea elephants. In searching for seals and sea elephants, they roamed the seas for new rookeries that had been undisturbed by man.

American whaling operations trace back to the early English colonists who had settled along the New England coasts. These New Englanders, however, had largely confined their whaling to coastal waters and the Atlantic. With the coming of independence, the New England whalers intensified their activities and widened their range of operations to more distant seas. New whaling grounds were opened up in the following order: the Brazil Banks, 1774; Madagascar, 1789; the Chilean coast, 1790; the mid-Pacific off-shore grounds, 5° to 10° south latitude to 125° west longitude, 1818; the Japan area, 1820; Zanzibar, 1828; the Kodiak grounds, 1835; Kamchatka, 1843; the Sea of Okhotsk, 1847; and Bering Sea and the Arctic Ocean, 1848.[17]

Nantucket was initially the principal center of whaling operations, but by 1818 New Bedford had challenged it in the number of whaling vessels, and afterward became the leading whaling center of the United States. Many other New England towns, however, participated in whaling operations. The incentive for whaling was the high price which the oil and bone of the whale commanded. In the early nineteenth century whale oil was a highly important commodity for illumination.

The first whaler to enter the southern Pacific was the *Amelia,* a British vessel manned by Nantucket men, which arrived off the coast of Chile in 1788. As a result of the information concerning this new whaling ground which the Nantucket crewmen passed on to their friends and relatives in Nantucket and New Bedford, these two towns fitted out five vessels for whaling expeditions to the coasts of Chile. The first American whaler to round Cape Horn was the *Beaver* of Nantucket, in August 1791, and the first to "fill ship" in the South Pacific was the *Rebecca* of New Bedford, which sailed for that area in September 1791 and returned to home port in February 1793.[18] A steadily increasing number of New England whalers began frequenting the waters off the Chilean coast and they began pushing their operations steadily northward until they reached the equator. In 1818 Captain Gardner of Nantucket discovered an excellent whaling area about 1,400 miles west of the Peruvian coast, and within two years some fifty whalers were hunting in these grounds.[19]

The Hawaiian Islands promptly attracted the whalemen as a rendez-vous and port of operation for whaling in waters of the northern Pacific which were known to abound with whales. The *Equator* of Nantucket and the *Balaena* of New Bedford rendezvoused at Honolulu in September 1819 and hence were the forerunners of the whaling fleets which utilized this port as a base of operations. It was another New England whaler, the *Maro* of Nantucket, which, together with the British vessel *Syren,* in 1819-20, discovered the excellent whaling grounds to the east of Japan in the North Pacific.[20] Thereafter American vessels frequented these waters in large numbers. No one really knows how many American whalers skirted by the coasts of the Japanese islands. In quest of whales, American whalemen discovered and frequented the Loochoo (Ryūkyū) and Bonin islands before they were known to other Westerners. In 1830 five white men and some native Hawaiians founded a colony on one of the Bonin Islands. When Commodore Perry visited these islands he found one of the white men, Nathaniel Savory of Essex County, Massachusetts, still alive and engaged in a profitable trade with visiting whalemen through the sale of vegetables, hogs, and distilled rum.[21]

Whaling operations in the Pacific, utilizing the Hawaiian Islands as a base, flourished for some three decades after 1820. In 1835 the *Ganges* of Nantucket opened up a new and highly profitable whaling area when it took whales off the coast of Alaska. Throughout the next decade and a half American whalers enjoyed a period of exceptional prosperity. During this period they hunted in three principal whaling grounds. The most important was the area off the coasts of Alaska and Kamchatka. The other two areas were the seas to the east of Japan in the North Pacific and the area south of the Hawaiian Islands along the equator.[22]

By the middle of the century Americans had opened up still another profitable whaling area, far north in the Arctic Ocean. The first American whaler to sail through Bering Strait and enter the Arctic Ocean was the *Superior,* in 1848, commanded by Captain Roys. The excellent catch made by this vessel lured large numbers of other American whalers to this area. The vessels engaged in this Arctic whaling regularly anchored off the coasts of Alaska, and even Siberia, to await the break-up of the icefields to the north, while the men would go ashore to trade with the natives. During this period of waiting they often stole the food and fuel supplies of the Eskimos, debauched them with liquor, and ruined their health by introducing the white man's diseases.[23] By 1853 nearly five hundred American whalers had visited this far-northern whaling area in one season. In June 1865, however, the Southern cruiser *Shenandoah* in one operation inflicted about two million dollars of damage on the Yankee whalers in the Arctic area.[24] Yankee whaling in the Arctic never fully recovered from this one great blow.

American whaling activities throughout the world reached their peak in 1846, when the fleet numbered 735 vessels consisting of 678 ships and barks, 35 brigs, and 22 schooners, with a total capacity of 233,189 tons and valued at $20,075,000, a not inconsiderable sum for that time.[25] In that year the American fleet comprised more than 76 percent of the world's aggregate whaling fleet of 965 vessels.

The discovery of petroleum in 1859 in Pennsylvania and its coming into use for illumination purposes marked the beginning of the decline of the New England whaler. Actually the use of gas for illumination some years earlier had created a crisis for the whaling industry, which was surmounted because of the continued demand for whalebone and for spermacetti oil as a high-grade lubricant. The Civil War dealt the first seriously noticeable setback to the whaling industry as a result of the large number of whalers which were sunk or heavily damaged during the course of the war. Thirty-nine whalers, for example, were scuttled to block up Charleston harbor at the outset of this war, and another 70 whalers were burnt by Southern privateers that roamed the seas in quest of Union prey. After the Civil War, whaling operations were resumed and continued profitable for many decades thereafter. In 1871, however, thirty-four American whaling vessels were crushed in the ice fields of Bering Strait. This was a single blow from which the American whaling fleet never recovered. By the end of the century the size of the fleet had greatly diminished, and by the end of the second decade of the twentieth century American whaling had practically come to a complete cessation.[26] By this time, moreover, New Englanders had become completely absorbed in the easier and more profitable challenge of industrialization.

A romantic chapter in the development of ever-widening American trade with the lands of the Far East and the Pacific was written by the advent of the clipper ships on the high seas. These sleek "greyhounds of the sea" were the nautical marvels of the time. Slender, lightly constructed, and with masts heavily laden with huge sails, these graceful ships in their day were synonymous with high speed, until steam navigation within a few decades relegated them to obsolescence. The peculiar significance of the clipper ships in the Far East trade was that they made tea, spices and other valuable items of China, India and the East Indies readily available to the consumers of America and Europe.

Precisely when the clipper ship made its appearance is difficult to determine, and the term was apparently not used in newspapers until 1835. No one man could claim it as the product of his own inventive genius. Between 1845 and 1865, at any rate, the term "clipper ship" came to have a definite meaning and connoted a sleek ship with peculiar characteristics and a capacity for high speed.[27] In the late 1840's and the 1850's the clipper ships comprised a substantial portion of the American merchant fleet engaged in the China, India and East Indies trades. New York came to be a kind of headquarters for the China trade, and Boston came to enjoy a similar position with regard to the Calcutta, or India, trade.

Tea had constituted an important part of the cargoes picked up by American vessels at Canton from the earliest years of the China trade. In recognition of the importance of the tea trade, the United States Government even gave it a measure of support by permitting the withholding of duty payments for as long as eighteen months. By the 1840's tea had become the principal American import from China, and American vessels were carrying to the United States some fifteen million pounds annually.[28] Light in bulk and relatively high in value, tea contributed significantly to the development of the speedy clipper ship.

The 1850's were in almost every respect a "golden age" of American maritime activity. The amazing upsurge of American maritime activity during this period was certainly greatly stimulated by the British Government's final nullification of remaining provisions of the old Navigation Acts in 1848. As a result of this action, American vessels were, for the first time since the establishment of the Republic, permitted to engage in commerce of foreign origin destined for the British Isles on terms of equality with those of British nationals. In the Far East this opportunity was seized upon by American entrepreneurs to outfit vessels for carrying tea from China to the British Isles. The first American clipper ship to carry tea from China to Britain was the *Oriental,* which departed from Whampoa on August 22, 1850, and arrived at London 104 days later on December 4, 1850. The speed of this voyage created a sensation in Europe and America.[29] Because of her known speed the clipper received an exceptionally high freightage for the tea she carried; and perhaps even more pleasing to her captain than the remarkable speed of the voyage was the profit of $48,000 that was made, a sum which equalled two thirds the cost of building the vessel.[30]

The advent of the American clipper ships in the China tea trade for a few years caused great financial loss to the lumbering British vessels engaged in this trade, which were ill-equipped to compete with them in speed. Writing on this subject, a British author in

1873 stated: "This new competition proved for a time most disastrous to British shipping, which was soon driven out of favor by the lofty spars, smart, rakish-looking hulls, and famed speed of the American ships, and caused the tea-trade of the London markets to pass almost out of the hands of the English ship-owner."[31] Within a few years, however, British clipper ships were also making the voyage to China and answering the American challenge. With the loss of their initial advantage, American clippers then turned to the rewarding challenge of bringing San Francisco closer to the East Coast. Historic records were also made on this run, the most famous being that of the *Flying Cloud,* built in East Boston, which in 1854 made the run from New York to San Francisco in 89 days, a record which was never surpassed, although twice equalled, by sailing vessels.

The high tide of American maritime enterprise was attained in 1855. In that year American shipping totalled 5,212,000 tons, of which less than 15 percent was in steamers. This was the greatest tonnage America had ever possessed, and more, relatively speaking in terms of the world's total tonnage, than she ever afterward acquired. Actually the American merchant fleet in 1855 was almost as large as that of Britain, and probably was considerably superior in efficiency. Certainly no other nation participated so extensively in the trade of the world as did the United States at that time. Even the Canton trade was dominated by American shipping. In 1855, for example, foreign shipping in China waters totalled 58,000 tons of which 24,000 was American, 18,000 was British, and the remainder was divided among other nations. Then came the Civil War, with its heavy damage to the fleet, and after that the almost fanatical absorption of the nation in the development of the West and the expansion of its industries. The once great zeal for the sea began to subside. The merchant fleet made a comeback, but as late as 1880 it had climbed back to only 4,000,000 tons. Not until the twentieth century did the nation's tonnage exceed that of 1855.[32] Thereafter the merchant fleet increased still further in absolute tonnage, but it never again came even close to acquiring that major share of the world's shipping which it had once possessed.

As has been indicated, early American interest in the Pacific area was initially confined to simple trading operations, which later were augmented by sealing and whaling. All of these operations were conducted by men and vessels based on the Atlantic seaboard. Although the capital accumulations of the individuals engaged in these activities contributed significantly to the early industrial development of the United States, the Government manifested a very limited interest in the Pacific area because of its remoteness and the relatively small number of Americans whose welfare and livelihood immediately depended on it. The overwhelming portion of American trade remained with Europe, and the Republic from its Atlantic seaboard faced the nations of Europe. It was but natural, then, that the national policy should have been mainly concerned with security from these nations and the promotion and protection of commerce with them.

Since the interests of the nation in the Pacific, as contrasted with those of the few, were very slight, the American Government initially gave very little attention to the development of a positive Far Eastern policy. The foundations of this policy were therefore perforce laid on the spot by the men who were actually engaged in the trading activities. These traders naturally desired nothing less than equal trading opportunities with their competitors. Hence they wanted most-favored-nation privileges.* They also did not want to see any of the governments of their trading rivals seize territories, particularly in China, because of the fear that they might be subjected to discriminations in them. Accordingly they favored the preservation of the territorial and administrative entity of the countries in which they traded. This was especially true of the traders in Canton. These on-the-spot policies of the early American traders in time became adopted by the United States Government when it felt compelled to support actively the commercial and other interests of Americans in China and other distant lands.

With the acquisition of California in 1848 the United States came into possession of an active Pacific Coast, and now faced west as well as east. Just as the Atlantic bound the nation to the countries of Europe, so did the vast Pacific now link it to the countries of Asia and its myriads of islands. Possession of a

*By virtue of most-favored-nation privileges a signatory to a treaty is entitled to any special right or advantage which may be granted to any other country.

Pacific Coast by the United States enabled American traders to conduct their operations more effectively and vigorously. The American Government also became concerned about the security of this new coast. Very naturally, then, the Government began to develop, consciously and fortuitously, a somewhat concrete Pacific policy.

By the eve of the American Civil War, the general outlines of this policy had been developed. With regard to the Pacific and its islands, the United States had developed a special policy for Hawaii. The basic principle of this particular policy was that because of the relative proximity of the Hawaiian Islands to the American West Coast, the United States regarded the permanence of their independence as imperative and would not tolerate an attempt by any power to seize them. As for the myriads of other islands, most of which had already been seized by various imperialist powers, the United States had no territorial ambitions and desired only that its citizens might engage in commercial activities with natives on conditions identical with those enjoyed by any other foreign nationals. Although the American people as a whole continued to regard colonialism with pronounced odium, the policy of the Government was that of respecting the *status quo* of all areas already under colonial domination. It did not seek to destroy or subvert the colonial system, much as it was incompatible with the lofty principles on which the Republic was based and nurtured. For itself, the Government did candidly disavow imperialism and the subjugation of helpless and so-called "backward" peoples for economic exploitation.

With regard to continental Asia, the fundamental policy had become based on the principles for which the early American traders had contended on their own initiative. The cornerstones of this policy were: (1) equal commercial opportunities and most-favored-nation privileges, and (2) the preservation of the territorial and administrative integrity of remaining sovereign countries, especially China and Japan. While this had become the basic policy, the United States had neither the vital interest nor the means to implement it by force if necessary. Its implementation depended almost exclusively on persuasive diplomacy.

CHAPTER TWO

Establishment of Treaty Relations with China

Until the sixteenth century knowledge of China in the West was largely confined to the celebrated *Book of Ser Marco Polo* and the accounts of Catholic missionaries. When the West entered upon its great age of navigation and exploration in the sixteenth century, China, then generally known as Cathay, was believed to be a fabulous world of its own whose opulence surpassed that of anything known to the Western world. There was more than a measure of justification for this belief. More impressive than the fancied riches of China, however, was the brilliant cultural achievement of the Chinese people who over the centuries had actually succeeded in developing one of the world's truly great civilizations. When Columbus set foot on the soil of the New World in 1492, China in its sum total was probably the most "civilized" country in the world, as well as its most opulent. Its imagined size awed the Europeans. It actually dwarfed all the Western European countries and was considerably larger than all of them combined. In addition, its teeming and industrious population then, as now, probably was a fifth of the world's total. Small wonder, then, that the Westerner from earliest times thrilled to the concept of "China" and envisioned it as a living El Dorado from which quick and fantastic profits might somehow be extracted.

It has been mistakenly assumed by many that the Great Wall of China symbolizes a traditional isolationist mentality of the Chinese people. This is hardly so. The Great Wall must be considered for what it actually was—a barrier erected of necessity, intended to contain the barbarians of the northwest and prevent them from pouring into and ravaging the fertile and prosperous valleys of China. Geography, rather than attitude, isolated ancient China from the rest of the world: in the north were the deserts of Mongolia, in the south the formidable Himalaya Mountains, and on the east the great ocean.[1] While it is true that the Chinese for centuries regarded themselves as the custodians of a superior civilization and considered that all others who did not embrace their civilization were "barbarians," the China of antiquity did not shut her doors to intercourse with the outside world. The character the Chinese employed to designate the "barbarians" was 夷 (transliterated as *i* but pronounced "yee") and it simply connoted one unfamiliar with the Chinese language, literature and decorum. Western accounts of the Chinese in the nineteenth century have generally interpreted *i* to mean "barbarian" with the intent of disparaging the Chinese and imputing to them an intolerable arrogance. The Japanese and Koreans, who employed the same character *i* in reference to Westerners, used it with much the same implication as the Chinese did.

Even before the Christian era, traders from the far west exchanged commodities with Chinese traders in the great cities of Central Asia which in those days were flourishing trading centers. Chinese merchants carried on trading activities almost continuously with the outside world until relatively recent times. Part of this trade was carried on through overland routes to Central Asia, part was carried on by sea from the coastal cities of China. It prospered or languished accordingly as war or brigandage prevailed.

Nestorian Christians, doubtless Syrians, reached China in 635 A.D., and although they were persecuted after 845 they remained active as late as the fourteenth century. Roman Catholic envoys reached northern China in the thirteenth century in the hope of enlisting the Great Khan against the Turks who were then threatening Western Europe and Christendom. They failed to obtain the assistance of the Khan, but they brought back to Europe fresh accounts of the magnificent civilization of China. The Venetian Marco Polo arrived at the court of the Great Khan in Cambaluc in 1275 and spent almost two decades in the service of the mighty Kublai Khan. After his return to Venice he dictated a book describing the marvels and fabulous wealth of China which stimulated a widespread interest in the Far East and its fancied treasures. Late in the thirteenth century Franciscan missionaries arrived in China and attempted to introduce Catholicism. They enjoyed some initial success, but by the end of the fourteenth century their efforts had practically ended in failure. While some of their Chinese converts remained loyal to the new faith, they numbered at the most only a few thousand in a land of millions.

During this long period of sporadic and limited intercourse with the West, the rulers and people of China customarily manifested friendliness and hospitality. Restrictions and persecutions generally resulted only after the foreigners had appeared to flout the laws and customs of the Empire or to disturb its tranquility.

Early in the sixteenth century the adventurous Portuguese, first of the Europeans to round the Cape of Good Hope and reach India, arrived in China. They probably reached Canton in 1515, and were well received by the local Chinese officials. The Portuguese at this time were among the most active and enterprising traders of the West, and they foresaw great profits in the opening up of a seaborn trade with China. Their tactlessness and disregard of the sensibilities of the Chinese, however, soon antagonized the local officials, and in 1557 they were required to confine their activities to a small island about 80 miles south of Canton (Kwangtung). There they established a permanent settlement, which they named Macao.* Other Westerners who followed on the heels of the Portuguese were also restricted to Macao after 1724, and until 1842, when the British obtained Hongkong, it served as the base of all Western trading activities in China. Russians also established contacts with the Chinese Empire, and were permitted to carry on a limited amount of trade by overland routes in northern China.

Following the Portuguese traders, Catholic missionaries arrived a second time in the latter part of the sixteenth century. The great Jesuit Matteo Ricci reached China in 1582, made his way to Peking, and there through tact, tolerance and an amazing understanding of Chinese culture ingratiated himself with the imperial court. Other Jesuits followed Ricci, and they in turn were followed

*Actually Macao is a small peninsula linked by a narrow neck of land to the island of Hsiang located in the delta of the Si River.

by Franciscan and Dominican missionaries. A bitter rivalry developed between the Jesuits on the one hand and the Franciscans and Dominicans on the other. This rivalry arose partly on doctrinal grounds, and partly because the Jesuits were under the protection of Portugal while the Franciscans and Dominicans were under the protection of rival Spain. Spain and Portugal at that time were maritime and commercial rivals. Annoyed by the rivalries and intrigues of the missionaries, the Manchu Emperor in 1724 expelled all except a few Jesuits who were permitted to remain in Peking because of their scientific attainments. The writings of these missionaries were translated into many languages and added to the West's growing but limited knowledge of China.

In the wake of the Portuguese traders came Spaniards from Manila in 1572, Dutch in 1622, who occupied Formosa (Taiwan) until 1661, Englishmen and others who were intent on sharing in the profits of the increasing China trade. Rivalries among these traders became intense and greatly disturbed the Chinese officials, who were primarily concerned with maintaining internal order and stability. As indicated above, all the traders after 1724 were restricted to Macao, over which the Portuguese had come to enjoy a limited degree of sovereignty.

The trade of the Europeans with China in the early part of the nineteenth century was on a treaty-less basis and confined to the Canton area. Treaties, of course, imply compacts among equals. Such compacts were unthinkable to the classically-trained mandarin officials of Imperial China. To them China was the only truly civilized nation and the Westerners engaged in trade at Canton were regarded as "barbarians." Trade with the Westerners was to be tolerated rather than encouraged, and their activities were to be closely regulated to prevent the moral contamination of the Chinese people and the perversion of Chinese culture.

China of the early nineteenth century was still based by an agrarian economy. The wants of her people were few and practically all of the necessities of life were obtainable within the confines of the Empire. The West had practically nothing to offer except luxuries. Hence there was also a practical reason why China tolerated rather than encouraged foreign intercourse.

Originally the China trade was based on the exchange of tea, silk, porcelain and other indigenous items for silver. As long as this trade resulted in an influx of the precious metal it was not unfavorably regarded, but by the beginning of the nineteenth century the importation of large quantities of opium from India upset the previously favorable balance of trade. Chinese products and the silver received in exchange for them were no longer of sufficient value to balance the opium imports. The country was consequently being drained of its precious metals to make up for the trade deficit.

Opium was first brought into China from India in 1700 by the Portuguese. The opium produced in the Indian province of Bengal was the most prized by the Chinese. After the British conquest of India and the establishment of British control over Bengal in the latter part of the eighteenth century, the opium trade became dominated by the British and it increased greatly in volume and value.

The use of opium by an increasing number of Chinese greatly alarmed the Chinese Government, and beginning in 1729 various edicts were issued against opium. In 1785 the export of silver as payment for opium was prohibited by the Emperor. In 1799 opium was declared contraband throughout all of China. An edict issued in the following year forbade the sale of opium, and another edict in 1809 specifically prohibited the import of opium.[2] All these measures, however, were of no avail. The harmful traffic continued because of the insatiable demands of the Chinese addicts, the corruption and connivance of local Chinese officials, and the defiance of the Westerners engaged in the profitable traffic.

Although the handling of opium was the most lucrative source of profit for Western traders in the first three decades of the nineteenth century, legitimate trading activities were of considerable importance. The restrictions imposed by the Imperial Government on these activities, however, were extremely vexatious. These restrictions were tolerated by the Westerners because of the handsome profits accruing from this trade and their unwillingness to risk its possible suspension by the Imperial Government. The traders were also aware that their respective governments were indifferent to the situation prevailing in China and that they could not count on them for support in the event of a serious conflict with the officials of the Chinese Government.

24

As has been indicated, all trading activity was confined to the Canton area. The principal official with responsibility for this area was a Viceroy, appointed by and directly accountable to the central government in Peking. Foreigners were required to reside in Macao. They were permitted to lease warehouses at Whampoa, an island twelve miles below Canton, but were allowed there only during the three months of the year when business was being conducted. Trade was arbitrarily regulated by a special imperial official, known to foreigners as the *hoppo,* which was a misrepresentation of *Hupu,* meaning the "Board of Population and Revenue," one of the six boards of the Imperial Government. The *hoppo* collected duties and fees and enforced commercial regulations. The foreign traders could deal with him only through Chinese intermediaries known as the *co-hong,* a merchant guild of a handful of traders who enjoyed a monopoly over all foreign trade at Canton. Actually *co-hong* was a Cantonese pronunciation of *chiu-hang,* whose literal meaning is "nine mercantile establishments." In accordance with the social custom of the Chinese, the *co-hong* were held responsible for all the acts of the traders with whom they conducted business. It was through the *co-hong* that the Viceroy was able to keep the foreigners in line. The most effective weapon employed by the Chinese Government was the threat to suspend the trade, or its actual suspension. To prevent the suspension of the trade, the foreign traders were willing to yield on any issue and comply with almost any demand put forth by the Government.

American trade with China was initiated on February 22, 1784, when the *Empress of China,* a trading vessel commanded by Captain John Greene, departed from New York for Canton via the Cape of Good Hope route. On board this vessel was Major Samuel Shaw, serving as "agent" for the group which sponsored the voyage. The vessel carried a cargo of ginseng, and it was anticipated that a handsome profit would be made from its sale in Canton. Apropos of the departure of this vessel, the *Maryland Journal and Baltimore Advertiser* noted that "the captain and crew, with several American adventurers" were "elated on being considered the first instruments, in the hands of Providence, who have undertaken to extend the commerce of the United States of

America to that distant, and to us unexplored country."[3] On August 23, 1784, six months after her departure, the *Empress of China* arrived at Canton harbor. After a stay of four months at Whampoa, during which time the ginseng was disposed of and cargoes of tea and nankeen were taken aboard, the vessel made the return trip to New York in 134 days. The owners of the vessel made a modest profit of $30,727, or slightly more than 25 percent on the total investment of $120,000.[4] The success of this venture encouraged other entrepreneurs to outfit vessels for the newly opened China trade.

Less than a year and a half after the conclusion of this historic voyage, the Congress on January 27, 1786, approved the appointment of Major Samuel Shaw to serve as consul in Canton "with neither salary nor perquisites." The Congress, of course, made no attempt to establish diplomatic relations with the Government of China. Shaw's title as consul was merely for the purpose of giving him status with the foreign merchants in China.[5] Shaw served as consul until his death in 1794. Other consuls were appointed after him, and they too served without remuneration from the Government. Until 1854 the consul actually was a merchant who received fees for whatever services he rendered.

Within a few years after the initial voyage of the *Empress of China,* the trading activities of Americans at Canton ranked second in importance to those of the British. In 1786 five American vessels arrived at Canton with cargoes valued at $2,500,000. By 1805 American exports to China had increased to $5,300,000, and imports amounted to $5,100,000.[6] Since the total volume of American foreign trade at that time was small, this trade amounted to a significant proportion of the total, probably about three percent. Prior to 1812 a considerable portion of the cargo picked up at Canton was reshipped from America to Europe. In 1803, for example, more than half the tea was reshipped to Europe.[7]

American trade with China continued to prosper until the outbreak of the War of 1812, when it was dealt a setback by British commerce raiders. With the termination of this war, however, the trade made a rapid recovery. By the 1820's the trade had taken on new characteristics. American firms with headquarters at Canton had replaced the supercargoes who had accompanied the captains of the vessels to handle the transactions at that port.

Large companies had also replaced the individual merchants who had provided the capital and initiative for the enterprises. In 1825, for example, some seven-eighths of the American trade at Canton was handled by four large firms: Perkins and Company of Boston, Archer of Philadelphia, James Oakford and Company of Philadelphia, and T. H. Smith of New York. New York came to dominate the Canton trade and became the center of the tea trade with China. From 1821 to 1841, a period when the China trade reached its full development, between twenty and thirty vessels sailed each year from American ports to Canton.[8]

The China trade reached its peak in absolute value between 1850 and 1855 when the fast-sailing American clipper ships, which had made their appearance in the 1840's, excited the admiration of the world and practically cornered the tea-carrying trade. During the Civil War the trade was seriously crippled by the Confederate commerce raiders, from whose depredations it never fully recovered. During the heyday of the trade, furs, particularly sea peltries, were the principal items exchanged for such Chinese goods as tea, silk, nankeens and chinaware.

The introduction of manufactured goods into the China trade in the years immediately preceding the outbreak of the Opium War in 1839 was of great significance for the future, as it placed China and her teeming millions in a new light. Traders now began to think of China as a limitless market for manufactured goods, particularly textiles, rather than primarily as a supplier of tea and other luxury items.[9] The first textile goods sold by Americans in China were obtained from England. English and other European textile goods imported into China by American vessels reached their peak in value around 1825, when they were valued at about $5,500,000. In that year American textile goods brought into China amounted only to about $160,000 in value.[10] By 1830, however, these goods had increased to more than $500,000 in value, and by 1845 they had exceeded $1,000,000 in value. By that time the importation of British and other European textile goods into China by American vessels had declined sharply. Although the total of all American trade with China in 1840 had amounted only to about $7,000,000, it was the future prospects rather than the then current volume that excited American entrepreneurs with interests in the China trade.[11]

27

Americans participated actively in the opium traffic, particularly between 1820, when the fur trade began to languish, and about 1830, by which time the importation of textile items was beginning to assume significant proportions. Americans picked up the opium in the Near East as well as in India. While the amounts of opium handled by Americans was considerable when the American traffic in this item was at its peak, it was small in comparison with the total being brought into China or that handled by the British alone.

After 1830 American participation in the opium traffic began to decline. This was partly a result of the increasing importance of textiles as import items, but there were other significant factors accounting for the decline. The American missionaries, for example, had continuously campaigned against the evils of the opium traffic on the ground it was incompatible with Christianity and that it injured the future prospects of Christianity in China. A considerable portion of the American commercial community in Canton consistently opposed the traffic on the usual moral grounds and even cooperated with the missionaries in the hope of bringing about its elimination. U.S. naval officers moreover issued frequent warnings to Americans that they would give no protection to men or vessels engaged in the illicit trade.[12] In 1839 American merchants in Canton voluntarily signed a pledge to abstain from the traffic.[13] Although the pledge was subsequently violated by many Americans, the participation of Americans in the opium traffic decreased markedly after the conclusion of the Opium War in 1842.

In the legitimate trade the early Americans were at a disadvantage in competing with the rival traders of imperialist nations like Great Britain, France, Portugal and the Netherlands, which had nearby possessions that could be utilized as bases of support. After the Opium War the governments of Great Britain and France, in particular, began to support their nationals actively and were able to take advantage of their possessions nearby China for making their military power felt. The United States, of course, possessed no territories beyond North America, and not until the late forties did it even possess a Pacific coast. Nevertheless the American Government was not unmindful of the value of the China trade. It was protected by Congress almost from its inception, and was subsidized until 1832 when duties on tea imported through foreigners were abolished.[14] *62447*

At Canton, however, the American traders received no positive support from the United States Government. Although a consul for Canton had been appointed as early as 1786, during a fifty-year period the regularly appointed consuls were actually resident at Canton for only fourteen years and invariably without any instructions from the Government.[15] Compelled to carry on their activities without the active support of their Government, the American traders consequently developed a policy of their own to protect their commercial interests in China. This policy was based on two fundamental principles: (1) the preservation of the territorial and administrative integrity of China, and (2) equal trading privileges with nationals of all other countries. These principles were ultimately adopted by the United States as the fundamental basis of its China and Far Eastern policies. The main concern of the American traders, as of other traders, was to keep the trade going and to do nothing that might antagonize the Chinese authorities and provoke them to suspend it.

The principal rivals of the American traders were the British. Initially the wealthy and powerful British East India Company enjoyed a monopoly over all British trade with China. After this company lost its monopoly in China, in 1833, individual British traders were supported by the positive and aggressive actions of the British Government. The British traders generally more than matched the arrogance of the Chinese officials, while the Americans were generally much more conciliatory. In the almost continuous squabbling between the British and Chinese the Americans sometimes sided with the British and sometimes with the Chinese, depending on the advantages to be gained at the particular moment.[16]

The Chinese regarded the American traders as "barbarians" in common with all Westerners. Americans nevertheless enjoyed a somewhat more favorable position with the Chinese primarily because the United States, unlike other Western powers, had never seized any territory in Asia. Individual Americans also tended to display greater consideration for the laws and sensibilities of the Chinese than did other foreigners. In the personal relations of Chinese and American traders there was even some degree of

29

mutual respect, and perhaps even of affection. Americans were often confused with the English, however, and many Chinese mistakenly assumed that Englishmen and Americans were the same people.[17] This was certainly a great disadvantage, for the Chinese officials apparently regarded the English with the utmost contempt as "overbearing and tyrannical," "unusually cunning," "by nature and appearance treacherous and unusually faithless," and "fundamentally not much different from dogs and sheep."[18] Being human, the American traders also chafed under the minute restrictions of the Chinese Government and the disdainful attitude of its officials, and like the other traders they came to look forward to the establishment of trade on a treaty basis.

To the American and European traders, *all* Chinese officials were "overbearing" and "arrogant." Since these traders were in China simply to make money and make it as fast as they could regardless of scruples, and inasmuch as they had not the slightest knowledge of China or its long-lived culture and cherished customs, this is understandable. But obviously there is another point of view. The Chinese officials were invariably scholars, deeply steeped in the values of Confucian culture and the very epitome of refinement. The traders, on the other hand, were too often uncouth, contemptuous of any law but that of their own country, and completely in the dark concerning the low status of the trader in this China, where the scholar was at the apex of the pyramid of status and the soldier was near the bottom.

During the period of early intercourse with China there was only one incident of a serious nature to disturb Sino-American relations. In 1821 an Italian seaman of the American vessel *Emily,* which was in the harbor of Canton, dropped a jar on a Chinese woman vendor who was in a small boat alongside the ship, causing her death. The Chinese claimed that the sailor, Francis Terranova, had deliberately thrown the jar and killed the woman. They demanded his surrender and trial under Chinese law. After some procrastination, Terranova was surrendered to the Chinese. He was given a farcical trial, condemned, and executed by strangulation. The British strongly denounced the American officials at Canton for having surrendered Terranova to trial by the Chinese, but it appears that the Americans hardly had any other alternative, as the Chinese threatened to suspend all trade unless he were delivered. To the Americans at Canton the continuation of the profitable trade was of paramount importance. In the absence of any tangible on-the-spot support from their Government, they were willing to yield to almost any Chinese demand when it was accompanied by the threat of suspending the trade.

The first Protestant missionary in China was the noted Dr. Robert Morrison, an Englishman, who arrived at Canton in 1807 and dedicated himself to translations and the compilation of a dictionary. Except for a brief period from 1813 to 1815, when he was joined by another Englishman, he was the only Protestant missionary in China until 1829 when David Abeel and Dr. Elijah C. Bridgman arrived at Canton to initiate American missionary activity. These two pioneer American missionaries were shortly afterward joined by such other noted American missionaries as S. Wells Williams and Dr. Peter Parker. By 1840 American Protestant missionaries outnumbered the British Protestant missionaries almost two to one.

The propagation of Protestantism in China became a matter of great concern to certain religious circles in the United States, and in a real sense American Protestantism came to have as great a stake in China as American commerce. Although neither the Protestants nor Catholics ever made any great inroads on China's millions, the influence of the American missionaries became reflected in American policy toward China. For one thing, American policy came to reflect the material interests of the missionaries with regard to favorable conditions for proselyting and conducting educational and philanthropic activities of a denominational nature. Certain altruistic aspects of American policy toward China, especially toward the end of the century, also partly reflected missionary influence. In the latter part of the nineteenth century the missionaries moreover inadvertently came to exert a noteworthy influence on revolutionary developments in China, for many of the Chinese reformists and revolutionists of this period were products of the mission schools, where they were exposed to concepts which to a great extent were antagonistic to traditional Chinese concepts of government and social organization.

From 1838 to 1848 the Imperial Government, disdainful of direct contacts with foreigners but mindful that their presence could not be ignored, entrusted the actual management of relations with foreign diplomats to especially appointed officials stationed at Canton, which during this period remained the great center of trade. After 1848 Shanghai began to displace Canton as the principal trading center of China, and relations with foreign diplomats were generally handled by the appropriate Chinese officials at that port. Lin Tse-hsü may be regarded as China's first "foreign minister," a function which he may be said to have discharged until his dismissal in 1842. The function of "foreign minister" may be said to have been subsequently exercised by Ch'i-ying,* from 1842 to 1848, and then by Yeh Ming-ch'en, from 1848 to 1858, after which relations with foreign diplomats were directly handled in Peking.[19]

On matters of unusual significance, all of the aforementioned were meticulously instructed by Peking on policy and courses of action. It was these three men who played prominent roles during the critical period of Western imperialism's initial frontal assault on China. Each of these men, incidentally, was a typical scholar-bureaucrat, learned in the classics and the epitome of refinement. It is perhaps of significance that Caleb Cushing, who negotiated the first American treaty with China through direct negotiations with Ch'i-ying, was impelled to note that he was "a Manchu of high qualities of head and heart, and of perfect accomplishment."[20]

From 1839 to 1842 China and Great Britain were involved in an armed conflict commonly known as the Opium War. Although the illegal importation of opium was a primary cause of friction between the Chinese Government and the foreigners, there were also other underlying causes. Principal among these was the persistent refusal of the Chinese officials to deal with representatives of the foreign powers as equals. Foreign representatives were not permitted to enter the capital in Peking and were restricted in their intercourse to local officials in Canton. These officials continually antagonized the foreign representatives by their haughtiness, procrastination and disdainful unfamiliarity with the trading and diplomatic practices of the West. Another underlying cause of the conflict lay in the absence of a treaty to specify the rights and privileges of foreigners engaged in trading activities. Added to these underlying causes was the lack of extraterritorial jurisdiction

*Western accounts dealing with this period usually refer to him as "Kiying."

by foreign governments which resulted in foreigners being liable to trial and punishment under the barbarous criminal code of China and the uneven and corrupt dispensation of justice on the part of Chinese officials.

Possessing the largest trading interests in China, Great Britain naturally took the lead in forcing the obstinate Chinese Government to grant diplomatic equality and conclude a treaty for the enlightened and practical regulation of trading activities. Several unsuccessful attempts had been made early in the nineteenth century by British, Russian and other envoys to conclude satisfactory arrangements, but in all instances the Chinese officials had arrogantly refused to make any changes in the traditional policy and practices of the Empire. Foreign envoys invariably had been regarded as tribute bearers and denied an imperial audience unless willing to perform the traditional "kowtow," a symbol of vassalage.

Serious trouble with the British Government began in 1834 when the monopolistic British East India Company withdrew from China and the China trade was opened to individual British traders on a competitive basis. This was of particular significance, for insults to British citizens were now regarded as affronts to the national honor whereas they had formerly been regarded merely as the normal difficulties of a trading company.[21] In that same year a three-man commission headed by Lord Robert Napier as Chief Superintendent of Trade was dispatched to Canton for the purpose of regulating the activities of the private British traders and their relations with the Chinese. Napier attempted to conclude trading arrangements with the local Chinese officials in Canton, but his efforts were high-handedly rebuffed and he was informed that he would have to withdraw to Macao and act through the co-hong merchants. In an effort to force Napier to comply with their demands, the Chinese also suspended foreign trade for a brief period. In no position to defy the Chinese, Napier retired to Macao, where he died in October 1834, bitterly disappointed and convinced that force would be necessary to compel the Chinese to respect the rights of Great Britain and her nationals. Tension mounted between the British and the Chinese, but the British Government was not yet prepared to employ force. The American consul in Macao believed that war between Britain and China was inevitable, and he counselled the State Department to stage a naval demonstration, in case of war, for the purpose of securing privileges equal to those which Britain might obtain.

Meanwhile, the importation of opium into China had reached alarming proportions. Practically all of the product came from British India and a large part of it was smuggled into China at various ports along the coast as far north as Tientsin. In 1835 more than 25,000 chests of opium were brought into China. By 1838 the amount had increased to 35,000 chests valued at $17,-000,000.[22]

Angered by the extent of this illegal traffic in defiance of the law of China, the Imperial Government in December 1838 appointed Lin Tse-hsü as High Commissioner to "go, investigate, and act" on the opium problem in Canton. The Imperial Government was doubtless as motivated by economic as by moral considerations, for the country was being drained of silver, which was used to pay for the opium imports that unbalanced the foreign trade. Lin acted swiftly. On March 18, 1839, he ordered all foreigners to withdraw from the illegal opium traffic, to hand over all stocks of opium within three days, and to post a bond as a guarantee they would bring no more opium into China. When the foreign merchants refused to surrender the opium in their possession, Lin suspended foreign trade. In addition, all foreigners in Canton were forbidden to leave the city, which was placed in a state of blockade by imperial forces. Lin's blockade was so effective that the foreigners trapped in Canton came close to the verge of starvation.[23]

Aware that Lin was in deadly earnest, the British Superintendent of trade, Captain Charles Elliot, in March 1839 surrendered under protest 20,283 chests of opium valued at $8,000,000 that had been placed in his custody.[24] Of this total, 1540 chests were owned by Americans, but the British Superintendent of Trade maintained that they were British property. To the astonishment of the foreigners who believed that Lin was bluffing, the entire lot of opium was mixed with lime and poured into the sea. Although the Chinese then lifted the blockade, Great Britain immediately began preparations for war on the ground that her representatives had been insulted, that her nationals had been mistreated, and that British property had been wrongfully confiscated. Meanwhile, other serious incidents involving Chinese and

British nationals contributed to the inevitability of war. Actual conflict broke out on November 3, 1839, when a naval skirmish took place at Chuenpi.

The issues were clear. To the Chinese it was primarily a question of destroying the illegal opium traffic and compelling respect for China's laws and traditions. To the British it was a question of obtaining payment for the confiscated opium, securing better trading conditions, and of acquiring recognition of diplomatic equality.[25]

On June 22, 1840, the British blockaded the port of Canton, and less than two weeks later demolished its fortifications by naval gunfire, although no declaration of war had been made. The city was spared from further destruction when the inhabitants of Canton paid a ransom of $8,000,000, the amount at which the confiscated opium was valued. Several coastal cities were subsequently seized by the British. In the military engagements that took place the Chinese war junks and the thousands of ill-armed Chinese troops were no match for the small force of British troops supported by powerful gunboats.

By 1842 the British were about to attack Nanking. At this point the Chinese realized the futility of continuing the struggle and sued for peace. On August 29 a treaty of peace was signed at Nanking aboard the flagship of the British fleet. By the terms of this settlement, known as the Treaty of Nanking, China was compelled to cede to Great Britain the island of Hongkong* and open five ports to trade on a treaty basis, namely Amoy, Ningpo, Foochow, Shanghai and Canton. China was also to abolish the trading monopoly of the *co-hong* merchants, establish a fixed tariff schedule, and pay a total indemnity of $21,000,000. Of the total indemnity, $6,000,000 was claimed as payment for the opium confiscated and destroyed by Lin Tse-hsü, $3,000,000 was for debts owed to British nationals by Chinese subjects, and the remaining $12,000,000 was for the cost of the war to Great Britain. Although the treaty implied a semblance of national equality in diplomatic relations, it did not provide for the establishment of direct diplomatic relations in Peking.[26]

*Hongkong had been ceded to Britain by a Chinese official at Canton in January 1841, but this cession had never been recognized by the Imperial Government.

The war had broken out largely because of the opium issue, but the treaty said nothing about it. The opium traffic continued on as large and shameful a scale as formerly, to the great moral and physical harm of the Chinese people.

On October 8, 1843, a second treaty was signed by Great Britain and China, known as the Treaty of the Bogue, which provided for a crude form of extraterritoriality, a conventional tariff of five percent *ad valorem,* and most-favored-nation privileges for Great Britain.[27] With the treaties of 1842 and 1843 the centuries-old status of foreign trade on a treaty-less basis came to an end. Other nations promptly concluded treaties with China whose provisions were similar to those negotiated by Great Britain.

Popular feeling in America was notably hostile to Britain during the Opium War, but the American merchants engaged in the China trade in general sympathized with Britain in her effort to compel China, through the use of force, to place trade on a treaty basis and to establish direct diplomatic relations on a basis of full equality. Actually the United States might have been able to exercise a restraining influence on Britain had she been willing to cooperate with her, but the feeling that Britain could do no right was so deeply ingrained in so many of the people that no Congressman would risk the loss of public favor by advocating such a role for the country. Consequently the entreaties of the China-trade merchants fell on relatively deaf ears, not because they were unworthy of consideration, but basically because to entertain them might entail a measure of cooperation with John Bull, the traditional whipping boy of the nationalists eager for public favor.

On May 25, 1839, eight American merchants resident at Canton drew up a noteworthy memorial, addressed to the U.S. Congress, which complained of the treatment received from the Chinese Government and protested against the Chinese "robbery committed upon British citizens." The memorial suggested that the United States singly or in concert with Great Britain, France, and Holland should take action "to establish commercial relations with this empire upon a safe and honorable footing, such as exists between all friendly powers." It specifically asked for Chinese acquiescence to such matters as the following: the stationing of foreign envoys near the Court at Peking; the promulgation of fixed tariffs on goods; freedom to trade in additional ports besides Canton; compensation for stoppages of legal trade; and criminal punishments for foreigners that would be no more severe than those provided by British or American law. The memorial concluded with the suggestion that all of the above might be obtained through a joint naval demonstration of the principal powers. To quote from the memorial: "In conclusion, we have but to express our candid conviction that the appearance of a naval force from the United States, England, and France, upon the coast of China, would, without bloodshed, obtain from this Government such acknowledgments and treaties as would not only place our country upon a secure footing, but would be mutually beneficial, and greatly increase the extent and importance of our relations with this empire."[28]

A few months later, Thomas Perkins and a group of Massachusetts merchants engaged in the China trade submitted a somewhat similar memorial, except that the unpopular suggestion of cooperation with Great Britain was omitted and a more cautious tone was adopted. This memorial asked the Government to dispatch naval forces to China, but at the same time warned against any action which might cause the Chinese to associate Americans with Englishmen in the impending war. These two memorials may have been responsible for the subsequent dispatch of Commodore Lawrence Kearny to Canton. The only action Congress took was to pass two resolutions asking for inquiries into the China situation. Meanwhile, however, hostilities had broken out between England and China.[29]

Caleb Cushing, a Massachusetts Congressman who later concluded the first American treaty with China, introduced one of the resolutions mentioned above. The views expressed in Cushing's resolution are interesting because they reflect the conventional political attitude toward Britain. "God forbid," he declaimed, "that I should entertain the idea of cooperating with the British Government in the purpose, if purpose it has, of upholding the base cupidity and violence and high-handed infraction of all law, human and divine, which have characterized the operation of the British, individually and collectively, in the seas of China." If England persisted in seeking "to coerce the Chinese by force of arms to submit to be poisoned with opium," he thundered with self-righteous indignation, she could never hope "to receive aid or countenance from the United States in that nefarious enterprise."[30]

Commodore Lawrence Kearny, in command of the frigate *Constellation,* arrived at Canton a few months before the end of the Opium War, ostensibly to protect American lives and property. One of his first actions was to announce through the American consul that the United States would not countenance any opium smuggling under the American flag.[31] This was a genuine gesture, and Kearny meant to enforce his threat. Acting firmly but without employing either threats or force, he was able to obtain payments through Viceroy Ch'i-ying that amounted to several hundred thousand dollars as compensation for Americans whose properties had been damaged or destroyed during the course of the war.

Upon learning that the British and Chinese were negotiating a tariff and trade agreement, Kearney on October 8, 1842, informed Ch'i-ying that he hoped American commercial interests would not be overlooked and that American citizens would "be placed upon the same footing as the merchants of the nation most favored."[32] A week later Ch'i-ying formally acknowledged receipt of Kearny's "polite communication" and noted that the American merchants "have been respectfully observant of the laws." This fact, explained Ch'i-ying, "the august Emperor has clearly recognized, and I, the governor, also well know." How then, declared Ch'i-ying, could he fail to show favor to them. "Decidedly," he pledged, "it shall not be permitted that the American merchants shall come to have a dry stick (that is, their interests shall be attended to)."[33] These were not mere words of procrastination. An imperial decree subsequently opened all the treaty ports to nationals of all countries on terms of perfect equality.

It is generally believed that the Chinese desired to grant most-favored treatment of their own volition for the safeguarding of China's interests, since they realized that the establishment of equal trading privileges for all might serve to restrain other nations from resorting to the employment of force to obtain concessions. Hence, in a very real sense, it was the Chinese themselves who laid down the principle of the most-favored nation and the Open Door policy in China, rather than the statesmen of any Western nations.

38

As a result of pressure from the merchants engaged in the China trade who were becoming extremely articulate about the protection of their profitable interests, President Tyler in 1843 appointed Caleb Cushing to head a special mission for the purpose of concluding a comprehensive commercial arrangement similar to the one negotiated by Great Britain. Congress somewhat begrudgingly appropriated $40,000 for this mission.

Unlike the British, who had had considerable experience in negotiating treaties with practically every state of Africa and Asia, Americans had accumulated very little in the way of wisdom and precedents for dealing with Asiatic peoples. Up to this time the United States had actually concluded only two treaties with Asiatic states. One of these treaties was with Siam and the other, with Muscat.[34] Each of these treaties had been negotiated by Edmond Roberts of New Hampshire.

Roberts had concluded the treaty with Siam in March 1833. Its provisions were similar to those of a treaty which the British had concluded with Siam in 1826. There were to be no duties of any kind, and no governmental interference with trading operations. No mention, however, was made of extraterritorial privileges. Despite the effort of Roberts to obtain the legalization of the opium trade, it was defined in the treaty as contraband. In September 1833 Roberts had also concluded on the island of Zanzibar the treaty with the Sultan of Muscat. This treaty provided for low import duties, no export duties, most-favored-nation privileges, and limited extraterritorial rights for the American consul. These two treaties had been ratified by the Senate in March 1835, and the ratifications had been duly exchanged by Roberts. Roberts died in Macao on June 12, 1836, and consequently was unable to carry out a proposed mission to Japan for the negotiation of a treaty.[35]

Cushing had eagerly solicited the China assignment, and gladly resigned from his Congressional seat to accept it. He assiduously prepared himself for the difficult mission by collecting and reading all available material on China, diplomacy and international law. He even made a strenuous effort to learn the Chinese language, which he abandoned because of its complexities, but he did actually succeed in learning Manchu and being able to speak it with some proficiency. He was deeply conscious of the historic nature of his mission and its direct bearing on the future of American trade with China. In a speech immediately prior to his departure, he explained that he was going to China "in behalf of civilization, and that, if possible, the doors of three hundred millions of Asiatic laborers may be opened to America."[36]

Cushing's instructions, dated May 8, 1843, and signed by Webster, were carefully prepared. He was specifically reminded that he was "a messenger of peace, sent from the greatest power in America to the greatest power in Asia." He was urged to point out to the Chinese the great dissimilarity between the overseas policies of the British and the Americans, and that China had nothing to fear from the United States in the way of aggression. He was cautioned not to do anything that might be construed as an act of subservience, and it was suggested that the threat of going directly to Peking might be very helpful in bringing the local Chinese officials to terms. The crux of the instructions, however, stipulated that he was to obtain most-favored-nation treatment for the United States. "Finally," stated the instructions, "you will signify, in decided terms and a most positive manner, that the Government of the United States would find it impossible to remain on terms of friendship and regard with the Emperor, if greater privileges or commercial facilities should be allowed to the subjects of any other government than should be granted to citizens of the United States."[37] These instructions may be properly regarded as the first official American declaration of a China policy.

Cushing arrived at Macao aboard the warship *Brandywine* on February 24, 1844. Accompanying the *Brandywine* were three other warships, the *Missouri,* the *St. Louis* and the *Perry.* These four warships mounted a total of more than two hundred guns, and there is no question but that they were intended to impress on China that the United States was also a powerful country. Dr. Peter Parker and Rev. E. C. Bridgman, missionaries fluent in the Chinese language, served as Cushing's interpreters.[38]

Cushing brought no gifts with him, for it was feared that they might be regarded as the traditional tribute of vassals, but he did bring along a number of scientific instruments to impress the Chinese with the advancement of the United States and what it had to offer toward the modernization of China. In addition, Cushing carried with him a remarkable letter, signed by President Tyler and addressed to the Emperor. For some reason this letter, apparently written by Webster, was couched in a child's language. "I hope your health is good," it stated. "China is a great empire, extending over a great part of the world. The Chinese are numerous. You have millions and millions of subjects. The twenty-six United States are as large as China, though our people are not as numerous." There was more of this child's talk, which concluded with the hope that the Emperor would conclude an appropriate treaty, signed in his own imperial hand, "so that nothing may happen to disturb the peace between China and America."[39]

Cushing's arrival at Macao was regarded with considerable misgivings by many of the American traders in the area, who feared that he might inadvertently disturb the tolerably satisfactory relations subsisting between them and the Chinese. They were moreover convinced that he could do nothing to improve these relations or obtain privileges which they did not already enjoy.

The presence of the grim American warships in Chinese waters naturally alarmed the Chinese, especially the imperial officials who by this time had come to associate the "barbarians" with flagrant aggression. These officials were extremely reluctant to be a party to the granting of any further concessions. Cushing encountered some initial procrastination and unfriendliness from the local Chinese officials. He did not hesitate to issue a veiled threat to the effect that in the West the refusal to receive envoys was considered "an act of national insult and a just cause for war." He also warned these officials that if authorized officials were not sent to discuss a treaty he would proceed immediately to Peking to deal directly with the Emperor. The threat worked, and special envoys headed by Ch'i-ying finally arrived at Macao to open treaty discussions with him on June 17. The negotiations proceeded without any untoward incidents, and a treaty was signed on July 3 at Wanghia, a suburb of Macao.* His mission completed, Cushing on August 24 departed for the United States, after having been in China for five months.

The Treaty of Wanghia was a comprehensive convention which contained sixteen provisions not included in the Treaty of Nanking that was dictated by the British. Among other things, it provided that American citizens were to have the right of residence and full trading privileges in all the treaty ports, in which there would be fixed tariff and tonnage charges. The most significant provision of

*"Wanghia" is actually a corruption of "Wang-hsia."

the treaty, however, was its clear definition of extraterritoriality*
and its extension to civil cases. This provision stipulated that in
criminal cases Chinese and American officials were to have jurisdiction over their respective nationals. In civil cases involving only
Americans, the American consuls would have full jurisdiction; and
in cases involving both Americans and Chinese, jurisdiction would
be shared jointly by American and Chinese officials.[40] The treaty
also stipulated that Americans involved in the opium traffic would
be tried by Chinese officials "without being entitled to any countenance or protection" from the United States.

The Treaty of Wanghia was a much more advantageous treaty
than the British Treaty of Nanking, and hence served as a model
or master treaty until 1858. Its advantages accrued to the other
nations by virtue of their most-favored-nation privileges. The fundamental principle underlying Cushing's treaty was that American
interests would be protected *ipso facto* by recognizing China as a
sovereign power. Subsequent events, however, were to demonstrate
that it was not enough to recognize China as a sovereign power
and that, on the contrary, it was necessary for China to act as a
responsible sovereign power.

One immediate result of the conclusion of the treaties described
above was the rise of foreign colonies in the five treaty ports. These
colonies were located in marked-out areas, generally known as foreign settlements or foreign concessions. In these areas the foreigners were permitted to establish their own municipal councils and
in general to regulate their own affairs. The most important of the
foreign areas was the International Settlement in Shanghai, which
started out as a British area but was later expanded to include all
foreigners. The French withdrew from it in 1862, however, and
established their own settlement in another quarter of the city.

*Extraterritoriality, or extraterritorial jurisdiction, is the privilege of a
state to have its nationals tried under its own laws and by its own representatives abroad, usually consuls. Only weak and backward countries, with
primitive and corrupt legal systems, granted this concession, and generally
under duress. In the case of the above treaty, however, the Chinese granted
the privilege of their own volition, for to them it seemed to comport with
the Chinese tradition and custom that a government should always assume
responsibility for the actions of its nationals abroad. Because of the length
of the term "extraterritoriality," it is sometimes shortened to "extrality."

With five ports opened to trade on a treaty basis and the most irksome of the restrictions now removed, trading activities increased considerably. Shanghai rapidly became the most important trading center for foreigners and Canton soon lost its former importance. Considerable trading activity also developed in Amoy, but Ningpo and Foochow failed to develop as important centers of foreign trade.

The Treaty of Wanghia, together with subsequent imperial edicts which promulgated religious toleration, opened the way for increased missionary activity. American missionaries were the most active in propagating the Protestant faith in the open ports. From 1807 to 1851 a total of 150 Protestant missionaries arrived in China, of whom 88 came from the United States, 47 from England, and 15 from continental Europe.[41] As has been mentioned,* the American missionaries came to exercise considerable influence on the molding of American policy with regard to China. Their hostility to the opium traffic, for example, strongly influenced the policy of the American Government.

Despite the general treaty settlement, China continued to regard herself as a nation above others. In actual practice the diplomatic equality desired by the Western powers remained to be obtained. Foreigners, including consuls and diplomats, were not permitted to set foot in the capital, Peking, and were confined to the treaty ports. The diplomatic relations with the "barbarians" continued to be handled by the especially appointed imperial high commissioners, stationed in the treaty ports.† Despite the abject military defeat China had suffered, these officials continued to manifest a disdainful attitude toward all foreign diplomats, who found it extremely difficult to obtain audiences with them, even on matters of great import and urgency. Perhaps this was decadent China's way, unrealistic as it was, of indicating to the "barbarians" that they were unwelcome and that the country wished to be rid of them.

Prior to the first general treaty settlement, the United States and other countries with China interests had been almost wholly guided by commercial considerations. As a result of the British

* *See* above, p. 31.
† *See* above, pp. 31-32.

occupation of Hongkong, the China policies of the interested nations now became deeply influenced by political considerations. In possession of Hongkong, Great Britain enjoyed a distinct advantage over her rivals who, in fact, became preoccupied lest this outpost might become a springboard for the transformation of China into another India.

Unable and unwilling to rely on the employment of force or the threat to use it like Great Britain, and to a lesser extent France, the United States was compelled to depend entirely on the utilization of skillful diplomacy for the protection and enhancement of American interests. Many Americans actually feared that China might be dismembered by Great Britain, either singly or in concert with France and other aggressive European powers, with the result that American merchants would be subjected to ruinous discrimination and perhaps even outright exclusion in the dismembered areas. The State Department consequently began to espouse the policy which had been developed by the early American traders, namely the preservation of the territorial and administrative integrity of China and equal trading privileges for the nationals of all countries.

In the 1850's the interest of the American Government in the entire Far East was more intense than at any other period in the nineteenth century except 1898, when the war with Spain was fought and the Philippines became an American problem. The territorial expansion of the United States to the Pacific coast had been completed. The Oregon Territory as far north as the forty-ninth parallel had been obtained as a result of the compromise treaty with Great Britain in 1846. The vast regions of California and New Mexico had been acquired in 1848 as a result of the victorious war against Mexico. The West Coast now seemed to truly bind the United States to the lands of the Far East, and China loomed ever larger in the dreams of American traders and manufacturers. To these elements the possession of the West Coast entailed a certain geographical advantage because of its relative proximity to the great potential markets of China, Japan and other populous Asiatic countries.

Meanwhile, the American share of the trade in Shanghai was increasing rapidly. Added to the enlarged interests of American merchants and their glowing expectations of the future were the

44

highly successful American Protestant missions which also had interests to safeguard and promote. The policy of the American Government naturally reflected these enlarged Pacific interests. In this reinvigorated policy the Government strove to open additional treaty ports in China, Japan and elsewhere, to secure more favorable trading arrangements, and to obtain coaling stations.

In the years immediately following the conclusion of the Opium War and the general treaty settlement, the Chinese and foreigners got along poorly. Despite the extensive concessions which had been obtained, the foreigners were far from satisfied and desired even greater privileges and rights. The Chinese, on the other hand, resented the extent of the concessions that had already been granted and generally refused to abide by them. The opening of the treaty ports, for example, was delayed by the Chinese; Canton was not opened until 1849. Even if the Chinese officials had been sincerely desirous of living up to the terms of the treaties, their task would have been extremely difficult because of the increasing anti-foreignism of the Chinese inhabiting the coastal areas who had been exposed to the rough contact of the Westerners. Unpleasant incidents between Chinese and foreigners became common occurrences. These disturbances were partly a result of the hatred and contempt of the Chinese who persisted in regarding all foreigners as "barbarians," and partly a result of the increasing arrogance of many foreigners, if not most of them, who looked down upon the Chinese as inferiors and manifested an almost flagrant disregard of Chinese laws and customs.

The most serious cause of friction was the refusal of the Chinese officials to abide by the terms of the treaties and to deal with the diplomatic representatives of the Western powers as equals. Especially galling to these representatives, including the American agent, was the arbitrary attitude of Yeh Ming-ch'en, who had been appointed special commissioner to handle relations with them.

It was doubtless as a result of their common resentment against China's refusal to respect the treaties and their distrust of each other's ulterior motives, not to mention other political factors, that the powers finally came around to the policy of a united diplomatic front against China, which usually goes by the name of the "cooperative policy." The desirability of such a policy to protect the true interests of the United States was ably argued by Humphrey Marshall, commissioner in China from 1852 to 1854, in his dispatches to the State Department. Above all, however, he stressed that "the higher interests of the United States are involved in sustaining China" rather than in permitting her to become "the theatre of a widespread anarchy, and ultimately the prey of European ambition."[42] The first American diplomatic agent to give full effect to the approved cooperative policy was Robert McLane, who succeeded Marshall in 1855 and served until 1857.

The first real test of the cooperative policy came with the question of treaty revision. The American and French treaties provided for revision after a twelve year period, and since Great Britain and Russia enjoyed most-favored-nation privileges they agreed to join in the united front for revision of all the treaties. Efforts to obtain Chinese acquiescence to treaty revision encountered the now familiar tactic of evasion and procrastination. In 1854 Yeh Ming-ch'en outrightly denied the validity of Britain's claim to treaty revision, notwithstanding her most-favored-nation clause.

Dr. Peter Parker, a medical missionary who had resided in China for some time and was then serving as a U.S. diplomatic representative, was instructed to make arrangements for the revision of the American treaty which would provide for right of residence at Peking for the American diplomatic agent and the elimination of all restrictions on individual liberties of foreign residents.[43] Parker arrived at Canton in December 1855 to open discussions with Yeh, but was not even able to obtain an interview with him. At Foochow Parker succeeded in holding discussions with the ranking Chinese official, but was unable to obtain a commitment on treaty revision.

Two serious incidents now occurred to worsen the strained relations between the foreign diplomatic representatives and the Chinese. In July 1856 a French missionary, Father Auguste Chapdelaine, was brutally murdered in the interior of Kwangsi province. The anger of the French was not in the least calmed by the Chinese contention that Father Chapdelaine had been murdered in the interior of the country, outside the treaty ports, where he had no right to be. Three months later, on October 8, Viceroy Yeh ordered the river police to seize some allegedly notorious pirates aboard the lorcha *Arrow*, a Chinese-owned vessel flying the Brit-

46

ish flag. As a result of the failure of Yeh to give adequate satisfaction for this affront to the British flag, a technical state of war came into existence between China and Great Britain on October 23. Because of the outbreak of the Indian Mutiny in May of the following year, 1857, the British were compelled to delay the initiation of military action. In the summer of 1857, however, they attacked the barrier forts of Canton and shelled the residence of the Viceroy.

In the course of these initial hostilities, the Chinese fired on a craft flying the American flag. Commodore James Armstrong immediately retaliated by bombarding the forts. The incident was happily closed when the Chinese offered a suitable apology. President Pierce was determined that American naval officers in Chinese waters should adhere to a policy of "forbearance." Upon learning of the incident he promptly condemned the action of Armstrong.

The American diplomatic representatives in China were much more sanguine than either the President or the Secretary of State. Prior to the *Arrow* incident Robert McLane had expressed the opinion that "Diplomatic intercourse can only be had with this government at the cannon's mouth."[44] Although the United States regarded the miltary objectives of the British as just and expedient, Secretary Marcy nevertheless informed Parker that their ulterior motives went beyond the legitimate interests of the United States. Marcy advocated a policy of protecting American citizens and their properties with naval forces, but at the same time insisted that the United States should have no part of the British quarrel with China. There should not be, he said, "any serious disturbance to our amicable relations with China."[45]

France now joined Britain in the war against China, and these two nations invited Russia and the United States to cooperate in the joint punitive expedition.* Both nations refused to employ force against China, but their diplomatic representatives in China were instructed to obtain by peaceful means whatever privileges the French and British might obtain by force. It was not until December 1857 that the French and British had assembled sufficient forces to launch full-scale military operations. Meanwhile,

*France and Great Britain, who had fought as allies against Russia in the Crimean War, were temporarily united by an unofficial entente.

Yeh had failed to recognize the great danger that was threatening China and he refused to take any steps of a conciliatory nature. In the fighting that followed, the Chinese forces once again were no match for the might of the West, and by January 1858 Canton was occupied. The French and British then moved northward and bombarded the Taku forts on May 20. These forts were easily demolished, and on May 30 Tientsin was occupied. With the Anglo-French forces now only some sixty miles from Peking, the alarmed Emperor hastily appointed commissioners to negotiate treaties in Tientsin.

Although the French and British had done the actual fighting, the Chinese negotiated the first treaty revisions with the Russian and American diplomatic representatives, perhaps in the hope of somehow dividing the Western powers. The American treaty was negotiated by William B. Reed, envoy extraordinary and minister plenipotentiary, and provided for the opening of two additional ports and toleration for the Christian religion. It also stipulated that if other powers obtained the right of stationing permanent diplomatic representatives in Peking, this right would also accrue to the United States. The British treaty, the most advantageous of all the treaties, was concluded last and signed on June 26.

Since all the powers were granted most-favored-nation privileges, the advantages of the British treaty accrued to each of them. The principal provisions of the Tientsin treaties enjoyed by all the powers in common granted the right to station resident ministers at Peking or at least their right to have access to the capital, the opening of nine additional treaty ports to trade, the right of foreign vessels to trade along the Yangtze River, and the right of foreigners to travel in the interior of China, provided passports issued by the foreign consuls were countersigned by local Chinese officials. Common to all of the powers was the provision granting complete religious liberty, stipulated as follows: "The principles of the Christian religion as professed by the Protestant and Roman Catholic churches, are recognized as teaching men to do good, and to do to others as they would have others do to them. Hereafter, those who quietly profess and teach these doctrines shall not be harassed or persecuted on account of their faith." This provision also stipulated that no foreigner "or Chinese convert" was to be "interferred with or molested."[46] The British treaty further provided for the payment by China of a total indemnity of 4,000,000 taels, while the French treaty provided for an indemnity payment of 2,000,000 taels.*

The provision guaranteeing freedom of religion to Christians had significant repercussions on China. In effect this provision amounted to the extraction of a guarantee that the Chinese Government would protect the missionaries and their converts. Hence it indirectly operated to make the Chinese Government a party, however unwilling, to the spread of Christianity and at the same time deprived it of a measure of control over its own Christian subjects. From the Chinese standpoint, Christianity was a disruptive influence inasmuch as its doctrine contradicted many of the traditional cultural and moral values which had long contributed to the stability of Chinese society. Many Chinese believed strongly that Christianity was a political as well as religious weapon of the West and that the aim of the missionaries was to make the culture of China subservient to Christianity.[47] Far from making the Chinese more amenable to the influx of Christianity, then, the effect of the Tientsin treaties was to intensify their hatred for the alien religion of the "barbarians."

A provision of the Tientsin treaties which has evoked considerable controversy among historians was the legalization of the opium trade. The attitude of William B. Reed, the envoy who negotiated the American treaty, is of interest in this connection. He had been instructed not to seek the legalization of the opium trade, and hence the treaty he negotiated made no mention of opium. Later, however, after having discussed the matter with Lord Elgin, the English diplomatic representative, he came to the view that "any course is better than that which is now pursued," and accordingly he accepted the legalization of the opium trade in principle. Actually the legalization of the opium trade was a result of British insistence. The British argument was that although the traffic in this drug was deplorable it could not be stopped, principally because of the inefficiency and corruption of the Chinese Government, and hence it was best to legalize it for the sake of better control and revenue.[48]

After the conclusion of the Tientsin treaties the diplomatic representatives of the four powers withdrew to Shanghai where addi-

*The tael was the equivalent of one and a third ounces of silver.

49

tional commercial and tariff regulations were agreed upon. It was also agreed that China should establish a uniform customs service at all the treaty ports. A British national was subsequently appointed director of the customs service, as an agent of the Chinese Government. The new customs service proved to be a model of efficiency and honesty, and it turned over a substantial revenue to the Chinese Government.

The Tientsin treaties did not bring peace to China, and the Chinese will to resist had not been broken by the West's display of its vastly superior military power. The Imperial Court continued to seethe with anti-foreign sentiment, while the local officials remained defiant and contemptuous of the Westerner who persisted in forcing himself deeper and deeper into China.

Because of the deliberate procrastination of the Chinese officials with regard to the exchange of the Tientsin treaty ratifications, the British and French again resorted to the use of force in what is sometimes referred to as the Second Anglo-French War on China. Hostilities were initiated in June 1859 when Admiral Sir James Hope tried to make his way up the Pei River to force the ratification of the English treaty at Peking. He was repulsed by the Chinese shore batteries, however, and wounded in the action. He might have suffered a catastrophic defeat had not Commodore Josiah Tattnall, aboard the U.S.S. *Toeywan,* which was in the area at the time, come to his prompt rescue, allegedly "not to assist him in the fight, but to give his sympathy to a wounded brother officer whom he saw about to suffer a most mortifying and unexpected defeat." Tattnall justified his unneutral act on the ground, "Blood is thicker than water."[49]

In August 1860 combined British and French forces battered the Taku forts and occupied the cities of Tientsin and Peking. Seeing that all was lost, and fearful of the "barbarian's" vengeance, the Emperor and his court fled to the neighboring province of Jehol. The enraged Anglo-French forces looted the ancient capital and burnt the historic old Summer Palace located on the outskirts. The order for the destruction of the Summer Palace was issued by Lord Elgin and the British military commander, who felt that some "great reprisal" was necessary to avenge alleged Chinese violations of the rules of civilized warfare. Of the wanton destruction, a noted Western authority on Peking has written: "The burning

50

palaces lighted the sky for two nights and sent black clouds of smoke drifting towards frightened Peking for two days, while the work of destruction was pushed to the farthest pavilions in the folds of the hills."[50] E. R. Scidmore, in *China, the Long-Lived Empire,* laments that "the Summer Palace held the greatest and richest collection of any art museum in the world when the soldiers were turned loose in it." As a result of the "senseless, brutal, ignorant destruction," he writes: "Not one-tenth of the treasures were saved to enrich the world; five-tenths of the precious fragilities were smashed by the butts of muskets or hurled about by skylarking soldiers, and the rest were consumed and shivered in the final explosions."[51]

The futility of resisting the vengeful might of the West now became apparent even to the most obstinate of the imperial advisers. Prince Kung, brother of the Emperor, hastened to sign a new treaty, the Peking Convention, with the plenipotentiaries of Britain and France. This convention stipulated that China would enforce all the articles of the Tientsin treaties and in addition pay all the costs of the Anglo-French expedition, amounting to 8,000,000 taels. China was further required to cede to Great Britain a strip of land on the mainland opposite Hongkong, known as Kowloon, and Tientsin was opened as a treaty port.

Although the United States and Russia had again abstained from participating in the fighting, their diplomatic representatives had been instructed to follow on the heels of the Anglo-French forces to obtain through negotiation any advantages that the belligerents might acquire. The refusal of the United States and Russia to employ force doubtless ingratiated these two powers with the Chinese, while the French and British naturally came to be regarded with increased odium and distrust. Actually the American diplomatic representatives in China from 1857 to 1860 were personally in favor of the use of force, and it was the State Department that insisted on a policy of ameliorating relations by conciliation and negotiation.

CHAPTER THREE

The Reopening of Japan to Western Intercourse

Stretching in a long arc some fifteen hundred miles in length off the coast of northeast Asia lie the mountainous islands of Japan. Although several hundred islands comprise the Japanese archipelago, the four largest islands account for about 95 percent of the total area, and one island alone, Honshu, has well over half the total area. At the dawn of the Christian era the Japanese people were in a state of barbarism, but beginning about the sixth century they came in broad contact with the resplendent civilization of China and within a few centuries had developed a civilization of a high order.

Japan was almost unknown to Americans in 1789, when the present American Republic was inaugurated. As American trade with China developed and expanded, and as American whaling and other seafaring operations grew to sizable proportions, large numbers of American vessels approached or passed through Japanese waters. Until the middle of the nineteenth century, however, Japan remained for most Americans an unknown land of mystery and at the same time fascination. Like the Kingdom of Korea, Japan was sealed off from the outside world by the rigid edicts of its rulers who were determined to keep the "barbarians," as the Westerners were then known, at a safe and respectable distance.

At the time American ships began approaching the shores of Japan in increasing numbers, the country was under a unique system of administration, commonly referred to as "dual government." This system had been firmly established by the Tokugawa clan early in the seventeenth century after it had succeeded in wresting military power from its rivals in the culmination of a long period of internal strife and bloodshed. Under the Tokugawa system actual power was exercised by the Tokugawas themselves, from their capital in Edo, now known as Tokyo. At the same time, the Emperor, residing in the ancient city of Kyoto,* was permitted to remain on his throne as a symbol of divine authority in whose name the Tokugawas theoretically exercised their dictatorial authority. In effect the Tokugawa system was one of centralized feudalism with the Tokugawa clan holding absolute military and political power. The Tokugawa dictator held the title of Shōgun, and his administrative system was known as the Bakufu, or, as it is commonly called by Westerners, the Shogunate.

During the two and a half centuries of Tokugawa rule, which came to an end in 1867, the country was regulated by a rigid policy of seclusion and exclusion whose fundamental purpose was to isolate Japan from the aggressive intentions of the West by hermetically sealing its shores and coastal areas. Under this policy no Japanese were permitted under any circumstances to leave the islands of Japan and no Japanese craft were permitted to engage in any operations other than coastal fishing and trade. Conversely, no foreigners were permitted to set foot on Japanese soil and even the profession of Christianity by Japanese was punishable by death. At the height of the enforcement of this policy, even foreign books were prohibited from circulation in the country.

The only exceptions to the inclusiveness of the above policy were the Dutch and Chinese, who were permitted to maintain small footholds in the Nagasaki area for the purpose of engaging in a limited amount of trade under minutely prescribed conditions. Since they were Westerners, the Dutch were subjected to particularly severe and humiliating restrictions, which they tolerated only because of the determination to preserve their commercial privilege. At the same time, however, the Dutch performed a service of a non-commercial nature, namely that of keeping the Bakufu reasonably well informed of political developments in the Western world. This service was not unappreciated by the Bakufu. It was from the Dutch, for example, that the Bakufu learned of the

* The transliteration of "Kyoto" should be "Kyōto" to preserve its correct pronunciation under the Hepburn system. To facilitate reading ease, however, this city and others in Japan that are well known to Americans are written without the long-vowel marks even though the Hepburn system may call for them.

Opium War between Great Britain and China and of other Western aggressions in Asia.

Actually the seclusion-exclusion policy, which dated from the establishment and consolidation of the Tokugawa system in the early years of the seventeenth century, had been in process of gradual disintegration since the latter part of the eighteenth century. Many of the powerful feudal lords (daimyō) of the western sections of Japan and the island of Kyūshū had begun to encourage the study of practical Western sciences and the Dutch language as a means of unlocking their secrets. Even the Bakufu had begun to somewhat relax its stern and inflexible enforcement of the policy. More significant than this weakening of the seclusion-exclusion policy, and doubtless a principal factor contributing to it, was the silent but inexorable economic change that had been taking place since the consolidation of Tokugawa rule. This was basically a change from a feudal rice economy to a handicraft economy, and in the process new classes of merchants and "financiers" had arisen who began to chafe under the minute and restraining feudal regulations of the Bakufu. By the middle of the nineteenth century, then, internal economic and social changes had in effect created conditions making for the collapse of the feudal system, the breakdown of the seclusion-exclusion policy, and the opening of the country to broad foreign intercourse. By that time, moreover, the Imperial Court and powerful western clans which had never become reconciled to the Tokugawa overlordship had become openly rebellious and were intriguing to bring about the demise of the Bakufu and the restoration of actual power to the Emperor.

It was not until the 1830's that the United States Government began to express concrete interest in breaching Japan's seclusion policy and establishing treaty relations with her. The first prominent American to hint at the inevitable opening of Japan to intercourse was John Quincy Adams, who declared it to be "the right, and even the duty, of Christian nations to open the ports of Japan, and the duty of Japan to assent, on the ground that no nation has a right more than any man has to withdraw its private contribution to the welfare of the whole."[1]

Long before the American Government became interested in

54

Japan, however, enterprising American seamen on their own initiative had sought to break through the heavy curtain of seclusion. An American ship may have entered Japanese waters as early as May 1, 1790, but nothing is known of its identity or any other details. Hence the first American vessels known to have passed through the Shōgun's seas were probably the *Lady Washington* and the *Grace* which sailed by the southern coast of Japan on May 6, 1791, en route to China.[2] It is recorded that they attempted, without any success, to dispose of some sea otter pelts to the Japanese.[3] Not until 1797 did another American ship enter Japanese waters, when the *Eliza,* commanded by Captain Stewart, arrived at Nagasaki as a chartered vessel of the Dutch, who were striving to circumvent the British blockade of the Netherlands because of her involvement in war against Britain on the side of Napoleon. In 1800, and again in 1803, Captain Stewart on his own account attempted to discharge some cargoes at Nagasaki, but on each of these occasions he was frustrated by officials who inflexibly enforced the edicts of the Shōgun to the effect that no trade would be conducted with any Westerners other than the Dutch.

To summarize, between 1791 and 1807 some fourteen American vessels are known to have put in at Japanese ports. Nine of these ships were in the chartered service of the Dutch, and the other five were engaged in private enterprise. For some thirty years, between 1808 and 1837, no American vessels are known to have appeared in Japanese waters. Between 1837 and 1845 only one American vessel attempted to put in at a Japanese port. After 1845, however, swarms of American vessels roamed the seas adjacent to Japan, and in a four-year period alone, between 1845 and 1849, at least twelve American vessels entered the forbidden Shōgun's seas for one purpose or another.[4]

By the decade of the 1830's, as has been indicated, the government in Washington was beginning to take a serious view of the necessity of breaking down Japan's seclusion and concluding a treaty with her. Andrew Jackson was the first president to take positive action toward that end, and in 1835 Edmund Roberts was commissioned to proceed to Japan and negotiate a treaty of amity and commerce. In that year Roberts departed from Washington on his mission. He carried with him a letter from President Jackson to the Emperor of Japan and a number of gifts together with authorization to spend an additional $10,000 for presents if it were necessary. Roberts was filled with enthusiasm at the prospect of being the first to unlock the doors of Japan, but that country was not to be easily unlocked, as many representatives of several nations had already found out, and as many more were to discover to their chagrin. On the way Roberts exchanged ratifications of treaties that had been concluded with Muscat and Siam, but en route to Japan he died at Macao in June 1836 and hence was unable to attempt the completion of his important mission.[5] Even had Providence given him more years, it is doubtful if he could have succeeded in completing his mission, for circumstances, which generally are the arbiter of things, had not yet decreed that the hour had arrived for this historic event.

Meanwhile, an American trader in China, C. W. King, a younger partner of one of the leading trading firms in Canton, Olyphant and Company, was dreaming private dreams of succeeding where others had failed. Utilizing seven shipwrecked Japanese nationals who had been assembled in Canton, King conceived the tempting idea of combining humanitarianism with religious propagation and commerce. His project was a simple one: to return the shipwrecked Japanese nationals to their homeland. His thought was that the Japanese authorities would be so grateful for this humanitarian action that they could be induced to open their country to commercial intercourse and permit the propagation of Christianity by Protestant missionaries. Under his initiative the *Morrison* was fitted and dispatched to Japan, carrying aboard the precious cargo of Japanese nationals. Although the ship carried no armaments and was on the most peaceful mission imaginable, it was fired upon by the Edo forts when it entered the bay. Unable to make a landing the ship withdrew and departed to southern Japan where it attempted to put in at Kagoshima, but it was again fired upon. Abandoning all hope of being able to land the shipwrecked Japanese nationals, the *Morrison* then returned to China.[6] Again the "barbarian" had been expelled from the Shōgun's seas.

Another notable attempt to return shipwrecked Japanese nationals was made by the whaler *Manhattan* in 1845. On this occasion the captain of the vessel, M. Cooper, had on board eleven Japanese nationals who had been picked up on a barren Pacific island. En route he had picked up another eleven Japanese who were clinging to a floating wreck.[7] This time the "barbarian" was courteously received in Edo Bay. The captain was permitted to discharge his cargo of Japanese nationals and the Japanese officials on their account gave him provisions and some lacquered ware and crockery. Although Captain Cooper was permitted to linger in the bay area for four days, none of his crew was permitted to set foot on shore. The vessel then sailed away and resumed its whaling operations.

By this time the large number of American vessels passing through or near Japanese waters had created a situation which the American Government could hardly ignore much longer. Some of these vessels were wrecked by storms or driven to the shores of Japan, with the result that many Americans were forced to seek haven and succor on Japanese soil. Since the law of Japan was specific and inexorable insofar as the presence of foreigners in Japan was concerned, regardless of whether an act of God had forced them on her shores, these unfortunates were invariably imprisoned and subjected to severe treatment and even indignities. The time had come when the American Government had no alternative but to recognize its obligation to take adequate steps for the protection of its nationals whose misfortune it might be to fall in Japanese hands. Added to this humanitarian concern was the pressure being exerted on Congressmen by the China-trade interests which were demanding measures that would make a legal port-of-call available in Japan as a stop-off center for the thriving China trade.

Partly reflecting the demands of the commercial interests, a resolution was introduced in the House of Representatives by Zedoc Pratt of New York in February 1845 which called for the immediate negotiation of treaties with Korea as well as Japan.* "The day and the hour have now arrived," said the resolution, "for turning the enterprise of our merchants and seamen into the harbors and markets of those long secluded countries." Pratt seems to have caught a vision of the great future importance of Japan. "With a population exceeding fifty millions (about thrice as numerous as the whole population of the United States)," declared his resolution, "the Japanese empire combines a degree of civilization and power that may well render it respectable and formidable among

---

*Korea at this time was also committed to a seclusion policy as strict as that of Japan. The opening of Korea to foreign intercourse is discussed in some detail in Chapter IX.

the nations of the world."[8] His estimate of Japan's population was greatly exaggerated, however, for at that time it was actually only about half of what he imagined.

Although Pratt's resolution was tabled, interest in Japan did not subside. By the spring of 1845 the American Government was prepared to undertake a serious effort at opening Japan to intercourse. In May of that year the State Department instructed Commodore James Biddle, commanding the East India squadron, to place his vessels at the disposal of the American diplomatic representative in China, Alexander Everett, should he deem it opportune to attempt the negotiation of a treaty with Japan and hence desire transport there. In ill health, Everett transferred his treaty-making powers to Biddle, who then proceeded with two vessels, the *Columbus* and the *Vincennes,* to Edo Bay, where he arrived on July 20, 1846. Contrary to what he had anticipated, Biddle was received in a most hostile manner and the Shōgun's officials informed him that it was pointless for him to talk of a treaty since the supreme law of Japan was clear and explicit on the point that no foreign intercourse would be tolerated with any Westerners other than the Dutch. A curt letter was handed to him, which stated: "The Emperor positively refuses the permission you desire. He earnestly advises you to depart immediately and to consult your own safety in not appearing again upon our coast."[9] On one occasion Biddle was struck or pushed by a lowly samurai, but he magnanimously refrained from retaliation of any sort. Finally realizing that nothing could be accomplished by further bickering with the officials, and at the same time doubtless recognizing that the "hour" had not yet arrived for attempting the breakdown of Japan's seclusion, Biddle departed from Japanese waters and returned to China.

Meanwhile, there was increasing concern for the welfare of shipwrecked American sailors who had been driven by fate to the shores of Japan and been imprisoned in accordance with the law of that land. Broad tales, most of them true but many a bit far-fetched, began to circulate widely to the effect that Americans imprisoned in Japan were being tortured and subjected to the grossest of indignities. In February 1848 Dr. Peter Parker, then in charge of the Peking legation, informed Secretary of State Buchanan that the survivors of the whaler *Lawrence,* which had been wrecked off the Kurile Islands in May 1846, had been held in confinement since July 1846 and subjected to extremely cruel treatment.[10] It was also learned from the Dutch consul in Canton that at least fifteen survivors of the whaler *Lagoda* were being held as prisoners in Japan.

In 1849 Commodore James Glynn arrived at Nagasaki in an aggressive mood in command of the *Preble* and succeeded, despite the efforts of the Japanese officials to frustrate him, in obtaining the release of thirteen survivors of the *Lagoda*.[11] He also took on board an American adventurer by the name of McDonald, who had made his way to Japan and found employment there as a teacher of English.[12] This McDonald may therefore be considered to have been the first American teacher of English in Japan. The rescued seamen, filled with bitterness, more than confirmed the reports of their cruel treatment, although it should be noted that their treatment had not been cruel by the Japanese standards of the time. In that same year, 1849, the survivors of the whaler *Trident,* which like the *Lagoda* had been wrecked off the Kuriles, were rescued through the assistance of the Dutch. Upon the completion of his assignment, Glynn returned to Washington, where he presented in writing to President Fillmore his suggestions concerning the opening of Japan to trade.[13]

By the 1850's the cumulative effect of the accounts of indignities and cruelties suffered by shipwrecked Americans imprisoned in Japan was beginning to be felt in Washington. The Executive Department of the Government was now beginning to feel that American honor as well as humanitarian concern for shipwrecked sailors was at stake and that forceful measures would be necessary to compel the Japanese authorities to comply with fundamental practices common in the "civilized" world.

The discovery of gold in California in 1848 and the rapid subsequent settlement of the Pacific Coast stimulated an accentuated and fresh interest in the Pacific and the Far East. With the acquisition of the entire Pacific Coast and the apparent fulfillment of continental "Manifest Destiny" the decade of the 1850's produced a new crop of expansionists who came to look upon the Pacific as the logical highway for the further and inevitable expansion of American power and influence. As has been indicated, American interest in the lands of the Pacific area attained an intensity in the 1850's which was not again equalled until the late 1890's. It was in the 1850's that American whaling operations in the North Pacific area reached their peak and it was in this decade that the China trade expanded to new volumes that seemed to presage an almost limitless future expansion. As a result of all this maritime activity, the Shōgun's seas became literally infested with American vessels. In one year alone, 1850, for example, a Japanese official is reported to have counted 86 American whaling vessels which passed in view from a single point in Japan.[14]

Biddle may have been correct in deducing in 1846 that the historic hour had not yet arrived for attempting the opening of Japan, but now it was apparent that the immutable destiny of America, together with silent but irresistible forces within Japan, were combining to strike the historic hour. Indeed the Washington Government had already taken steps to satisfy the demands of vested American interests and at the same time to protect the nation's honor and answer the call of destiny. After serious discussions had been held on the cabinet level, President Fillmore instructed his Secretary of State, Daniel Webster, to take immediate steps to bring about the conclusion of a treaty of amity and commerce with Japan. On June 10, 1851, Secretary Webster commissioned Commodore John H. Aulick, Commander of the East India Squadron, to attempt the conclusion of such a treaty. Glynn had hoped for this assignment, but he was apparently passed over in favor of Aulick because the latter outranked him in naval seniority. [15]

Aulick had personally requested this assignment. Fired with enthusiasm, he departed for Canton on June 8, 1851, in command of the new steam frigate *Susquehanna*. He spent some time at Canton assembling from the vessels in Asian waters a squadron of sufficient size to awe the Japanese, but before he was able to proceed to Japan he received a curt notification that his commission had been withdrawn and that he was to return to Washington to answer certain charges concerning breach of decorum. These charges were apparently the work of an enemy in the consular service.[16] Ill and broken in spirits, Aulick early in 1853 took passage on a British mail steamer for the return home via London. He was subsequently cleared of the charges against him, but mean-

60

while Commodore Perry had not only been commissioned to replace him but had sailed for Japan.[17]

In recalling Aulick, Washington had doubtless concluded that the success of the Japan mission demanded more thorough preparations. Among other reasons for the de-commissioning of Aulick, moreover, Washington had apparently given sober second thought to the personal qualifications required of the man heading such an important mission. It was decided that Commodore Matthew Calbraith Perry, because of his temperament and experience, was much better qualified to insure the success of the historic mission.

Perry coveted this assignment, partly because of his personal desire for additional fame, but also because of his nationalist conviction that the destiny of America lay in the Pacific and that the opening of Japan constituted but one, albeit an extremely important, step in the fulfillment of the country's destiny in that area.

The most thorough preparations were made, for Perry was not the type of man to undertake any mission that might end in failure because of any shortcomings or omissions on his part. Specialists were carefully selected, books of every description dealing with Japan were collected and studied, and navigation charts were purchased from the Dutch. Even American manufacturers were called on for samples of their products, which might be given to the Japanese with the object of arousing their admiration for American technological development and at the same time stimulate their desire to obtain them through trade.

Perry's instructions, originally intended for Aulick, were signed by the ad interim Secretary of State, C. M. Conrad. They throbbed with historical consciousness and the exuberance of a young and vigorous nation: "Recent events—the navigation of the ocean by steam, the acquisition and rapid settlement by this country of a vast territory on the Pacific, the discovery of gold in that region, the rapid communication established across the isthmus which separates the two oceans—have practically brought the countries of the east in closer proximity to our own; although the consequences of these events have scarcely begun to be felt, the intercourse between them has already greatly increased, and no limits can be assigned to its future extension." The instructions stressed that the Japanese were to be reminded that Japan and the United States had in effect become neighbors, and that it was up to Japan whether they would be friendly neighbors.[18]

Perry's instructions stipulated that the aim of the mission was to obtain a treaty which would (1) guarantee protection for shipwrecked American seamen, (2) make available ports for refitting and refuelling of vessels, and (3) open one or more ports for the conduct of trade on a dignified basis. The instructions stressed the pacific nature of the mission and urged Perry to be courteous and conciliatory with the Japanese. At the same time, he was to be firm on fundamental points, and if the Japanese refused to at least guarantee protection and humane treatment for shipwrecked Americans and to otherwise relax the seclusion policy, he was to warn them that the United States of its own accord would insist on humane treatment for shipwrecked Americans and that cruelties inflicted on them would bring prompt American retaliation.[19]

On November 14, 1852, the indomitable Commodore weighed anchor at Norfolk, Virginia, and set forth on his epoch-making mission. In his possession were his credentials signed by President Fillmore together with a letter from the President to the Emperor of Japan.* In addition he carried along a number of gifts and samples of American-manufactured articles. At Canton he took on board the noted Dr. Samuel Wells Williams to serve as his chief interpreter.

On May 23, 1853, Perry arrived with his squadron at the port of Naha (Napha) on the island of Okinawa of the Ryūkyū group. He remained in this area for some time, encountering considerable opposition, which was overcome, however, through his policy of firmness. While sojourning at Okinawa, he took the *Susquehanna* to the Bonin Islands, where he conducted surveys for a naval base and coaling station.[20] He finally weighed anchor at Naha on July 2, 1853, and sailed for Japan to execute the main purpose of his mission.

On July 8, 1853, nearly eight months after his departure from Norfolk, Perry arrived in Edo Bay with a formidable squadron of four warships, the decks of all cleared for action. The squadron passed in view of the forts on the mainland and dropped anchor off the village of Uraga without any incidents. However, a large number of Japanese boats soon pressed around his ships, much to

*Perry and the U.S. Government were manifestly in considerable ignorance with respect to the exact nature of the dual government then in existence in Japan and particularly of the actual relationship between the Shōgun and the Emperor.

62

the annoyance of Perry, who immediately issued a warning that if they did not promptly withdraw he would order his guns to open fire on them. The threat sufficed to keep the craft at a distance.

The arrival of Perry's ships threw the city of Edo and the neighboring areas into an uproar. The thick black smoke belching from the flagship *Susquehanna* greatly awed the Japanese, as it was the first time they had seen a steamer. It was apparent to the onlooking Japanese that these grim-looking vessels were on no ordinary mission and that destiny had brought them face to face with the visible symbols of a mighty overseas force.

Perry's first contacts were with minor Japanese officials, whom he refused to see personally because of his predetermined tactics of refusing to negotiate with anyone whose rank was not commensurate with his. When these officials informed Perry that he was violating the law of Japan by remaining in the bay and that he had best proceed immediately to Nagasaki, he firmly had them informed that he intended to remain where he was until persons of suitable rank had conferred with him and received from his hands his credentials and copies of the presidential letter for the Emperor. Finally on July 14, 1853, his demands were met and he came ashore with a large and impressive escort to confer in a pavilion especially prepared for the occasion. There he conferred with two officials of the Bakufu and in a dramatic and impressive ceremony presented his credentials and the presidential letter. On receiving these items the officials then urged him to depart immediately for Nagasaki. Again Perry made it clear that he was determined to carry out fully the instructions he had received from his Government, and he explained that while he would weigh anchor in a few days it was his intention to return in the spring, accompanied perhaps by an even larger squadron of warships, at which time he would anticipate that the Japanese would have had ample time to study the presidential letter and be prepared to enter into negotiations for a treaty which would establish relations befitting civilized nations. On July 17, eight days after his historic arrival, Perry's vessels weighed anchor. Perry then proceeded to China, where he intended to spend the winter months and at the same time have his warships at hand to give aid and protection to the Americans in China, if necessary.*

*The great civil war, known as the Taiping Rebellion, was raging in China at this time.

En route to China Perry authorized what practically amounted to the seizure of Peel Island, in the Bonin group, and urged his Government to annex it as a coaling station. He also suggested that the Ryūkyū Islands might be seized and held as hostages in case Japan hesitated to conclude a treaty or declined to furnish satisfactory guarantees with respect to the protection of shipwrecked Americans. These suggestions were turned down by Washington.

Perry and his squadron had created an excitement among the Japanese that rapidly spread throughout the country. He personally had deeply impressed the Japanese by his dignified bearing, his directness and measured aggressiveness, and his calculated reasonableness. Moreover, several of Perry's "tactical maneuvers" had been very effective, such as his demanding the withdrawal of the Japanese boats which initially crowded around his vessels, his compelling the highest officials in the area to confer with him, his surveying of the bay area and deliberately creating the impression that he might advance as far as Edo itself, and his adamantly refusing even to discuss the possibility of a withdrawal to Nagasaki.

The Japanese emissaries had promptly delivered the presidential letter to the Shōgun. This letter was signed by President Fillmore and Edward Everett, the Secretary of State. In addition to the customary salutations and good wishes, the letter candidly stated that the United States desired a treaty which would include the provisions embodied in the instructions consigned to Perry (mentioned above). The President's letter declared: "I have directed Commodore Perry to assure Your Imperial Majesty that I entertain the kindest feelings toward Your Majesty's person and government, and that I have no other object in sending him to Japan but to propose to Your Imperial Majesty that the United States and Japan should live in friendship and have commercial intercourse with each other." The letter suggested: "If Your Imperial Majesty is not satisfied that it would be safe to abrogate the ancient laws which forbid foreign trade, they might be suspended for five or ten years, so as to try the experiment. If it does not prove as beneficial as was hoped the ancient laws can be restored." The letter urged that shipwrecked Americans should receive protection until they could be rescued by American vessels and that American ships should be permitted to call at Japanese ports to obtain fuel, provisions and water.[21]

The presidential requests placed the Bakufu in a dilemma. If they were complied with, the powerful and rebellious elements hostile to the Tokugawas would deliberately represent the action as outright subservience to a foreign power with the result that a civil war might break out in the country. On the other hand, if the requests were denied there was the distinct possibility that Perry might employ armed force, as he had intimated, in which case Japan might easily be crushed because of the vastly superior military power of the American intruders.

Deeply conscious of the gravity of the problem, the Bakufu decided on taking the unprecedented step of forwarding copies of the presidential letter to the Emperor and the highest nobles in the land with the object of soliciting their advice. The Imperial Court, which was then dominated by anti-Tokugawa elements, insisted on a firm continuation of the long-established seclusion policy and the blunt denial of the American requests even if such an action entailed armed conflict. This view was shared by most of the nobles who were consulted, although a small minority did counsel that it would be the part of wisdom to negotiate a treaty with the Americans that might be put into effect for a short and temporary trial period.[22] Much better informed than any other elements in Japan, the government of the Shōgun finally decided that the interests and security of Japan would best be served by meeting Perry's demands.

In the meantime feverish military preparations were made to resist Perry should he resort to force on his return. Probably not one Japanese in a thousand viewed Perry's visit as a peaceful or friendly one. The forts in the Edo Bay area were strengthened and new fortifications were hastily thrown up. Bells of monasteries and metal articles contributed by wealthy patriots were melted and cast into cannon. Some three hundred thousand samurai warriors allegedly flocked to Edo in a fanatical outburst of patriotism to offer their lives, if need be, for the defense of the land of the gods.

Shortly after Perry arrived in Edo Bay the Russian Admiral Poutiatin had called at Nagasaki and made an unsuccessful attempt to conclude for his government a treaty of amity and commerce. The rebuffed Admiral then proceeded to Shanghai where he at-

65

tempted to induce Perry to agree to a joint Russo-American mission to secure a common treaty since the objectives of their respective countries appeared to be similar. Perry politely rejected this overture on the ground that established American policy did not permit entangling alliances or arrangements with foreign countries. Actually he had not the slightest desire to share the honor of opening Japan with any other official even had he the authority to do so. Moreover, Perry was obsessed with the conviction that the opening of Japan by the United States would be a historic milestone in the expansion of her power and influence in the farther regions of the mighty Pacific which washed her western shores and by destiny linked her to these distant lands. Perry furthermore had a deep distrust of Russia and believed that at some not too distant date the interests of the two countries would clash in the very area in which he was striving to bring new glory and advantages to the nation he represented.

While Perry was wintering in China, two events occurred to which he attached considerable significance: (1) the death of the Shōgun, and (2) the outbreak of the Crimean War which brought Russia into armed conflict with England and France. Perry of course was under the impression that the Emperor had died, and his great concern was that the passing of the sovereign might bring about a new situation in Japan characterized by unrest and a firmer attitude against his mission. As for the Crimean War, Perry feared that its hostilities might spread to the Far East and that the belligerents might even seize areas in Japan for use as military bases, in which case the chances of success for his mission would also be jeopardized. These two developments together with the overtures of Poutiatin influenced Perry to believe that it would be unwise to defer the completion of his mission any longer, even though the Chinese civil war was still raging and all American ships in Far Eastern waters were needed in the China area to meet possible emergencies.

On February 12, 1854, Commodore Perry arrived in Edo Bay for the second time and with twice as many warships as on the occasion of his first visit. Again the vessels anchored off Uraga. More procrastination was to test the tenacity and patience of the resolute Commodore. When informed by the Japanese envoys that the government of the Shōgun was prepared to enter into discussions but that they should be conducted in nearby Kamakura, Perry inflexibly stated that this site was unacceptable and that he would not move from his present anchorage until an appropriate place suitable for the nearby presence of his vessels was selected. He warned that he was not prepared to endure further procrastinations and that if necessary for the fulfillment of his mission he could immediately increase the size of his already formidable fleet to fifty warships and that as many more could be summoned from California. Fully convinced by now that the Commodore was not to be trifled with, the Japanese then informed him that preparations would be made to hold the discussions at Kanagawa, a village just outside Yokohama, where the bay was of such a depth that his vessels could anchor nearby. This arrangement was acceptable to Perry.

In addition to the realization that Perry could not be induced to abandon his mission, it seems that the Bakufu was also reasonably well informed, presumably by the Dutch, of the outbreak of the Crimean War and hence was greatly concerned about the possibility of the nations engaged in that war seizing Japanese areas for bases or other warlike purposes. Of its own initiative the Bakufu apparently concluded that a negotiated treaty with Perry, in which only his minimum demands would be met, might contribute toward preserving the independence and territorial integrity of Japan, since the other powers might readily be induced to accept as much, but no more, than had been granted to Perry.

At any rate, the treaty discussions began on March 8 between Perry and the representatives of the Shōgun, comprising a plenipotentiary and four others of very high rank. Perry had proceeded to the conference site in impressive fashion, escorted by five hundred armed officers, sailors and marines, while offshore his grim warships lay at anchor with their guns bristling.

A measure of amity characterized the discussions, but Perry was in firm command from beginning to end, never at any moment deviating in the least from his predetermined objectives. The Japanese representatives presented Perry the Shōgun's reply to the presidential letter, which stated that the requests of the President were acceptable. On March 11 Perry delivered the many presents and articles he had brought with him, which included such diversified items as perfumes, firearms, a telegraph set, and a miniature railroad set. Twelve days later the Japanese in turn presented a number of gifts to Perry for himself, the President and the members of his staff participating in the discussions. On March 27, after the terms of the treaty had been agreed upon, Commodore Perry gave an elaborate reception to the Japanese on the deck of the *Powhattan*. Drink was apparently as plentiful as food. One of the Japanese officials, Matsusaki, became inebriated and in an outburst of fellowship threw his arms around Perry's neck, inadvertently crushing his epaulets, and exclaimed, "Nippon and America, all the same heart!"[23]

Each article of the treaty was discussed point by point. On none of them did Perry deviate in the least from what he considered to be the minimum requirements of his Government. Only on minor points did he make concessions, and these were made only after his major points had been obtained. It seems that Perry was particularly sensitive about the humiliating restrictions and conditions imposed on the Dutch and Chinese at Nagasaki and he took especial pains to make it perfectly clear to the Japanese that his Government would not tolerate such humiliations and conditions even in the slightest degree.

On March 31 the finalized treaty was signed. This treaty, known as the Treaty of Kanagawa, stipulated that between the two countries there would be established a "perfect, permanent, and universal peace and sincere and cordial amity." Trade was to be conducted on a cash and carry basis at two ports, Shimoda and Hakodate, which might also be utilized by American vessels for refitting and refuelling. Neither of these sites, incidentally, was very useful as a port. Shimoda was located in an unimportant area of Japan, far removed from Edo, while Hakodate was in the far north on the then thinly settled and almost totally undeveloped island of Hokkaido. The treaty further stipulated that shipwrecked American sailors were to be humanely treated and that their properties were to be protected. An American consul or agent might also be stationed in Shimoda after eighteen months. A provision of the treaty also gave most-favored-nation privileges to the United States. Perry attached particular importance to this provision, since he anticipated that the English, Russians and others would immediately conclude treaties with Japan which would undoubtedly contain more advantageous provisions than his treaty.

After the conclusion of the Treaty of Kanagawa, Perry departed for Shimoda and Hakodate to investigate personally these areas with the view of determining what further safeguards were needed to assure the workable operation of the treaty. As a result of his observations at these two sites, a supplementary agreement, known as the "Additional Regulations," was concluded on June 17 which contained additional minor concessions and privileges. His mission now successfully completed, Perry departed from Japan on June 28 for China. En route he stopped at the Ryūkyū Islands and at Naha on July 11 concluded an arrangement with the authorities of the islands which guaranteed courteous treatment to American nationals who might call at the islands for one purpose or another. At Hongkong Perry boarded a British mail steamer and arrived in New York on January 12, 1855, after an absence of two years and two months from the United States.

The treaty of Kanagawa was promptly submitted by the President to the Senate, which ratified it unanimously. Ratifications were exchanged in Japan by Commodore Adams early in 1855. Adams encountered difficulties in effecting the exchange of ratifications, primarily because of misunderstandings on the part of the Japanese concerning the exact meaning of some of the treaty's provisions. He easily overcame the recalcitrance of the Japanese, however, by displaying some of the tenacity and astuteness of Perry.

While the Treaty of Kanagawa was inadequate as it said nothing about extraterritoriality, the right of permanent residence for Americans, and other vital matters, it nevertheless ended the long period of Japanese seclusion and exclusion. For better or for worse, Japan had opened her doors and there no longer existed any possibility of her again shutting them to the outside world. Just as Perry had anticipated, the other powers shortly after concluded similar treaties. Admiral James Sterling of Britain obtained a treaty in October 1854, ratified a year later, which contained crude extraterritorial privileges, provided for freedom of religion for British subjects, opened Nagasaki and Hakodate to British ships, and also provided for most-favored-nation treatment. A Russian treaty, concluded by Admiral Poutiatin in February 1855, closely resembled the Perry treaty and provided for the use of three ports, Nagasaki, Hakodate and Shimoda. The Russian treaty, moreover, provided for mutual extraterritorial rights. A Dutch treaty, signed in November of that year, was largely concerned with the removal of the long-standing restrictions on Dutch trade, but it also contained crude extraterritorial privileges and a most-favored-nation clause. Since the United States enjoyed most-favored-nation privileges, its rights were represented by the sum total of all these treaties.

In successfully negotiating the Treaty of Kanagawa Perry had not performed any routine or ordinary diplomatic function. He had in fact achieved a brilliant diplomatic success which must be accorded a place of honor in the annals of American diplomatic history. What were the fundamental reasons for this success, for this achievement where so many others had failed so dismally?

Perry of course had the advantage of a powerful military force behind him, whereas the Japanese had no such power to support their position. In diplomacy, as is well known, the strength of a nation's hand is fundamentally determined by the effective military power at its disposal. This factor Perry exploited to the full. Perry moreover instinctively understood and penetrated the political personality of the officials and government with whom he dealt. He furthermore by disposition and training was possessed of the personality characteristics so vitally necessary in a mission of the type he was called upon to fulfill.

The basic reasons for Perry's success are revealed in his own words. In his official report, for example, Perry wrote: "I was convinced that if I receded in the least from the position first assumed by me, it would be considered by the Japanese an advantage gained; and, finding that I could be induced to change a premeditated intention in one instance, they might rely on prevailing on me, by dint of perseverance, to waver in most other cases." Hence, wrote Perry, "it seemed to be the true policy to hold out at all hazards, and rather to establish for myself a character for unreasonable obstinacy than that of a yielding disposition."[24] More light is disclosed in the dispatch he sent to the Navy Department when he left Edo Bay to winter in China and to give the Japanese an opportunity to mull over the presidential letter. "It is very certain," he wrote in this dispatch, "that the Japanese can be brought to reason only through the influence of their fears, and when they find that their coast is entirely at the mercy of a strong naval force they will be induced, I confidently hope, to concede all that will be asked of them; and I feel assured that, even if they can not be brought to any treaty arrangement, strangers who may hereafter be thrown upon their shores will be treated with kindness."[25]

Perry the nationalist was deeply conscious of the honor of his country. "It struck me," he wrote, "that it was better to have no treaty than one that would in the least compromise the dignity of the American character, and to agree to any arrangement that would recognize, in the remotest degree, the restrictions submitted to by the Dutch could not for a moment be thought of." Nevertheless, there was a chivalrous side to Perry and an inner, even if somewhat suppressed, feeling of sympathy for the Japanese. This seems apparent from one of his communications to the Japanese concerning his desire for the ultimate opening of additional ports. "I feel assured," he declared, "that in a short period experience will satisfy everyone that no injury will result to Japan from such arrangement, but rather that the empire will be benefited by the adoption of laws more congenial to the spirit of the times."[26]

At the same time, however, it needs to be noted that Perry was driven by a fierce personal ambition and that by disposition he was not reluctant to employ force when it served his ends. The civilian authority of the Government was not unaware of this side of Perry. In a note dated November 14, 1853, the Secretary of the Navy, James C. Dobbin, firmly informed Perry that the President, "while he would be happy to see your interesting mission crowned with success, and would aid you as far as he can legitimately, desires to impress you with the conviction that the great end should be attained, not only with credit to the United States, but without wrong to Japan." Dobbin emphatically reminded him that "no violence should be resorted to except for defense." Apparently reflecting a lack of complete faith in Perry's determination to shun the use of force, Dobbin thought it necessary to point out that warmaking was the exclusive power of Congress. "It is very desirable to make our navy an efficient branch of the government, both in extending and protecting commerce and trade," Dobbin wrote, "but as Congress alone has the power to declare war, too much prudence cannot be exercised, even in the great work in which you are engaged."[27]

The name of Perry will doubtless command attention as long as diplomatic history is studied. Although Japan was ripe for the reopening of intercourse with the outside world, and although it can be assumed that if it had not been Perry it would have been someone else, the fact remains that it was he who succeeded in reopening Japan to Western intercourse. Moreover, while some of his tactics appear high-handed, it cannot be gainsaid that in reopening Japan at the precise moment that he did the country was undoubtedly spared from internal bloodshed and foreign aggressions.

Secretary Dobbin wrote Perry as follows on the completion of his mission: "You have won additional fame for yourself, reflected new honor upon the very honorable service to which you belong, and, we all hope, have secured for your country, for commerce, and for civilization, a triumph the blessing of which may be enjoyed by generations yet unborn."[28] Abroad, as well as at home, Perry's achievement was recognized as an outstanding event of the time.

The fullest recognition and honors have probably been bestowed on Perry by the Japanese. When the ratifications of the Treaty of Kanagawa were exchanged in February 1855, the Japanese commissioners with whom Perry had conducted the negotiations proclaimed that "his name would live forever in the history of Japan." At the turn of the century a group of Japanese organized a society for the erection of a fitting monument to the memory of Perry, whose visit they described as "the most memorable event in our annals—an event which enabled the country to enter upon an unprecedented era of national ascendancy in which we are now living." All classes of Japanese society, including the Emperor, eagerly contributed money for the monument, which was dedicated on July 14, 1901, the forty-eighth anniversary of Perry's initial landing in Japan. In a dedication address the president of the Perry society that had made the monument possible declared that "it was at this spot that the modern civilization of our empire had its beginning" and that the monument "is erected to preserve on stone our determination never to forget the friendship of the United States that sent Commodore Perry to induce us in a peaceful way to have intercourse with foreign powers."

CHAPTER FOUR

The Acquisition of Alaska

The Russians were the first to discover the vast region now known as Alaska and its natural appendage comprising the Aleutian Islands. The Russian discovery was a culmination of the irresistible eastward movement of the pioneer Russian traders, the *promyshleniki,* who had crossed the Ural Mountains in the sixteenth century and reached the Amur River as early as 1650. By the middle of the seventeenth century these pioneer traders had reached the Pacific coast of Siberia, and by 1713 they were exploring the Kamchatka peninsula.[1] From Kamchatka they pushed on to discover the huge northwestern bulge of North America, to which was given the name Alaska, an Aleut word meaning "Great Land."[2]

The Russian drive to Alaska was but a phase of the massive expansionist movement which characterized Russia since the days of Peter the Great. At the outset of the nineteenth century Russian policy was clearly to utilize Alaska as a base for the consolidation of Russian influence in North America. It was only after Britain and the United States indirectly interposed themselves that this ambition was abandoned.[3] Apropos of the imperialism of the Tsars, the distinguished American historian Bancroft in 1866 noted: "In the great seizure and partition of America by European powers there was no reason why Russia should not have a share. She was mistress in the east and north as were France and Spain in the west and south; she was as grasping as Portugal and as cruel as England; and because she owned so much of Europe and Asia in the Arctic, the desire was only increased thereby to extend her broad belt quite round the world. It was but a step across from one continent to the other, and intercourse between the primitive peoples of the two had been common from time immemorial. It was but natural, I say, in the gigantic robbery of half a world, that Russia should have a share; and had she been quicker about it, the belt might have been continued to Greenland and Iceland."[4]

Vitus Bering, a Dane in the naval service of the Tsar, may be considered to be the discoverer of Alaska. Bering commanded two pioneer Russian expeditions to the Alaska area. On his first voyage, which began from Kamchatka in July 1728, he passed through the strait that now bears his name and ascertained to his satisfaction that Asia and America were not parts of the same continent. He actually came close to the coast of Alaska, but could not see it because of poor visibility conditions. It was on his second voyage that Lt. Alexei Chirikov, in command of one of the two vessels that comprised his expedition, discovered the coast of Alaska north of Cape Muzon on July 15, 1741. The Bering expedition netted a profit of some $100,000 on the furs that were acquired, and this stimulated other trader-adventurers to undertake the exploitation of the Alaska area fur resources. The passage from Kamchatka, their continental base, to the Alaska area became one of the most active sea lanes of the time.[5]

Russian fur-trading was initially concentrated on obtaining sea otter pelts and largely confined to the Aleutian Islands. The furs were obtained by barter, by robbing the natives, or by hunting.[6] It was not until 1761 that Russians again reached the Alaskan mainland, impelled by the diminishing of the fur resources on the Aleutian Islands. A Russian settlement was founded on Kodiak Island in 1783, but the extensive exploitation of Alaskan furs did not begin until around the turn of the century.[7] In a real sense, then, it was the quest of the sea otter's fur that lured the Russian trader-adventurers to North America. From 1743 to 1799 the Russian traders are reported to have obtained 186,754 sea otter pelts, with some one hundred vessels engaged in the trade.[8]

With the accession of the mystic Alexander I to the throne of Russia in 1801, the activities of the fur traders became more extensive, and the coasts of Alaska were explored by several Russians between 1807 and 1820. It was not until 1835 and 1843, however, that explorations of the Alaskan interior along the Yukon River were made by Malakhov and Zagoshin respectively.[9]

Meanwhile Alaska had not escaped the attention of explorers

74

and navigators of other nations. Their motivation was the search for the Northwest Passage which had been initiated by Martin Frobisher in 1586. Among the many noted British explorers who searched for this passage in vain were John Davis, Henry Hudson, William Baffin, and James Cook. The nearest a British explorer came to completing the passage was in 1847 when Sir John Franklin came within ninety miles of its successful completion. Actually it was not until 1906 that Roald Amundsen successfully sailed the *Gjoa* from the Atlantic to the Pacific through Bering Strait. The first Englishman to sail into the Arctic from the Pacific was Captain Cook in 1778, but he was compelled to turn back because of impassable ice barriers. George Vancouver, one of Cook's lieutenants, visited Alaska in 1791 and explored and charted certain areas so accurately that most of our knowledge of them rested on his findings for about a hundred years. Spanish and French navigators also visited parts of Alaska during the last two decades of the eighteenth century.[10] Russia based her claims to Alaska, which came to be recognized by the powers, on the voyages of Bering.

The Russian hold on Alaska was secured largely by the efforts of two men, Grigory Shelikhov and Alexander A. Baranov. It was in the last decade of the eighteenth century that Shelikhov organized a trading company known as Shelikhov-Golikov and then headed a trading expedition to Alaska. After his return to St. Petersburg in 1787, he obtained a charter from Catherine II which gave his company favored trading privileges in Alaska. In 1797 the firm of Shelikhov-Golikov merged with another prominent firm engaged in the Alaska trade to form the famous Russian-American Company. This company was modelled after such enterprises as the British East India Company and the Hudson Bay Company. Its avowed purpose was to spread the Christian religion and engage in such other activities as developing trade, building vessels, exploring new lands, colonizing, and discovering new peoples. In 1799 the company received a charter from the Russian Government which conferred upon it a monopoly of the Alaskan trade for a twenty-year period. A few months later this company moved its headquarters from Irkutsk, in the interior of Siberia, to St. Petersburg. The Tsar was moreover made a stockholder.[11] The company was originally capitalized at $500,000, subsequently increased to $1,000,000.[12]

Baranov was made the general manager of the company's operations in Alaska. He established his headquarters at Sitka, and under his able and energetic direction the company prospered. He governed his subordinates with an iron hand and treated the natives ruthlessly. No compunctions restrained him, for, as he put it, "God is in Heaven and St. Petersburg is a long way off." He established a factory far to the south in California and named it Fort Ross.* This action was resented by the Spaniards as an intrusion in their domains, but Baranov subscribed to the Russian position that Spanish sovereignty did not extend north of San Francisco. Baranov was not only a clever trader but a dreamer of empire as well, and at one time he seriously considered seizing the Hawaiian Islands.

Baranov served as the general manager of the Russian-American Company until 1818. Thereafter the history of the company was one of generally declining fortunes. It became unable to meet the competition of American and British traders in the gathering and sale of furs, and during its last years became an unprofitable venture. When the Tsarist Government at last perceived that the company was no longer useful in its design to expand in the Western Hemisphere, it took action to liquidate it. The company nonetheless played a unique role in history comparable to that of the more famous British East India Company, the Hudson Bay and other similar commercial companies. It might be noted, also, that between 1804 and 1840 the company outfitted thirteen round-the-world voyages, many of which contributed greatly to the knowledge of the world.[13]

American interest in Alaska may be said to date from as early as 1798 when Captain Gray discovered the Columbia River and became acquainted with the extensive fur resources of the Northwest Coast. Thereafter Americans frequented the Alaskan coasts to trade and obtain furs. The Americans, willing and able to pay higher prices for the furs of the natives, in a short time practically confined the activities of the Russian-American Company to the

*"Ross" is a corruption of the original "Rus." Fort Ross and the interests of the Russian-American Company were subsequently sold for $30,000 to John A. Sutter of "gold-strike" fame. The Russians evacuated the area in 1842. (Henry W. Clark, *History of Alaska,* pp. 53, 55.)

hunting stations operated by the natives who were dependent on the company. To the officials of the company these American trading activities constituted "smuggling," but they lacked the military power to suppress them.

In May 1812 the company, with the approval of St. Petersburg, concluded a trade agreement with John Jacob Astor which gave him the right to transport Russian furs to Canton and supply the Russian colonies in Alaska with provisions. In concluding this agreement the company hoped that Astor's influence with the traders and with government officials of the United States might be instrumental in bringing about a cessation of American "smuggling." The agreement did not work out to the benefit of the company, however, for Astor charged shipping rates that it considered abnormally high and moreover supplied the colonies with provisions that were not needed. Notwithstanding the agreement with Astor, the American traders continued to engage in widespread trading with the Alaskan natives. According to the company's calculations, apparently made in the year 1817, an average of fifteen American vessels were trading along the coasts of Alaska and exporting some 10,000 to 15,000 otter furs annually.[14] Russian warships on round-the-world cruises visited Alaska every two or three years, but they made no effort to suppress the American traders.

By the end of the second decade of the nineteenth century the officials of the Russian-American Company, powerless to keep Americans and other foreigners out of Alaska, complained to the Tsar and asked for increased support. Among the many complaints of the company was one to the effect that Americans sold firearms to the natives and taught them how to use them "to the detriment of our traders." In August 1820 the company on its own initiative forbade its colonies to engage in any barter with foreigners. By this time, however, the policy of St. Petersburg was greatly changed, and the company was conceived as a screen to further Russian ambitions for the establishment of empire over the entire Pacific, north of the Hawaiian Islands.[15] In the following year the Tsar renewed the company's charter for another twenty-year period and gave it jurisdiction over all territory north of 51° north latitude, including the Aleutians and most of the Kuriles. The chief manager of the company was given the same status as the imperial governors of Siberia, and military and naval officers, together with civil service officials, were given special inducements to serve with the company.[16]

On September 4, 1821, the Tsar issued a celebrated *ukaz* or imperial decree which prohibited any foreign vessel from approaching to within one hundred Italian miles of the coast north of 51° north latitude. The pretext for the decree is to be found in its preamble wherein the Tsar complained that "the trade of our subjects on the Aleutian Islands and on the northwest coast appertaining to Russia" suffered "oppression and impediments" because of "secret and illicit traffic."[17]

The Tsar's *ukaz* greatly displeased the American and British traders who had been carrying on a substantial and profitable trade with the islands off the southeastern coasts of Alaska. Great Britain made a strong protest, but the *ukaz* did not initially alarm the American Government to any appreciable extent because of the remoteness of Russia, the almost equal remoteness of the area concerned, and the absence of any vital national interest in the area. Moreover the Tsar had consistently maintained a friendly policy and attitude toward the United States, and hence his action was not interpreted as hostile. By 1823, however, Secretary Adams had developed a strong interest in safeguarding American claims to the whole of the Oregon region, upon which the Tsar's *ukaz* had encroached. In July of that year he informed the Russian minister in Washington, Baron Tuyll, that the extension of Russian sovereignty in North America was not looked upon with favor and that "the American continents are no longer subjects for any new European colonial establishments." This principle was restated by President Monroe in his annual message to Congress four months later which came to constitute a part of the Monroe Doctrine.

Friendly discussions followed in Washington, however, between Baron Tuyll and Secretary Adams, and in 1824 a Russo-American treaty was concluded which established the southern limit of Russian America at 54°40' north latitude. Russia hence relinquished all her claims to any portion of the Oregon territory, which at that time was in serious dispute between the United States and Great Britain. By the terms of the treaty Americans were moreover granted for a ten-year period unimpeded right of entry to all inland waters of the Russian-American territories for the purpose of fishing or fur trading. A similar treaty was concluded by Russia and Great Britain in the following year, 1825. These treaties placed the Russian-American Company in a difficult position with regard to suppressing "smuggling" inasmuch as it legitimized fur trading.

With the expiration of the Russo-American treaty in 1834, Americans were denied the right of further intercourse with any part of Russian America on the ground that they had abused the privileges accorded them by the treaty. The new prohibition was not enforced, however, and American traders continued to visit the coasts of Alaska.

In 1842 the charter of the Russian-American Company was renewed for another twenty-year period, but by this time its fortunes had declined abjectly. One reason was the disadvantage at which it operated in competition with the rival American and British traders who were willing to pay higher prices for furs because of their easier access to items for barter and the greater ease with which they were able to transport the furs to the profitable Canton market. The natives naturally took advantage of the higher prices offered by the company's competitors and hence preferred to sell to them. Many elements in St. Petersburg were also displeased with the company's bad record with regard to promoting the welfare of the natives. This, of course, was a responsibility of the company since it enjoyed a monopoly over every phase of administration. In 1862 the Tsar refused to renew the company's charter, and thereafter it operated without one. By that time, however, the company was nearly bankrupt and the Tsar had moreover decided to rid himself of his Alaskan possession at the appropriate opportunity.

The Russian Government had been greatly disturbed by Polk's slogan of "fifty-four forty or fight" during the 1846 election campaign. This slogan expressed determination to occupy all of the disputed Oregon territory up to the southern limits of Russian America. As a result of Polk's expansionist ambitions, relations between the United States and Great Britain became severely strained and even threatened to errupt into open war. The Tsar was consequently constrained to believe that it was only a matter of time before Britain or the United States would covet Alaska. Certainly, there was no reason for the Tsar to feel completely at ease,

79

considering the statement made by R. J. Walker who upon accepting the post of Secretary of the Treasury declared that "in the event of success in the Oregon question this would leave no European power upon our Pacific Coast except Russia, whose well known friendship to us would, it is to be hoped, induce her to cede to us her North American territory."[18]

The exigencies of the Crimean War (1853-55), during which Russia was aligned against the mighty naval power of Britain, had convinced most influential Russians that it would be impossible to hold on to Alaska indefinitely and that it would fall easily to Britain in the event of a future war with her.* In the hope of improving the security of Alaska, the Russian Government had, long before the Crimean War, considered placing it under imperial rule, but it was concluded that the cost of maintaining a colonial establishment in distant Alaska was not warranted by the value of the region.[19] Within a few years after the Crimean War, then, the Tsar's advisers and officials had almost unanimously agreed that there was no alternative but to sell the vast territory.

Grand Duke Constantine, the Tsar's brother, seems to have been the earliest influential advocate of the idea of selling Alaska. He suggested it as early as 1857. He explained to Foreign Minister Gorchakov that "The United States of America should, in the natural course of events, be eager to conquer all of North America, and will therefore, meet us sooner or later, and there is not the slightest doubt that it will seize our colonies without great effort, and we shall never be in a position to recover them." Constantine further proposed selling Alaska to the United States, thereby "solving in a friendly fashion and in a way that would be profitable to us a problem which will otherwise be solved in a way disadvantageous to us and in addition by conquest."[20] The feeling of the Foreign Minister at that time, however, was that although the sale of the territory was desirable it was inadvisable because of the

*In 1853 Russian officials actually drew up a fictitious contract for the sale of the company to a San Francisco firm. Baron Stoeckl even consulted Secretary Marcy on the advisability of publishing an account of the bogus sale, but Marcy advised him that this would be futile because the British would easily detect the fiction. (S. B. Okun, *The Russian-American Company*, pp. 237-238; V. J. Farrar, *The Annexation of Russian America by the United States*, pp. 1-2.)

grave offense it might give Britain. It was therefore agreed to postpone action until after January 1, 1862, when the charter of the Russian-American Company expired.[21] In 1858-59 when Baron Edouard de Stoeckl, the minister to Washington, was on leave in St. Petersburg, he added his concurrence to the belief that the sale of Alaska to the United States was advisable because that country would inevitably covet and possibly even seize it.

The basic reason for St. Petersburg desiring to sell Alaska was actually more fundamental than the fear of future American covetousness. Between 1847 and 1861 the extremely able Nikolai N. Muraviev served as governor-general of eastern Siberia. Combining the skill of an explorer with that of a statesman, he established the foundations of a great empire for the Tsar in eastern Asia. In 1858 he occupied the mouth of the Amur River in defiance of a Russo-Chinese treaty of 1689 and extended Russian control to the borders of Korea. Two years later, in 1860, he founded Vladivostok, and the very name he gave it, "Dominator of the East," revealed the heights of his imperial ambitions. Muraviev fervently believed that the destiny of Russia in Asia lay to the south, not to the east, and that Alaska was not worth the effort and expense of safeguarding it from American and British cupidity. Muraviev's ideas came to find favor with the Tsar and some of his most influential advisers and officials, and they came to be reflected in Russian foreign policy.[22]

Of the many reasons which impelled Russia to sell Alaska, the principal ones may then be summarized as follows: (1) her inability to defend it in case of war with a naval power, (2) her inability to defend it even during a protracted period of peace because of widespread rumors which were circulating to the effect that the territory abounded with gold, which might inevitably lead to a heavy influx of fortune seekers, and (3) the calculated shift of Russian policy to develop its interests on the Asian mainland, and hence the desire to be unincumbered by so distant and untenable a possession as Alaska. There were some reasons inherent in the Russian-American Company itself. Since this company was not, for example, in actual possession of the territory but merely the occupier of a few posts, it was helpless to check the exploitation of the vast uncontrolled areas by foreigners operating under the guise of leases.[23] Among other reasons which might be given for Russia's desire to sell the territory were her need for money, the belief that Alaska was of little or no economic value, the feeling that its retention might lead to needless friction with the expanding United States, and finally the possible desire to "humble" Great Britain by contributing to the rising power of her greatest rival in North America just as Napoleon had done in 1803 by ceding the vast Louisiana territory to the then infant American Republic.

An American offer to purchase Alaska was made by Senator Gwin of California in 1859 when, professing to speak for President Buchanan and Assistant Secretary of State Appleton, he suggested to Stoeckl that the United States might be willing to pay five million dollars for the territory. This offer was taken under serious consideration by the Russian Government, but before much could be done about it the United States was in the turmoil of a heated presidential election and on the verge of civil war. In July 1861 Stoeckl, reporting to his Government, advised the suspension of negotiations until after the United States had settled its internal problems.[24] Negotiations were thereupon terminated and not resumed until after the Civil War. That Alaska would soon, at the opportune time, become a territory of the United States was clearly foreshadowed, however, in September 1860 when Secretary Seward declared, in commenting on Russian activity in that area: "Go on, and build up your outposts all along the coast and even up to the Arctic Ocean—they will yet become the outposts of my own country—monuments to the civilization of the United States in the northwest."[25]

An episode of the Civil War contributed indirectly to smoothing the way for the purchase of Alaska afterward. In 1861 Russia dispatched two fleets, each comprised of six vessels, to San Francisco and New York. Gullible Americans, worried about British intentions, interpreted the Russian fleet movement as a warning to Britain that Russia would come to the assistance of the United States if she intervened in the Civil War. Not until a half century later was it known that Russia's real motive was to prevent these vessels from being bottled up in Russian ports in the event of a general European war, which seemed possible at that time over the Polish question. After the Civil War, when the treaty providing for the purchase of Alaska was being bitterly opposed by Congressmen and the press, supporters of the treaty harped on the Civil War episode and argued that failure to carry it through would be an act of base ingratitude to a nation that had shown her friendship at a time of need.[26]

In 1866 Russia took the initiative in bringing about formal negotiations for the transfer of Alaska to the United States by purchase. By-passing the cautious Foreign Minister, Grand Duke Constantine convinced the Tsar that it was to Russia's best interest to consummate the sale of Alaska immediately. Baron Stoeckl was then instructed to begin negotiations at once with the American Government. There seems to be some uncertainty as to the price Stoeckl initially requested and the price Seward offered. In any event, they were considerably apart on the price to be paid when the negotiations started. According to Stoeckl, he "gradually brought Mr. Seward up to six and a half million, but he would go no higher. The negotiations were broken off temporarily, but I stood my ground, and the Secretary yielded."[27] It was finally agreed that $7,000,000 would be a fair price, to which would be added an additional $200,000 for the settlement of the Russian-American Company's outstanding obligations. President Johnson had no interest whatsoever in acquiring Alaska, but he gave his "unenthusiastic approval" to the negotiations. Upon the completion of the negotiations, Stoeckl cabled the Emperor for approval of the terms.

There has been much speculation by historians as to why the United States purchased Alaska. All available evidence seems to indicate that the territory was acquired simply because Seward wanted it. Certainly there was no popular movement or clamor for its purchase. In this connection, it is pertinent to note that back in 1852 when he was a member of the Senate, Seward had ventured to predict that the interests of the United States in the Atlantic would "relatively sink in importance, while the Pacific Ocean, its islands, and the vest regions beyond" would become "the chief theatre of the world's great hereafter."[28] Alaska with its thousands of miles of Pacific coastline and its great chain of Aleutian islands projecting far into the Pacific offered opportunities for the establishment of meaningful naval bases and hence fitted neatly into this type of imperialist thinking. Seward was also apparently motivated by the determination to prevent Alaska from possibly falling into British hands and at the same time to increase the influence of the United States in British Columbia, which was then sparsely settled and an area of possible future American expansion. Seward was in fact of the conviction that all Canada would ultimately become a part of the United States and that there would be serious friction with Britain until this union was consummated.

A report dated May 18, 1868, of the Senate Foreign Relations Committee, headed by Charles Sumner, explained the motives for the purchase of Alaska as follows: "They were, first, the laudable desire of citizens of the Pacific coast to share in the prolific fisheries of the oceans, seas, bays, and rivers of the western world; the refusal of Russia to renew the charter of the Russian-American Fur Company in 1866; the friendship of Russia for the United States; the necessity of preventing the transfer, by any possible chance, of the north-west coast of America to an unfriendly power; the creation of new industrial interests on the Pacific coast necessary to the supremacy of our empire on the sea and land; and finally, to facilitate and secure the advantages of an unlimited commerce with the friendly powers of Japan and China."[29] The first three factors mentioned by this report are far-fetched and even somewhat spurious. The last three factors mentioned, while not cogent, may have carried some weight with the senators who were asked to vote approval of the purchase treaty inasmuch as they squared up with the "big talk" which characterized the Manifest Destiny feeling of the time.[30]

The actual drafting of the treaty providing for the transfer of Alaska has the elements of a Hollywood production. On Friday evening, March 29, 1867, according to Seward's son, Baron Stoeckl called at the Seward home while the Secretary was playing whist with members of his family and declared: "I have a dispatch, Mr. Seward, from my government, by cable. The Emperor gives his consent to the cession. Tomorrow, if you like, I will come to the Department, and we can enter upon the treaty." To which Seward promptly replied: "Why wait till tomorrow, Mr. Stoeckl? Let us make the treaty tonight."[31] The secretaries were then summoned to the State Department building and, with Senator Sumner present, the instrument of transfer was drawn up in an atmosphere of great secrecy and signed at four o'clock in the morning of March 30.

Fearing that the special session of the Senate might adjourn at any moment, Seward promptly presented the treaty to that body and relied on Senator Sumner to obtain its speedy ratification. In the Senate the treaty encountered strong initial opposition. This opposition was actually more to Seward than to the treaty. There was also the suspicion that the transaction was tainted with corruption.[32] Sumner knew nothing about Alaska, and at first had been unenthusiastic about acquiring it. Having decided to support it, however, he spared no effort to obtain its ratification. Hastily reading all available material on Alaska, he delivered an amazing three-hour talk in the Senate and sounded like one of the world's experts on the region. In explaining his support of the treaty, Sumner later declared: "Abstractly I am against further accessions of territory but this question was so perplexed by considerations of politics and comity and the engagements already entered into by this government, I hesitated to take the responsibility of defeating it."[33] The treaty was finally ratified after a secret session of the Senate by a comfortable margin of 37-2 on April 9.

On October 18, 1867, at Sitka, Captain Alexei Petchourov formally transferred the sovereignty of Russian America to General Lovell H. Rousseau. Commenting on the transfer ceremonies, a correspondent of the San Francisco newspaper *Alta California* enthusiastically wrote: "The Russian eagle has now given place to the American, and the national colors floated over a new widespread territory. Our dominion now borders on a new ocean and almost touches the old continent—Asia. Democratic institutions now extend over an area hitherto the possession of a despotic government."[34] Such is the intoxication of the wine of imperialism. The natives of Alaska, on the contrary, were soon to discover that they had, without having been consulted, merely changed one despotism for another.

Although the United States was now in physical possession of the vast Alaskan territory, it did not make provision for the cession payment until nine months later. Because of the exigencies of domestic politics, the presidential request for the necessary financial appropriation was not presented to the House until May of the following year, 1868. Debate on the appropriation bill did not actually begin until June 30. The bill encountered formidable opposition, based on the reluctance to acquire non-contiguous territory, the belief that Alaska was worthless, and the unwillingness to incur additional expenditures at a time when the nation's finances were severely strained. Not until July 14 did the House vote the necessary appropriation, 113 to 43, with 44 not voting. The strong support which Thaddeus Stevens gave the bill was chiefly responsible for the substantial majority. Those opposing the bill labelled it "an outrage on the Constitution" and "the senseless endorsement of a worthless land of ice." The opposition papers vied with each other in ridiculing Alaska by coining such labels for it as "Icebergia," "Polaria," "Seward's Icebox," "Seward's Folly," and "Walrussia." The New York *Herald,* for example, characterized Alaska as "an ice house, a worthless desert with which to enable the Secretary of State to cover up the mortification and defeats he has suffered with the shipwrecked Southern policy of Andrew Johnson."[35] To still other opposition elements, Alaska was "a barren, worthless, God-forsaken region," a country of "icebergs and polar bears," a land where the ground was "frozen six feet deep" and "the streams were glaciers."[36] Is it any wonder, in view of this damning initial appraisal, that it has taken Americans nearly a century to recognize that Alaska, far from being worthless and icebound, is a land abounding in natural resources of every description and susceptible to extensive economic development!

The Russian Government never received the full amount of $7,200,000 specified by the treaty. It actually only received $7,065,000. The remaining $135,000 was utilized by Baron Stoeckl to "pay off" several Americans for "services rendered" of one type or another in influencing the ratification of the treaty and the House appropriation bill. There is no longer any doubt that bribery was employed by Stoeckl to obtain Congressional approval. According to Foster Rhea Dulles, "The whole transaction was tainted with the aroma of corruption which was to become so familiar to post-war Washington."[37] While it is still not known to whom Stoeckl made all his disbursements, evidence indicates that he paid $30,000 to John W. Forney, an influential newspaperman who supported the bill; $20,000 to R. J. Walker, his chief lobbyist, and E. P. Stanton; $10,000 to Thaddeus Stevens, the majority leader in the House; and $8,000 to N. P. Banks, the chairman of the House Committee on Foreign Affairs.[38] At any rate, the corruption which permeated the transaction was too much for Stoeckl to stomach, for after the appropriation bill was approved and the money payments were made he asked his Government for a transfer so that he might "breathe an atmosphere purer than that of Washington."

The acquisition of Alaska marked a step along a new and untried path for the United States. Hitherto territories had been acquired with the view of their ultimate admission into the Union as states. Alaska was acquired with no such thought in mind. The acquisition of Alaska was also significant because it marked the first time in the history of the Republic that an inhabited non-contiguous area was annexed to the United States.

The annexation of Alaska added a domain of 586,400 square miles to the United States. In size, then, Alaska almost equals one fifth the entire continental area of the country. For decades the vast Alaskan territory remained neglected and considered relatively worthless because of its far-northern latitude. Actually the climate of most of Alaska is not much different than that of such states as Montana and the Dakotas. With regard to its economic value, geologists have disclosed that it contains one of the greatest variety of minerals of any region in the entire world. It is reputed to have more gold than California and Colorado combined, more copper than Arizona and Montana, and more coal than Pennsylvania, West Virginia and Ohio. Recent disclosures also indicate that Alaska may contain extensive deposits of oil. The vast forest reserves have scarcely been tapped. The fisheries resources, of course, are now well known and appreciated. With regard to agriculture, it is the opinion of experts that Alaska can raise all the crops necessary to support a population many times its present size.[39]

With the annexation of Alaska to the United States, the region ceases to fall within the scope of this book. Its subsequent history under American control may be succinctly summarized, however, simply by noting the section titles of a book written in 1954 by Ernest Gruening, who served as governor of the territory from 1939 to April 1953. In this book, *The State of Alaska*, Gruening divides the long period of American control into the following phases: the Era of Total Neglect (1867-1884), the Era of Flagrant Neglect (1884-1898), the Era of Mild but Enlightened

Interest (1898-1912), the Era of Indifference and Unconcern (1912-1933), and finally, the Era of Growing Awareness (1933-1954).

Despite a steady and increasing demand for statehood on the part of most Alaskans, it did not come until 1958. Let it suffice in this volume merely to indicate the steps that led to it. In 1906 Congress authorized the people of Alaska to elect a Delegate to Congress without voting privileges. The first territorial legislature convened in 1913 at Juneau, which has since remained the capital of Alaska. The first bid for statehood was made in 1916 when James Wickersham, the Delegate to Congress, introduced a bill to that end, but it failed to find support. The movement for statehood gained momentum in 1946, however, when a referendum in Alaska indicated that its citizens favored statehood by a ratio of five to three. Another bill for statehood was introduced in 1947 to the eightieth Congress by the Delegate, E. L. Bartlett, and every Congress thereafter down to 1958 gave consideration to statehood. Statehood finally came in 1958. On May 28 of that year the House approved it by a vote of 208-166, and the Senate concurred on June 30 by a vote of 64-20. President Eisenhower formally signed the statehood bill on July 7, and the people of Alaska on August 27 voted in a plebiscite to accept statehood by a ratio of five to one. Were Gruening to revise his notable book today, he would doubtless add a new section and perhaps entitle it, "The New Promise—Statehood."

CHAPTER FIVE

Relations with China From 1861 to 1894

From 1850 to 1865 China was in the convulsions of a bloody uprising known as the Taiping Rebellion.* The leader of this rebellion was a fanatic mystic, Hung Hsiu-ch'üan, with perverted ideas of Christianity who professed to be Heaven-sent to establish a new dynasty and bring a new era of happiness and well-being to the Chinese people. He took the title of T'ien Wang, or Prince of Heaven, and the new order he purported to establish he called the Taiping, or Great Peace. His followers are known as the Taipings.

Actually China was ripe for a successful rebellion, principally because of the progressively weakening power of the decadent Manchu dynasty, the increasing corruption in government, and the widespread unrest resulting from a series of famines and the chronic troubles with foreigners. Large numbers of dissatisfied Chinese, including the adventurous and the lawless, flocked to the cause of the Taipings. For a time it appeared as though the Taiping leader would succeed in the achievement of his aims. At the height of his military success, in 1853, about half of China had been seized from the Manchus, the historic city of Nanking had been made the provisional capital, and assaults were being prepared on Tientsin and Peking.

---

*Because of the familiarity of most Americans with this name it is spelled "Taiping," as it appears in standard American dictionaries. It should be spelled "T'ai-p'ing," however, to represent its correct pronunciation in accordance with the Wade system of transliterating Chinese names.

The Taipings might have succeeded in gaining the final victory but for the assistance given the Imperial Government by foreign adventurers and the official support of the British and French governments. It was an American soldier of fortune, Frederick Ward of Massachusetts, who organized the famous "Ever-Victorious Army" of foreign volunteers which fought for the Imperial Government. This army won a succession of victories over the Taipings and for a time appeared invincible in battle. Hence the name which was bestowed upon it by the Emperor. After Ward's death in action, in September 1862, the command of this army fell to an Englishman, Major Charles "Chinese" Gordon, whose victorious exploits equalled those of Ward. The grateful Manchu Government conferred high honors on both Ward (posthumously) and Gordon.

During the initial stages of the rebellion most Westerners, ignorant of the real nature of the Taipings, were highly sympathetic to them because of the belief that they were fundamentally Christians and that under them better and more advantageous commercial relations might be established. Even President Pierce, in his annual message of December 1853, expressed the hope that improved commercial relations might result from a Taiping victory. Said Pierce, "The condition of China at this time renders it probable that some important changes will occur in that vast Empire which will lead to more unrestrained intercourse with it." It was not long, however, before the true nature of the Taipings and their sham Christianity became known to all. Thereafter the sympathies of most of the foreigners resident in China switched to the Manchus.

The position of the State Department during this protracted civil war was one of neutrality, but the American diplomatic representatives stationed in China favored positive support of the Manchu regime in its effort to destroy the Taipings. They believed that the United States should not stand by idly and allow events to take their course, as such a policy might result in the imperialist Western powers taking advantage of China's turmoil to obtain territorial concessions that could not but have an adverse effect on American commercial interests. Humphrey Marshall feared that Russian intervention on the side of the Manchus would "probably end in China passing under a Russian protectorate," while the

Russian boundaries might be pushed as far south as the Yellow River or the Yangtze. He also feared that if Great Britain joined Russia in an intervention, these two powers would probably partition China between them. He accordingly warned the State Department that "almost any sacrifice should be made by the United States to keep Russia from spreading her Pacific boundary, and to avoid her coming directly to interference in Chinese domestic affairs." He admonished that "the highest interests of the United States are involved in sustaining China."[1]

When Robert McLane, Marshall's successor, was instructed to investigate the desirability of extending *de facto* recognition to the Taipings when they were near their pinnacle of success, he reported that the Taipings "neither profess nor apprehend Christianity" and that "intercourse cannot be established or maintained on terms of equality with them."[2] After the outbreak of the American Civil War, the general policy of the United States was to extend full moral support to the Manchu regime with emphasis on the preservation of the territorial integrity of China. Meanwhile, Great Britain and France in 1860 had decided to frankly support the Manchu Government.

By 1864 the imperial forces, thanks to British and French support, had succeeded in breaking the back of the rebellion by capturing the Nanking stronghold. In June of that year, his cause now hopeless, Hung Hsiu-ch'üan committed suicide. By the end of the year the revolt was practically crushed and thousands of captured Taipings were slaughtered in reprisals. The last die-hard Taipings were not wiped out, however, until May of the following year.

Probably no single happening of the nineteenth century so weakened China and the power and prestige of the Manchu dynasty as did the Taiping Rebellion. It is estimated that as many as twenty millions lost their lives as a result of the rebellion.[3] The damage to the economy of China was incalculable. Unfortunately for the Chinese, the great uprising came at a critical time when the nation needed to conserve its resources and present a united front to the relentless encroachment of the West.

The easy victories of the French and British during the conflict which lasted from 1856 to 1860 and the extreme difficulty of the Manchu Government in quelling the rebellion of the Taipings revealed the utter weakness and disunity of Imperial China. A wave of European spoliations followed which detached extensive border areas in the north and south that had been regarded as vassals of the Chinese Emperor. By treaties concluded in 1858 and 1860, the Russians obtained a huge area south of the Amur and east of the Ussuri rivers. As a result of wars on weak vassal states in Indochina, France established protectorates over Annam and Tonkin in 1862 and over Cochin China in 1867. Britain subsequently invaded Burma, and annexed it to India in 1884. Britain also established protectorates over Nepal and Bhutan, northern neighbors of India. The loss of these areas deprived China of her outer layer of buffer states. However China proper, except for Hongkong and Kowloon, remained intact and tempting to the aggressive and powerful imperialist states of the West. With the United States, Great Britain and Russia now actively engaged in Far Eastern activities, their relations with one another became a phase of the politics of the West.[4]

The Anglo-French invasion and occupation of Peking, the venerated capital, together with the overwhelming reverses and problems created by the Taiping Rebellion, had in 1860-61 resulted in the temporary eclipse of the extreme anti-foreign, conservative elements at the Imperial Court. Most influential of the new element that came into positions of influence was the able Prince Kung, who took charge of foreign affairs. Although devoted to the culture and traditions of imperial China, he recognized that the Westerners could not be expelled and that there was no alternative but to make the necessary accommodations to their presence. Although unwilling and unable to meet the broad intent of the treaties that had been dictated, he strove to enforce compliance with their literal provisions. His efforts were only partially successful, for he was continuously hampered by the intrigues of the die-hard conservatives and the jealousies and obstructionist tactics of the local officials.[5]

The Tsungli Yamen, the new Chinese equivalent of a foreign office, was established in 1861 and initiated a relatively efficient conduct of relations with the diplomatic representatives who had taken up their posts in Peking in accordance with provisions of the Tientsin treaties. Fortunately for China, several of the principal members of the Tsungli Yamen were men of exceptional ability and hospitable to the idea of direct diplomatic intercourse with the foreign powers. China remained, however, without diplomatic representatives abroad, for she had not yet become convinced of the desirability of having such representatives. Actually, the first Chinese diplomatic representative, Kuo Sung-tao, was not sent abroad to London until 1877.

Anson Burlingame was the first American minister to take up residence in Peking with the responsibility of dealing directly with the Imperial Government under the changed conditions. Burlingame was a man of wide experience and had served as Congressman from Massachusetts. He failed of reelection in the 1860 campaign, and as a reward for his loyal political service he was commissioned minister to Austria. The Austrian Government refused to receive him, however, because of the moral support he had given to Hungarian and Italian nationalists who were fighting for the liberation of their countrymen from Austrian rule.[6] He was then offered the post of minister to China, which he accepted somewhat reluctantly.

Burlingame reached Canton in October 1861. Because of the lateness of the year, he spent a number of months at the various treaty ports in the south familiarizing himself with specific problems and conditions. He arrived at Peking in July 1862 and remained in China until 1865, when he returned to the United States on leave. After an absence of fifteen months he returned to China, but in November 1867 resigned from his post to accept a diplomatic assignment with the Chinese Government. During his stay in China he was rendered invaluable service by the noted S. Wells Williams, who served as interpreter and acting secretary of the legation during his absences. Williams had a profound knowledge of China, and it appears that his ideas greatly influenced Burlingame.

Burlingame was a man of great charm and by nature was understanding, sympathetic and tactful. He almost immediately gained the respect and confidence of both the Chinese and the other diplomatic representatives stationed in Peking. Although he could hardly understand a word of Chinese, his rapidly acquired familiarity with Chinese problems resulted in the Chinese Government occasionally soliciting his assistance as an unofficial adviser. During most of the period of his stay in China the United States was preoccupied with the critical problems of the Civil War and Secretary Seward practically allowed him a free hand. Hence American policy toward China from 1861 to 1867 was in effect the policy of Burlingame. Fortunately for him, the new British minister to China, Sir Frederick Bruce, was "a man of his own cheerful temperament and breadth of view."[7]

During Burlingame's tour of duty in Peking no important issues arose between China and the great powers. One of his outstanding achievements, however, was to obtain a pledge from the other diplomatic representatives that their governments would respect the territorial integrity of China and cooperate with one another to that end. In doing this, of course, Burlingame was implementing the so-called "policy of cooperation" which had been initiated by the State Department some years previously. Hitherto, however, this policy had been vague and highly theoretical, whereas under Burlingame it became concrete and practical.[8] In a dispatch of June 1862 to Secretary Seward, Burlingame contended that "if the treaty powers could agree among themselves to the neutrality of China, and together secure order in the treaty ports, and give their moral support to that party in China, in favor of order, the interests of humanity would be subserved." Burlingame's views were apparently in full accord with those of the representatives of Britain, France and Russia, who readily agreed to consult and cooperate on all matters. In this same dispatch Burlingame reported that these representatives had agreed "that while we claim our treaty right to buy and sell and hire in the treaty ports, subject, in respect to our rights of property and person, to the jurisdiction of our own governments, we will not ask for, nor take possession of, territory in the treaty ports, or in any way interfere with the jurisdiction of the Chinese Government over its own people, nor ever menace the territorial integrity of the Chinese Empire."[9]

Burlingame's policy received the full endorsement of President Lincoln and Secretary Seward, although the latter feared that the policy, while good and desirable, would probably fall into disuse when the intelligent and able diplomatic representatives then in China became replaced by others. In this judgment Seward was quite correct, for the effectiveness of the policy depended on personalities and in later years it lapsed into ineffectiveness when new and less able foreign representatives appeared on the scene in China.

In 1867 Burlingame resigned his post as minister and accepted a commission from the Chinese Government to head a special Chinese mission to be sent abroad for the purpose of revising the Tientsin treaties of 1858. The Chinese Government apparently felt that Burlingame would be able to obtain concessions which they themselves could never hope to obtain. Accompanied by a staff of two high-ranking mandarin officials and thirty others, including a Frenchman and an Englishman as secretaries, Burlingame arrived at Washington in May 1868. The mission had received an enthusiastic welcome in San Francisco the previous month, and it was as enthusiastically received in Washington, and later in New York and Boston. President Johnson personally received the mission and both Houses of Congress held receptions in its honor.

Burlingame personally felt that although China was backward in material things she was great in culture and capable of working out a solution to her problems, particularly if left unmolested by the great powers. In a speech at New York he declared that "there is not a spot on earth where there has been greater progress made within the past few years than in the Empire of China."[10] This faith in China was expressed despite the then recent Taiping Rebellion which had cost the lives of millions of Chinese and contributed to the further weakening of the decadent Manchu Government. Needless to say, it was not shared by most of the "old China hands," that is to say, those who knew China intimately from long years of residence and experience there. Nevertheless, Burlingame's opinions greatly influenced official Washington, and a treaty, or rather an amendment to the Treaty of Tientsin, was signed by Burlingame and Secretary Seward at Washington on July 28, 1868. Although called the Burlingame Treaty, Seward actually drafted it and desired it even more than Burlingame.

The Burlingame Treaty substituted reciprocal privileges for the old unilateral privileges of the Treaty of Tientsin. In the new treaty the United States pledged to respect the territorial and administrative integrity of China and granted most-favored-nation privileges to China. The United States further pledged not to interfere in any way with China's internal economic development. One of the most important provisions of the treaty concerned the voluntary emigration of Chinese laborers to the United States. This provision stated that the two countries recognized "the inherent and inalienable right of man to change his home and allegiance, and also the mutual advantage of the free navigation and emigration of their citizens and subjects respectively from one country to the other for the purposes of curiosity, of trade, or as permanent residents." This clause was inserted on the initiative of Secretary Seward and had for its purpose the accelerated emigration of Chinese laborers to the West Coast, where they were sorely needed as "cheap labor."

To Burlingame the treaty was much more than a mere instrument to facilitate the flow of "cheap labor." In a speech at Boston he contended that it recognized China "as an equal among the nations, in opposition to the old doctrine that because she was not a Christian nation, she could not be placed in the roll of nations." He denounced "the habit of foreigners in China to lecture the Chinese and to say what they should do and should not do." This treaty recognized, on the contrary, "that it is for the Chinese themselves to determine when they will institute reforms, that they are masters of their own affairs, that it is for them to make commercial regulations and do whatever they will, which is not in violation of the law of nations, within their own territory." He was fully aware, he explained, that the treaty would be "attacked by the spirit of the old indigo planters in India" and that it would be "resisted by the spirit of the old opium smuggler in China."[11]

The action of the United States in concluding this generous treaty revision with China somewhat disquieted the European treaty powers, who felt that the United States in acting independently on this matter was breaking away from the unofficial united front against China. It was even intimated in some European capitals that the treaty was concluded by the United States to curry special favor with the Chinese Government.

After the conclusion of the treaty in Washington, the Burlingame mission proceeded to London. Although it did not receive as warm a welcome there as in Washington, the British Government expressed sentiments of goodwill to China and pledged that it would cooperate in the policy of conciliation. In a letter to Burlingame, the British Foreign Minister, Lord Clarendon, stated that "The Chinese Government is fully entitled to count upon the forbearance of the foreign nations, and the British Government has neither a desire nor intention to apply unfriendly pressure to China to induce her government to advance more rapidly in her intercourse with foreign nations than is consistent with safety and with due and reasonable regard for the feelings of her subjects."[12] Clarendon made it clear, however, that China was expected to observe the treaties and protect British subjects within her Empire.

From London the mission went on to Paris, Stockholm, Copenhagen, The Hague, Berlin, and finally St. Petersburg, where Burlingame fell ill of pneumonia and died on February 23, 1870. In Paris, Berlin and St. Petersburg, the three principal capitals on the European continent, Burlingame was unable to obtain the abnegation pledges which he had received in London and Washington. Following the death of Burlingame, the mission returned to China.

Although Burlingame had failed to negotiate treaty revisions with any nation other than the United States, his efforts were greatly appreciated by the Chinese Government, which honored his memory and decreed tablets in his memory for having died in the service of China. No more fitting tribute has been paid to Burlingame than that which Frederick W. Williams penned in 1912: "It was he who first declared abroad the necessity of assisting China to find herself, and of elevating the diplomacy of Western powers in Asia to something higher than securing for their traders the largest possible advantages in a secular struggle for profits."[13] Actually Burlingame was far in advance of his time, for imperialism was not to be discredited in the West until after the conclusion of World War II, three quarters of a century after his death. The sad truth is that even today there are many Westerners who still believe, under one guise or another, that imperialism is proper.

An immediate effect of Burlingame's diplomatic mission was to encourage the Chinese Government to stiffen its resistence to the encroachment of the West.[14] Certainly China had every justification for so doing. She had at the point of a gun been victimized and forced to grant concessions which no Western power would on any account concede to other nations. The injuries that the Chinese people had suffered were far too great to be easily for-

97

gotten, and it was apparent that as long as there was a will to resist, China could not become reconciled to the position of distinct inferiority that had been imposed on her by brute force.

Despite his sincerity in eloquently portraying China as a nation capable of progress and working out its own problems if left unmolested by the Western powers, Burlingame had underestimated the deep-seated hatred of most Chinese for Westerners. Shortly after the conclusion of the Burlingame Treaty of 1868, J. Ross Brown, the American minister in Peking, warned the State Department that the impression which had been created in America to the effect that China was friendly to the United States was not based on reality. On the contrary, he stated, "The dominant feeling is antipathy and distrust towards all who have come in to disturb the administration of its domestic affairs." In a later dispatch he contended that since the United States had insisted on obtaining all that the British and French had secured through the use of force, the Chinese regarded the United States as an accomplice "in the acts of hostility committed by those powers."[15]

Anti-missionary sentiment had been aroused in China from the moment the foreign missionaries, well meaning as they may have been, began proselyting among the Chinese. The anti-missionary feeling of the Chinese was characterized by hatred of both the missionaries and their doctrines. The missionaries were hated because of their zealous determination to proselyte even in violation of the laws of China and against the opposition of the Chinese people as a whole. The doctrines of the missionaries were hated, as has been mentioned, because they contradicted or even denounced many of the cherished traditional values of Chinese society.[16]

In 1869 Prince Kung declared to the British minister, Sir Rutherford Alcock, "Take away your opium and your missionaries, and you will be welcome."[17] By this statement Kung did not mean to imply that the missionaries were linked with opium, but merely that the missionaries and the opium traffic were the two principal grievances of China against the West. The statement moreover implied that China was now prepared to accept legitimate commercial intercourse with the West in conformity with internationally recognized procedures.

Mention has been made of the Chinese feeling that the missionaries were a political as well as religious weapon of the West.* Actually the United States and Britain had arrogated the role of protectors of Protestant missions, while France had arrogated a similar role with regard to the protection of Catholic missions. In assuming the role of protectors of missions, these governments in effect took the position that missionaries had the "right" to proselyte and that when the "right" did not exist they were justified in demanding it. The Chinese, on the other hand, took the contrary position that the proselyting of alien missionaries was not a "right" but a "privilege" which a government might or might not extend. Eventually, however, the Chinese Government was compelled to yield completely to the Western position.

Between 1867 and 1870 several attacks of a serious nature were made on missionaries and their establishments. On June 21, 1870, however, the confidence in China which Burlingame had disseminated abroad was completely shattered when a mob in Tientsin, enraged by anti-French and anti-missionary sentiment, attacked the French consulate and a Catholic orphanage and cathedral. Eighteen French nationals, three Russians who may have been mistaken for Frenchmen, and some forty Chinese converts were brutally murdered. The French dead included ten nuns and two priests, whose bodies were badly mutilated. The frenzied mob also plundered four British and American chapels.

Upon hearing of this outrage, the foreign envoys at Peking promptly presented a collective note to the Tsungli Yamen deploring the inadequate protection accorded to foreigners by local Chinese officials and demanding that justice should be done. On the day following the receipt of this protest, on June 25, the Imperial Government instructed the viceroy of the Tientsin area to investigate and punish the guilty. The investigation did not proceed rapidly enough or satisfactorily, for within a month five French warships, as well as one American and three British warships, were at Tientsin. But for the critically strained relations with Prussia which resulted in a war with her a few weeks later, France might possibly have launched a major punitive expedition against China. Instead she apparently welcomed the opportunity of obtaining full

* See above, p. 49.

satisfaction without resort to arms, although her diplomatic representative did not hesitate to present extreme demands.

Two imperial decrees of October 5 and 9 finally provided for the settlement of the incident on terms that were accepted by France. In compliance with these decrees twenty Chinese were decapitated for alleged complicity in the murders, and another thirty-one were banished to remote areas of China for periods of three or ten years. China also paid an idemnity of 250,000 taels to the French Government and offered an official apology.

In 1873 the young Emperor T'ung Chih became of age and assumed the rights of the throne. With his coming of age the foreign diplomatic representatives reopened the old issue of an audience under conditions acceptable to Western practice and sensibilities. The Tsungli Yamen, while willing to arrange an audience, insisted that the foreign representatives in meeting the Emperor should kneel before him. This the foreign representatives were unwilling to do on the ground that such an action was degrading to the agents of sovereign countries that were fully the equal of China. The American minister, Frederick F. Low, was instructed by Secretary Fish to attempt by conciliatory methods to reach an agreement "with due regard for the inveterate prejudices and the grotesque conceit of the Chinese courtiers."[18] The issue was partly resolved when the Chinese consented to accept three bows as a gesture of proper respect to the Emperor. With this understanding the reception was held, but unfortunately it was held in the so-called Pavilion of Purple Light, a hall formerly used to receive the representatives of vassal states. This subterfuge, of course, provoked considerable ill feeling.

The Emperor T'ung Chih died in 1875, and since his successor was another minor the imperial audience issue did not arise again until 1891 when he assumed the rights of the throne under the name Kuang Hsu. Once again the advisers of the Emperor procrastinated on the issue of an imperial audience under conditions acceptable to the foreign diplomats. Not until China had again been thoroughly chastised by the Japanese in the Sino-Japanese War of 1894-95 and by a combination of allied powers in the Boxer Rebellion of 1900 was the issue resolved to the full satisfaction of the foreign diplomatic representatives.

Despite the persistent and intense anti-foreignism of most

Chinese living in the coastal areas, the United States Government continued to manifest a friendly attitude and to abstain from territorial encroachments or advancing demands for compromising concessions. Many of the progressive Chinese were not unaware of the somewhat consistently sympathetic attitude of the United States. Partly in recognition of American friendliness, the Chinese Government shortly after the Tientsin massacre sent more than a hundred youths to the United States for study. This action was indicative of a liberal influence operating in the Chinese Government and of an incipient force striving to bridge the gap between East and West. In 1883 all of these students were recalled, however. The precise reasons for this action are not known, but they were doubtless connected with the fact that the liberal elements had fallen out of favor at the Imperial Court, which had reverted to a policy of pronounced anti-foreignism and reaction.

Chinese from southern China had emigrated abroad long before the nineteenth century. Most of these emigrants had gone to the Philippines, Indochina, Siam, Java and the Malay peninsula. In the nineteenth century a demand for cheap Chinese coolie labor arose in Peru, Cuba, Brazil and other countries of the New World, particularly for toil in plantations, mines and construction projects. As a result of this new demand for cheap Chinese labor, a so-called coolie trade came into existence. It reached significant proportions as early as 1854.[19]

The Imperial Government of China consistently took a negative attitude toward the emigration of its subjects. The law actually provided that no Chinese could leave the country without a permit, and a special reason was required for it. The power of the central government had become so enfeebled by the middle of the nineteenth century, however, that the law was not enforced and it was not a difficult matter for a Chinese to leave the country.[20]

Westerners became deeply involved in the coolie trade and made huge profits from it. The principal beneficiaries of this trade were the entrepreneurs who bought and sold the coolie contracts, and the shipowners of ocean-going vessels who were paid handsome fees for each coolie transported. Although American vessels participated in this trade, they did not transport coolies to the Pacific Coast or any other part of the United States. The Chinese who entered the United States came essentially as "free" laborers, and

101

they should not be confused with the victims of the coolie traffic.

Coolies from southern China were induced to emigrate abroad on the basis of contracts which provided for a stipulated number of years of service as contract laborers, generally eight years, and for fixed but low payments. In actual practice the contracts signed by the coolies were sold by auction at prices ranging from $400 to $1,000. Recruiting agents invariably misrepresented the contracts to the ignorant and unsuspecting coolies, and the conditions under which they were transported to their destinations in filthy and overcrowded holds of vessels were abominable. Large numbers died en route in the holds of ships. The mortality rate on vessels putting in at Havana, for example, was nearly 10 percent for American ships and more than 38 percent for Portuguese ships.[21] Conditions aboard the vessels were so unbearable that coolies often committed suicide and not infrequently mutinied and even killed the captains of their vessels.[22] Those unfortunates who survived to be carted off to a plantation or mine were brutally treated and subjected to virtual slavery. The profits of this shameful trade became so lucrative and the demand for the coolies increased to such an extent that the coolie traders even resorted to kidnapping helpless Chinese and forcing them to board vessels sailing for countries in which coolie labor was in demand.

At first the Chinese Government was unconcerned about the evils of this barbarous traffic, for its traditional policy had been that Chinese who emigrated abroad were no concern of the government. However, when the traffic swelled to outrageous proportions and the abuses attendant to it became so scandalous that even Western nations were shocked, the Chinese Government finally took an interest in the problem and sought to end its most vicious aspects. Some years after he had retired from office as Secretary of State, Seward remarked that the coolie traffic was "an abomination scarcely less execrable than the African slave trade." It is estimated that more than a hundred thousand coolies were transported to Peru and that another one hundred and fifty thousand were transported to Cuba alone.

Great Britain was the first Western nation to take action against the traffic in 1855 when Parliament prohibited British vessels from participating in the trade. The United States did not take action until seven years later, when Congress passed a law which forbade American vessels to transport coolies and authorized the U.S.

Navy to search American vessels suspected of violating the law. The law and the vigilance of the U.S. Navy were sufficient to drive American vessels out of the traffic and to prevent the introduction of coolie labor in the United States.[23] Moreover, American laws did not permit the existence of coolie contracts, and hence even if coolie laborers had entered the country their contracts would have been invalidated. As has been mentioned, the large number of Chinese laborers who did emigrate to California and other areas of the United States labored essentially as free men, although at jobs which were then unwanted by white laborers.

Chinese immigration to the United States began shortly after the discovery of gold in California in 1848. Large numbers of Chinese settled in the mining towns, and some were able to accumulate small fortunes. When the gold rush subsided in the mining towns, a fresh demand arose for large numbers of cheap Chinese laborers for unskilled work in railroad construction. These laborers signed their contracts either in China or in California, after their arrival there. They contracted to work for a stipulated number of years, and in general the contracts were heavily weighted against them. The management of Chinese laborers later fell into the hands of Chinese companies, whose methods of operation and financing, while proper in China, were alien to America.[24]

For a time the number of Chinese immigrants increased somewhat rapidly. In 1848 there were probably not more than fifty Chinese in the United States; by 1852 there were 25,000; and by 1867 the number had increased to about 50,000,[25] almost half of whom were located on the Pacific Coast, largely in California. The first phase of Chinese immigration, which lasted until about 1870 when the heavy demand for cheap labor ended, was generally looked upon with approval by Americans of the West Coast. The newspaper *Alta California,* for example, commented on May 12, 1852: "Scarcely a ship arrives that does not bring an increase to this worthy integer of our population. The China boys will yet vote at the same polls, study at the same schools and bow at the same altar as our own countrymen."[26] These sentiments were a far cry from those of later generations of Californians.

After the conclusion of the Burlingame Treaty of 1868 the number of Chinese increased to such an extent as to alarm native Americans on the Pacific Coast and to give rise to violent and shameful acts of anti-Orientalism. The animosity of the American whites was due to a number of factors. The thrifty and hard-working Chinese, willing to put up with a low standard of living to which they were accustomed, demonstrated a marked ability to succeed under conditions intolerable to most whites. The low wages for which they were willing to work were represented as a menace to the American standard of living. Even the East Coast *New York Nation* jeeringly commented that the Chinese immigrants had "disgusting habits of thrift, industry, and self-denial."[27] The Chinese practice of living in colonies of their own, which was but natural, and their apparent unassimilability were castigated by white agitators as un-American and likely to result in the Pacific Coast becoming an Oriental outpost.* Equally exploited by the agitators were the strange customs of the unassimilated Chinese and their non-Christian beliefs which were represented as threats to American moral standards. Yielding to the widespread animosity and clamor, several states passed laws which outrightly discriminated against the Chinese; but when tested in the courts these laws were declared unconstitutional.

The Burlingame Treaty was concluded at the time the first transcontinental railroad was completed. Shortly afterward, the thousands who had been employed on this work, ninety percent of whom were Chinese, were released and forced to seek employment elsewhere. This led to severe competition for jobs in California, at a time when the "gold rush" prosperity had run its course and a period of economic dislocation and readjustment was underway. It was inevitable that the Chinese minority would be made the scapegoat. Animosity towards the Chinese was perhaps strongest among native American laborers, with whom the Chinese competed for jobs. Chinese immigration consequently became a leading issue in California politics.

By the late 1870's anti-Chinese feeling reached unfortunate extremes, especially in California, where Chinese laborers, thrown out of work, began to concentrate. In 1880 there were probably 75,000 Chinese in California, representing about nine percent of the state's total population at that time. Since the gold-rush pros-

---

*The agitators, of course, completely disregarded the elementary fact that the Chinese could only be assimilated to the extent Americans allowed and encouraged them to become assimilated.

perity had completely petered out by this time, it was inevitable that rabble-rousers would work on the emotions of unemployed whites. The most notorious of the rabble rousers was Denis Kearny, an Irish-born naturalized citizen, who in 1876 mobilized the resentment. One of his more notorious manifestoes declared that "the Chinaman must leave our shores" and that "death is preferable to life on a par with the Chinaman."[28] Goaded by Kearny and others like him, gangs of self-styled "Americans" perpetrated every imaginable outrage against the helpless, law-abiding Chinese. Some of these outrages were merely despicable, such as throwing fresh laundry into the mud, setting dogs upon the Chinese, or seizing them and shearing their pigtails. But all too often the gangs stoned the Chinese, beat them, burnt their houses, and even killed them. Ironically enough, many of Kearny's followers were recent immigrants who probably had not been in the country as long as some of the Chinese they persecuted. As Thomas A. Bailey puts it in his inimitable way, the Irish adherents of Kearny supported him with shouts of, "Immeriky fur Immerikans, bejabers!"[29]

The crusading anti-Chinese spirit aroused by Kearney and his henchmen spread to other states of the Pacific Coast and even eastward as far as Colorado. On a Christian Sunday, October 31, 1880, a mob of drunken whites attacked some Chinese who were gambling and allegedly smoking opium. One of the Chinese was killed and several others injured. A general riot then broke out and the police rushed some 400 Chinese to the county jail for safety, but while they were there members of the mob broke into 141 Chinese homes and stole property valued at $53,655.[30] The Chinese minister at Washington lodged a formal protest, but he was informed that the United States Government did not have jurisdiction and that it could do nothing more than see that the Chinese had the same legal recourse as the citizens of the state concerned.

The most outrageous crime against the Chinese, however, was the massacre at Rock Springs, Wyoming, on September 2, 1885. On that day a white mob attacked some 500 inoffensive Chinese coal miners in an orgy that resulted in the killing of nineteen Chinese, the wounding of many more, and the flight of some 400 frightened Chinese from the town.[31] Again the Chinese Government protested, and the United States offered to pay $147,749 as indemnification to the injured Chinese. The United States Government made it clear, however, that it was not making the settlement because of any "obligation of treaty or principle of international law, but solely from a sentiment of generosity and pity to an innocent and unfortunate body of men" who had been "so shockingly outraged."[32]

As a result of pressure from California, as well as the concern of responsible men in Washington, Congress appointed a joint committee in 1876 to make an on-the-spot investigation of the Chinese problem on the Pacific Coast. The committee was headed by Senator Oliver Morton of Indiana. Morton became ill after the mission had completed its survey and he was unable to submit the majority report. The majority report was therefore submitted by Senator Sargent of California, in February 1877. It reiterated the hackneyed complaints against the Chinese and recommended the adoption of measures by the United States Government to revise the Burlingame Treaty, confine Chinese immigration to merchants, and legislate against all Asian immigration. A minority report, based on the findings of the then-ill Senator Morton, refuted most of Sargent's allegations and reminded all concerned of the sanctity of the Burlingame Treaty and of the inalienable right of all men to change their domicile and allegiance. The report described the inalienable right of emigration as "the great American doctrine."

Pressure from the West Coast was winning the battle, however, and in 1879 Congress passed a bill which flagrantly violated the emigration clause of the Burlingame Treaty and fell just short of excluding all Chinese from entering the United States. *Inter alia,* the bill permitted not more than fifteen Chinese to obtain passage on any vessel bound for the West Coast. The bill was rightly vetoed by President Hayes. In his message to Congress he pointed out that while the Burlingame Treaty had not worked out well because of changed conditions, it was nevertheless the responsibility of the United States to respect its provisions as long as it remained in effect.

Aware that the Californians would be content with nothing less than the actual exclusion of Chinese immigrants, Hayes in 1880 appointed a special three-man mission to negotiate at Peking a revision of the controversial Burlingame Treaty that would make this possible without hurting the pride or offending the sensibilities of the Chinese Government. The members of the mission were Dr. James B. Angell of the University of Michigan, former Assistant-Secretary of State William H. Trescott, and John F. Swift of California. They were hospitably received by the Chinese Government and encountered no difficulty in obtaining the desired changes. The new treaty, concluded on November 18, recognized that the United States "may regulate, limit, or suspend" Chinese immigration "but may not absolutely prohibit it."[33] It was suggested that this stipulation was to apply only to Chinese laborers and not to others who might desire entry into the United States for business reasons or educational purposes. The treaty also provided that Chinese laborers in the United States who desired to visit China would be assured of reentry.

In a reciprocal gesture, the American mission consented to negotiate a new commercial treaty, one of whose provisions stipulated that appropriate legislation would be enacted in the United States to the effect that "citizens of the United States shall not be permitted to import opium into any of the open ports of China, to transport it from one open port to another open port, or to buy and sell opium in any of the open ports of China."[34] This gesture certainly pleased the Chinese, for they had never become reconciled to the opium traffic, notwithstanding its legalization by the 1858 Rules of Trade to which they had been compelled to subscribe. The Chinese position was doubtless sincerely expressed by Li Hung-Chang, China's foremost statesman of the nineteenth century, in a letter of May 24, 1881, addressed to the British Society for the Suppression of the Opium Trade. In this letter Li declared that "the single aim of the government in taxing opium will be in the future, as it has always been in the past, to repress the traffic, never the desire to gain revenue from such a source.[35]

Actually several years passed before Congress passed the necessary legislation to implement the anti-opium treaty pledge, and some American vessels continued to engage in opium smuggling. The authority to enforce the pledge was finally embodied in an act of Congress, approved on February 23, 1887. The anti-opium pledge of the United States may well have been the price paid for the attainment of its major objective, the effective exclusion of

Chinese immigrants.[36] The American action was nevertheless appreciated by the Chinese Government, especially since the British continued to insist on the legality of the opium trade as defined by treaty.

The West Coast was far from satisfied with the 1880 immigration treaty, however, and Congress in 1882 passed an act suspending the immigration of Chinese laborers for twenty years. President Arthur courageously vetoed the measure on the ground that the suspension of Chinese immigration for twenty years was not in consonance with the assurances given the Chinese Government by the American mission which had negotiated the treaty of 1880. Congress respected the President's position, and amended the act to provide for the suspension of immigration for only a ten-year period. The new bill, however, provided that "no state court or court of the United States shall admit Chinese to citizenship." The West Coast apparently felt that the new bill did not go far enough, and a Congressman of that area sneeringly remarked that President Arthur manifestly wanted to "empty the teeming slave pens of China upon the soil of California."[37] Meanwhile, on the West Coast the legislatures further discriminated against the Chinese and violence continued unabated.

The United States Government had no alternative but to appease the West Coast, and in 1888 another treaty was concluded with China which provided that Chinese nationals in the United States could not visit China and return to America unless they had property worth $1,000 or had a wife and children in the United States. Primarily because of the amendments desired by both the United States and China, the treaty failed of ratification. Meanwhile, under heavy pressure from various elements in California, particularly the labor unions, Congress passed the Scott Act which prohibited rather than suspended the immigration of Chinese laborers. This act violated the treaty with China that was in force, but President Cleveland signed it on the ground that China had failed to ratify the newly negotiated treaty of 1888. In 1892 Congress extended for another ten years the provisions of the bill of 1882 and tightened up the definition of those eligible to enter the country as businessmen, students and tourists. The Chinese minister in Washington denounced the measure as "a violation of every principle of justice, equity, reason and fair dealing between two friendly powers."[38]

108

Anxious to have an agreement that would square up with the new conditions, President Cleveland instructed Secretary Gresham to begin negotiations with the Chinese minister in Washington for a new treaty. The negotiations proceeded successfully, and a treaty was signed in 1894. In general its provisions restated those of the unratified treaty of 1888. It again stipulated that the immigration of Chinese laborers was to be suspended for ten years, but was amended to provide more leniency for those eligible to enter the country. Following the expiration of this treaty in 1904 and the refusal of China to negotiate a new treaty which would perpetuate exclusion, Congress reenacted, without a time limit, all existing laws suspending the immigration of Chinese laborers. Thus the immigration of Chinese laborers came to a definitive end, and the Chinese population in the United States subsequently declined markedly. Whereas in 1882 there had been 132,000 Chinese in the United States, by 1930 they had declined to 74,954, of whom 30,868 were born in the United States and hence American citizens.

The arbitrary exclusion legislation of Congress produced a short period of intense anti-Americanism in China and resulted in the first and only boycott of American goods in 1904 and 1905. The boycott was finally terminated as a result of the protests of the United States Government and the merchants of Shanghai.[39]

Although the Chinese immigration policy was forced on the country by the West Coast, the tactless manner in which the Chinese problem was handled was a deep stain on our record of traditionally good and reasonably honorable relations with China. The immigration act of 1924 placed Chinese on the same basis as other Orientals, all of whom were excluded from the country. Not until 1943 was the immigration of Chinese placed on the same basis as European immigration, that is, on a quota basis. This quota allowed the Chinese 105 immigrants annually. In asking Congress for support of this measure, President Roosevelt explained that "We must be big enough to acknowledge our past mistakes and to correct them." Actually, however, this concession to Chinese immigration was a wartime measure of expediency to keep China fighting on our side against Japan; it hardly represented a sincere and moral approach to a just solution of the problem of Asiatic immigration.

CHAPTER SIX

Relations with Japan, 1856–1894

While Perry's mission was a considerable diplomatic success and succeeded in opening the door that had long closed Japan to the outside world, it did not result in the peaceful overnight transition of Japan from a policy of seclusion to one of open intercourse with foreign countries. The domestic enemies of the Bakufu made political capital of the concessions that had been made and for political reasons encouraged the intensification of anti-foreignism as a means of embarrassing the Bakufu and further weakening it for the final assault. Moreover, it was too much to expect that the seclusion mentality which had been assiduously cultivated over a long period of two and a half centuries could be easily and smoothly transformed without incidents and some turmoil. With the conclusion of Perry's mission and the signing of the subsequent treaties with the other powers, there consequently followed a period of more than a decade during which Japan seethed with the possibility of civil war and widespread violence against the foreigner who had in effect forced himself upon Japan.

In accordance with a provision of the Treaty of Kanagawa, the United States Government in August 1855 commissioned Townsend Harris as the first American consul general to reside in Shimoda. Harris was instructed to exert every effort toward securing full protection for Americans frequenting Shimoda, if possible to obtain an audience with the Shōgun, and, failing in that, to attempt to convince the Bakufu of the desirability of enlarging commercial intercourse between the United States and Japan.[1]

Although his formal schooling was limited, Harris was well informed and had acquired a knowledge of Spanish, French and

Italian. He had had some experience in public affairs, had been a merchant in New York, and had also served as a supercargo and merchant in China where he had acquired a first-hand knowledge of the Far East. He was a man of great tact, unusual ability, great fortitude and high moral principles. Indicative of his conscientiousness and sincerity is the entry he made in his journal as he approached the Japanese coast and caught his first view of majestic Mount Fuji: "I shall be the first recognized agent from a civilized power to reside in Japan. This forms an epoch in my life and may be the beginning of a new order of things in Japan. I hope I may so conduct myself that I may have honorable mention in the histories which will be written on Japan and its future destiny."[2]

Harris arrived at Shimoda aboard the warship *San Jacinto* on August 21, 1856. En route he had stopped at Siam, where he negotiated a treaty with the government of that country.

As a result of his first meetings with the Japanese, Harris was very favorably impressed by them and significantly wrote in his journal that "they are superior to any people east of the Cape of Good Hope." Nevertheless, from the very outset Harris encountered obstacles and a hostility that doubtless would have discouraged a man of lesser fortitude and courage. The magistrate (*bugyō*) of Shimoda, for example, promptly informed him that the arrival of a consul had not been anticipated and consequently no preparations had been made to receive or accommodate one. The governor suggested that it would be very advisable to return to the United States. Harris was indignant at this suggestion. After being warned by Harris that if he were not properly treated in Shimoda he would proceed at once to Edo in the *San Jacinto,* the governor reluctantly agreed to provide a temple for living quarters. An offer to furnish some men "to aid and protect him" was rejected by Harris, who suspected that they would be employed to spy on him. After taking up residence in the temple, Harris was confronted with further vexations and annoyances. Japanese guards were stationed around the temple and even his servants were obstructed when they went shopping for food and supplies. By means of patience and tact, however, Harris gradually gained the confidence of the Japanese and won their respect for his rights as a consul.

It is of interest to note that in general Harris was a good observer and that he learned much about Japanese customs, although many of them puzzled him. Noting that the Japanese were "a clean people" and that they all, rich and poor, bathed every day, he was shocked to observe that males and females bathed together in the nude in the public bathhouses that were to be found all over the country. "I cannot account for so indelicate a proceeding on the part of a people so generally correct," he wrote in his journal.[3]

Although commissioned as a consul general, Harris had been vested with full diplomatic powers and the authority to engage in treaty discussions. Shortly after his arrival he therefore informed the Shōgun's minister of foreign affairs that he was prepared to begin discussions with the view of concluding a treaty which would be more adequate than the one in effect. Discussions for this purpose were carried on in Shimoda over a protracted period of time, during which Harris was compelled to tolerate the most vexatious procrastination and obstructionism. There were times when even the persevering Harris doubted that he could win the Japanese over to his arguments. Added to these difficulties, Harris was in poor health and completely isolated from his home government, from which he did not receive a single communication until more than a year after his arrival in Shimoda.[4]

Success finally came to Harris, however, and on June 17, 1857, ten months after his arrival in Japan, he and officials of the Bakufu affixed their signatures to the Convention of Shimoda, concluded "for the purpose of further regulating the intercourse of American citizens within the Empire of Japan." This convention clarified some of the misconceptions resulting from the Perry treaty and also embodied all that had accrued to the United States by virtue of its most-favored-nation privileges. The convention opened the port of Nagasaki for the procurement of supplies, specifically granted Americans the right of permanent residence in the treaty ports, fixed the rate of exchange for American currency at its actual value, granted extraterritorial jurisdiction to American consuls, and more clearly defined the rights and privileges of American consuls in Japan. Although Harris was ailing and somewhat discouraged when this convention was concluded, it nevertheless was a very considerable diplomatic achievement, an achievement due entirely to his own sincerity and persuasiveness without threats or military backing.[5]

In October 1857 the Dutch also concluded a new treaty with the Japanese which, *inter alia,* provided for a temporary import tariff of 35 percent, authorized freedom of religion for Dutch nationals within their premises, and significantly forbade the importation of opium. A Russian treaty concluded in the same month also prohibited the importation of opium. The Dutch and Russian "anti-opium" clauses rendered a singular service to Japan; it is very likely, however, that the Dutch and Russians were more motivated by a desire to strike at a key product in Britain's envied trade rather than by sincere moral convictions.[6]

The Convention of Shimoda, while a noteworthy improvement on the Perry treaty, nevertheless was too limited in scope and details to meet the legitimate requirements of the United States at that time. Harris' next move, therefore, was to begin negotiations for a truly comprehensive treaty. Harris had in his possession a letter from the President of the United States, addressed to the Emperor, which he wished to deliver in person. Initially Harris was apparently ignorant of the exact nature of the dual government then prevailing in Japan and of the fact that the actual ruler was the Shōgun rather than the Emperor. It was not long, however, before Harris became well informed of the actual state of affairs. He then insisted on being permitted to deliver the letter personally to the Shōgun's court in Edo. The Bakufu was at first strongly opposed to this suggestion, but finally consented for fear that Harris might employ warships to deliver the letter personally by force.

Harris made the long journey from Shimoda to Edo on horseback in November 1857, accompanied by a retinue of some 350 guards and attendants. The trip of 180 miles was made over the ancient Tokaidō (the main highway) and required seven days. The Bakufu had made careful preparations for the trip of Harris and his retinue. Huge crowds assembled along the route to catch a glimpse of the "great man." No incidents of any kind took place until Harris reached the outlying districts of Edo, where the officials of the Shōgun insisted on examining his baggage in accordance with provisions of the law. Harris firmly refused to permit this examination on the ground that it would be a violation of his rights as a consul. Somewhat chagrined, the officials did not press the matter and permitted Harris to continue his journey unmolested, his baggage untouched. Harris arrived in Edo on a Sunday, and hundreds of thousands of curious Japanese observed the pompous entrance in silence. A devout Protestant, Harris refused to conduct any business on that day since it was the Sabbath. "Ever since I have been in this country," he wrote in his journal, "I have refused to transact any business on that day." The Japanese apparently understood his motive and respected him for it.

Harris' arrival in Edo was of historic significance, since it marked the first time since 1613* that a foreign representative had been received in audience by the Shōgun. After calling on the principal ministers of state, Harris was presented to the Shōgun,† to whom he personally delivered the President's letter. After the audience, in which the Japanese were greatly impressed by his dignified bearing, Harris retired to his apartment and there was the recipient of a special elaborate dinner sent by the Shōgun. The usual presents were then exchanged, and thereafter Harris set to work in earnest to discuss the comprehensive treaty desired by his government.

Although the Japanese had ceased to be hostile and by this time had actually come to have a very high regard for Harris, his task was not easy, primarily because of the almost total ignorance of the Japanese concerning the nature of diplomatic relations on a basis of equality. Aware of this ignorance, to which they frankly confessed and for which they begged enlightenment, Harris obligingly and painstakingly explained many things to them, such as the rank of a minister, his duties, the fundamental principles of international law, and the characteristics of Western governments and economic systems. The following entry in his journal is particularly interesting and refreshing: "I may be said to be engaged in teaching the elements of political economy to the Japanese. They said they were in the dark on these points, and were like children; therefore I must have patience with them."

By means of patience, sympathetic understanding, tact and political acumen, Harris finally succeeded in overcoming the hesita-

*In that year the British envoy Captain Saris had been received in audience by the Shōgun.

† Prior to the audience Harris had obtained the consent of the Shōgun's officials for the substitution of three bows, as was customary in European receptions, for the traditional kowtow expected of all when presented to the Shōgun.

tion of the Japanese. His candidness and sincerity gained the complete confidence of the Japanese officials, and he further ingratiated himself with them by yielding on a number of minor points which he knew they could concede only with the greatest difficulty, if at all. Harris clinched his objective, however, by skillfully playing on the fears of the Japanese concerning the intentions of the avidly imperialistic powers, such as Great Britain, France and Russia. He warned Lord Hotta, the Shōgun's enlightened prime minister, that as soon as the British and the French concluded the war they were then waging against China (the Arrow War) they would dispatch fleets to Japan and demand important concessions. He suggested that Japan could best protect herself by establishing full treaty relations with the Western powers, who would then serve as a check on the aggressive intentions of each other in Japan. The United States, he reassuringly and correctly pointed out, did not permit the acquisition of territory overseas. Moreover, he argued, there was no danger whatsoever of the United States and Japan becoming enemies, regardless of whether or not the desired treaty was concluded. He cautioned, however, that if Japan failed to establish satisfactory treaty relations with the Western powers, she might become the victim of grave misfortunes, caused not by the United States but by the other less scrupulous Western powers. "If you accept the treaty I now offer you, no other country will demand more," he explained to Lord Hotta. "If I display the treaty to the Europeans, they will desire to conclude similar treaties, and the matter will be settled by the mere sending over of a minister."

The Imperial Court in Kyoto, which, as has been indicated, was strongly influenced by powerful daimyōs now openly hostile to the Tokugawa Bakufu, was opposed to the treaty and refused to sanction it. In effect this was the first time in the history of the Tokugawa Bakufu that it had failed to obtain imperial approval of any of its actions. Seemingly an impasse had been reached, since the Bakufu, conscious of its waning power and prestige, dared not oppose what purported to be the imperial will. On the other hand, the Bakufu was fully aware of the grave danger threatening Japan and the necessity of establishing satisfactory relations as a means of forestalling acts of aggression by the foreign powers, as Harris had explained. So vitally important was the imperial sanction of the treaty considered by the Bakufu that Lord Hotta in March

1858 went to Kyoto and made a personal appeal. Reflecting some of Harris' ideas, he argued strenuously that the treaty would be instrumental in aiding Japan to protect herself from Western aggression. "When our power and national standing have come to be recognized," he pleaded, "we should take the lead in punishing the nation which may act contrary to the principle of international interests; and in so doing, we should join hands with the nations whose principles may be found identical with those of our country."[7] His arguments, though sound, were in vain, however, and he was unable to sway the Imperial Court, which was dominated by elements hostile to the Bakufu who hoped to embarrass it by making a national issue of the Harris treaty.

Returning to Edo early in June, Lord Hotta invited Harris to his mansion and frankly informed him of the critical state of affairs which admonished postponing the signing of the treaty. He tried to make Harris understand that an immediate attempt to open the country would plunge it into bloody civil war. Patiently he pleaded for a postponement of the signing of the treaty. Harris was bitterly disappointed, and even hinted that he would go directly to Kyoto if, as Hotta seemed to imply, the real authority was located there. Despite his chagrin, however, Harris consented to the postponement.[8]

During Hotta's absence from Edo, the Shōgun's Court had seethed with intrigue concerning a successor to the Shōgun Iesada, who was dying. It was finally agreed to accept as his successor a mere youth, and Lord Naosuke Ii was appointed Tairō, or Regent. With his appointment to this office, Lord Ii took over the management of foreign affairs, and Hotta ceased to exercise any real influence. A man of strong character and political perspicacity, Lord Ii believed that failure to sign the treaty would be blind folly and a needless invitation to disaster, but he hoped that the signing might be delayed until imperial approval could be obtained. Late in July an American vessel arrived at Shimoda and brought news that the powers had forcibly compelled China to sign new treaties and that British and French warships were on their way to Japan to demand concessions. This news greatly alarmed the Bakufu, and at a meeting of its highest officials a majority voted to have the Harris treaty signed immediately.

Bowing to the will of the majority, Lord Ii assumed full responsibility and ordered the Harris treaty to be signed regardless of the refusal of the Imperial Court to sanction it. Because of this bold and seemingly defiant action, he incurred the intense hatred of the pro-imperialists and anti-foreigners. He was subsequently assassinated, partly because of the hatred he had aroused in concluding the treaty without imperial authorization. Nonetheless, he deserves to be remembered as one of the courageous men of modern Japan who rendered that nation a great service in a critical hour.

The Harris treaty was at length signed in Edo Bay aboard the U.S.S. *Powhattan,* on July 29, 1858. It was the first real treaty of commerce concluded by Japan since the beginning of the seventeenth century, and served as a model for treaties subsequently negotiated by the other powers. It provided for the opening of three ports to trade and two others to visitation and residence, the establishment of an American ministry in Edo, extraterritorial jurisdiction for American consuls, and freedom of religion for Americans resident in Japan. The treaty also invited the Japanese to study naval construction in the United States, and a clause, common in American treaties with Asian countries at that time, provided for the mediation of the President of the United States between Japan and other powers should the occasion arise and should it be requested. Either government could request the revision of the treaty after July 4, 1871. The commercial regulations which supplemented the treaty provided for a sliding scale of duties on imports and a flat five percent duty on all exports. The duties could be revised in 1864 upon the request of the Japanese Government.

It may be of interest to note the extraterritorial provision of the treaty, which stipulated: "Americans committing offenses against Japanese shall be tried by American Consular courts, and, when guilty, shall be punished according to American law. Japanese committing offences against Americans shall be tried by the Japanese authorities and punished according to Japanese law."[9] Harris had reluctantly insisted upon the inclusion of this provision, and he subsequently stated that its inclusion in the treaty was against his conscience and that he hoped it would some day be abolished. Actually, however, the Bakufu was not reluctant to grant extraterritoriality, for at the time it seemed to comport with the ancient tradition that the national laws were sacred and therefore not to be applied to "barbarians."[10]

Without the support of warships or armaments of any kind and without invoking threats, either open or veiled, Harris had succeeded through tact and brilliant diplomacy alone in achieving one of the most outstanding successes in the annals of the foreign service of the State Department. Whereas Perry was the first to break the hard shell of Tokugawa seclusion-exclusion, Harris paved the way for the establishment of full commercial relations with the nations of the West on a basis of reasonableness and dignity. In a sense, too, Harris prepared the way for the eventual admission of Japan as an equal member in the comity of nations.

Treaties similar to the one negotiated by Harris were immediately concluded by Great Britain, France, Russia and the Netherlands. The British treaty was negotiated by the illustrious Lord Elgin, who called on Harris at Shimoda to secure a copy of his treaty for use as a model and also to employ on a temporary basis his secretary, Henry Heusken, as an interpreter. The British treaty, however, provided for the reduction of import tariffs on cotton and woolen manufactured goods from twenty to five percent. It is to be noted that this provision, when implemented, caused great injury to the native textile industry and greatly handicapped its modernization, since Japanese producers could not compete with the low cost of the industrially produced British products. All the treaties concluded by the Bakufu were approved by imperial edict on February 2, 1859, as temporary measures to keep the foreigners at a safe distance and to serve merely as a prelude to the ultimate restoration of the ruptured seclusion policy.[11]

The Harris treaty provided for the exchange of ratifications in Washington. In February 1860 a Japanese mission consisting of 71 persons sailed from Japan aboard the American warship *Powhattan* to exchange the ratifications and also to make a study of American institutions. The members of the mission were warmly welcomed in San Francisco and Washington. The keen intelligence and gentlemanly comportment of the Japanese greatly impressed the Americans who came in contact with them. The American press noted that "they were quite as dignified, intelligent, and well bred as any gentlemen in any country or time."[12]

After the American ratification of the treaty, Harris was commissioned as Minister to Japan, a post he held until 1862 when he was relieved at his own request. He gave as his reasons for resigning the following: "The extraordinary life of isolation I have been compelled to lead has greatly impaired my health, and this, joined to my advancing years, warns me that it is time for me to give up all public employment." Many years later, on December 18, 1936, the Japanese honored the name of Townsend Harris by the erection of a monument to his memory in Tokyo.

The attempt of the Bakufu to enforce the treaties of 1858 and open the country to widened intercourse with the world accentuated the discontent that had been smoldering for some time against the Tokugawa Government. Part of this discontent was directed against the rapidly weakening Bakufu, and part was directed against the foreigner. Forces hostile to the Bakufu, particularly the Imperial Court in Kyoto and certain rebellious clan leaders, notably the daimyō of Mito, capitalized on the unpopularity of the treaties and the apparent responsibility of the Bakufu for their conclusion. Indeed, during this critical period anti-Tokugawaism and anti-foreignism were almost synonymous terms. "Revere the Emperor and expel the barbarians" became a popular catchphrase which epitomized the explosive unrest of the time.

The period of intense anti-foreignism lasted from the time of the conclusion of the treaties of 1858 to about 1865 when the Emperor sanctioned the treaties. From then until 1868 the fury of anti-foreignism abated considerably. After the overthrow of the Tokugawa Government in 1868, the Imperial Government switched from its former apparent support of anti-foreignism to a policy of assiduously favoring increased foreign intercourse. With this change in imperial policy, however, anti-foreignism did not immediately die down completely. Actually it remained as a force of considerable importance, although a minor and decreasing one, until about 1894. It ought to be noted, however, that suspicion and distrust of foreigners remained a strong characteristic in the Japanese character.

During the period of intense anti-foreignism the Bakufu apparently acted in good faith and attempted to do all it could to comply with the provisions of the treaties. Harris understood the dilemma

119

and difficulties of the Bakufu, and he refused to hold it responsible for the lawless acts of individuals over whom it actually had little if any control under the changed conditions that had come into existence. The other foreign representatives did not, however, share Harris' view and in general they favored a tough policy. Secretary Seward also advocated a tough policy, and he believed that there was a real danger the foreigners might be expelled from some or all of the treaty ports. He informed Harris that "very large interests, not of our own country, but of the civilized world, are involved in retaining the foothold of foreign nations already acquired in the Empire of Japan."[13] Happily for all concerned, Harris adroitly softened the toughness advocated by his superior, the Secretary of State.

The first serious anti-foreign outbreak occurred in 1859 on the occasion of the visit of a Russian fleet to Yokohama when an officer and two sailors were attacked in the streets. The officer and one of the sailors were killed. In the following year the interpreter of the Russian legation was mortally wounded and the captains of two Dutch vessels were hacked to pieces. It was in March of that year that Naosuki Ii was assassinated by a band of *rōnin,* or "masterless samurai," allegedly for "making foreign intercourse his chief aim."

In January 1861 Henry Heusken, Harris' interpreter, was murdered in the streets of Edo. On learning of this outrage, Secretary Seward suggested a joint naval demonstration by the United States, France, Great Britain and Russia to compel Japan to honor the stipulations of the treaties. Harris wisely disapproved the suggestion, and Seward reluctantly abandoned it. Nevertheless, on December 13, 1862, Seward instructed Harris to advise Japan that she "can only have friendship or even peace with the United States by protecting the citizens and subjects of foreign powers from domestic violence."[14] It is difficult to determine precisely how much of this "toughness" in Seward should be attributed to the exigencies of the American Civil War then raging and his compelling desire to remain on the friendliest terms possible with the great European powers, whose governments were in general sympathetic to the South.[15] He was particularly concerned about the neutrality of Britain and France, which had extensive interests in Japan and were being courted by the South.

In 1862 the British legation was attacked and two of its Japanese guards were killed. In that same year an arrogant Englishman, Charles Richardson, was assaulted and murdered by some retainers of the Daimyō of Satsuma. The British Government held the Bakufu responsible for this act and demanded and obtained from it an indemnity of $500,000. In addition, the British bombarded Kagoshima, the capital of the recalcitrant daimyō, and forced him to pay an additional indemnity of $125,000.

As an immediate result of the Richardson incident, the foreign diplomatic representatives stationed in Edo withdrew to Yokohama, where they could be protected by the guns of the foreign warships at anchor in the harbor. Harris, however, refused to leave Edo. In his attitude toward the anti-foreign outbreaks he differed sharply with his diplomatic colleagues. He insisted that the harassed Bakufu was doing everything it could to honor its treaty responsibilities while the foreign diplomats, on their part, were expecting too much and the impossible under the circumstances then prevailing. He strongly maintained that none of the foreign powers should expoit the chaotic situation and the compromised position of the Bakufu to press unreasonable demands or resort to actions that would further compromise or weaken the Bakufu. In a note to Sir Rutherford Alcock, the British minister, he lamented: "I had hoped that the page of future history might record the great fact that in one spot in the Eastern world the advent of Christian civilization did not bring with it its usual attendants of rapine and bloodshed; this fond hope, I fear, is to be disappointed. I would sooner see all the treaties with this country torn up, and Japan return to its old state of isolation, than witness the horrors of war inflicted on this peaceful and happy land."[16]

The British bombardment of Kagoshima failed to intimidate the Japanese or put an end to the anti-foreign outbreaks. In 1863 the American legation in Edo was mysteriously burned. The captain of the U.S.S. *Wyoming,* then in Japanese waters, was instructed to employ whatever force was necessary to protect American lives.[17] Robert Pruyn, who had replaced Harris, then reluctantly left Edo and joined his colleagues in Yokohama, where British and French troops had just been landed. A conscientious and able diplomat, Pruyn like Harris took a position of sympathetic understanding regarding the Bakufu and its vexatious problems. He nevertheless exerted the fullest effort to protect American rights. By negotiation he was able to obtain from the Bakufu an indemnity of $10,000 for the burning of the legation and an additional $10,000 as indemnification for the Dutch mother of the murdered Heusken.

Meanwhile, in compliance with a demand of the Emperor, the Shōgun made a personal appearance at the Imperial Court in Kyoto. This action was a further indication of the rapidly deteriorating position of the Bakufu, for it marked the first time since 1634 that a Shōgun had made an appearance at the court in Kyoto.[18] The Shōgun departed for Kyoto in March 1863. Shortly after his arrival in Kyoto, a council of nobles decided that July 25, 1863, would be established as the day for beginning action to close the country and expel the foreigners. The Shōgun was detained in Kyoto for nearly three months against his will, but he finally managed to get away and returned to Edo late in July.[19] On July 24, the day before the target date for beginning the expulsion of foreigners, the Bakufu, acting in compliance with the alleged imperial will, informed the foreign diplomatic representatives that imperial instructions had been received to close the ports and expel the foreigners. The Shōgun, immediately after his return to Edo, conscientiously dispatched a memorial to the Emperor in which he advised that the time was inopportune to attempt the expulsion of the foreigners. The more enlightened members of the Imperial Court shared these views, but the chauvinistic elements were only further provoked. At any rate, the Shōgun hesitated to enforce the order.

When informed by the Shōgun's officials of the expulsion order, the foreign diplomats warned that their governments were prepared to engage in whatever military action might be necessary.[20] On this issue Pruyn sided with his diplomatic colleagues, and he cautioned the Bakufu that the closing of the ports would mean war with the United States as well as with the other powers. In so informing the Bakufu, Pruyn was carrying out the specific instructions of Secretary Seward to the effect "You will represent to the minister of foreign affairs that it is not at all to be expected that any of the maritime powers will consent to the suspension of their treaties, and that the United States will cooperate with them in all necessary means to maintain and secure the fulfillment of the treaties on the part of the Japanese government."[21]

One of the most serious anti-foreign outbreaks occurred in June and July 1863 when the Daimyō of Chōshū, in giving concrete support to the Emperor's alleged desire to suspend foreign intercourse, closed the straits of Shimonoseki to foreign traffic and fired on American, French and Dutch ships in that area. The American warship *Wyoming* happened to be in Yokohama at the time and its captain obtained the approval of Minister Pruyn to engage in retaliatory action. Proceeding to the Shimonoseki area, the *Wyoming* sank an armed steamer and a brig belonging to the Daimyō of Chōshū, at a cost of four killed and seven wounded. Pruyn incidentally believed that this action strengthened the hand of the Bakufu and that it moreover would discourage other anti-foreign daimyōs from engaging in similar acts of provocation. The defiant daimyō remained unchastened until September 1863, however, when an allied expedition of seventeen vessels, only one of which was American, heavily bombarded Shimonoseki.*

With one of its most inveterate and influential enemies thus humbled, the Bakufu drew fresh courage and informed the foreign diplomats that temporizing was no longer necessary and that the treaties would be fully respected. The Bakufu of its own volition assumed full responsibility for the Chōshū incident, and in October 1864 concluded a convention with the injured nations which provided for the payment of an indemnity of $3,000,000, of which $750,000 was to accrue to the United States.

On November 24, 1865, the Bakufu happily informed the foreign diplomats that the Emperor had at last fully sanctioned the treaties of 1858 and that the tariffs would be revised downward as desired by their governments. This development was of great significance, for it weakened the anti-foreign elements and also to a considerable degree lessened the dependence of the foreign diplomats on the Bakufu.

The Shimonoseki indemnity remained unappropriated in the United States Treasury until 1883 when Congress, its conscience awakened, voted to return it to Japan. By this time the Bakufu had

*Nine of these warships were British, four Dutch, and three French. The American ship, the *Pembroke,* was a chartered merchant vessel and mounted only one gun.

been overthrown and the Emperor had been restored to nominal power. The Imperial Government expressed its profound gratitude and the hope that this instance of traditional American generosity would "tend to strengthen the mutual confidence and the feeling of good-will and friendship which at present happily subsists between the peoples of our respective countries."

In 1868 the Bakufu was overthrown in a relatively bloodless revolution and the boy emperor, Mutsuhito, was ostensibly restored as the real ruler of Japan.* Actually the governing power was merely transferred from the Tokugawas to the leading clansmen of the west and the imperial nobility. The Emperor remained essentially a figurehead, and his power was fundamentally restricted to the theory that the new Government administered for him and in accordance with his wishes. Be that as it may, the new Government demonstrated a remarkable vitality, ability and open-mindedness in dealing with the vastly changed situation in which Japan found herself. Gone was most of the blind conservatism and xenophobia which had seemingly once animated many of the elements now included in the Government. The new Government promptly and intelligently applied itself to the task of modernizing Japan so that she might take her place among the great nations of the world and be able to defend herself and promote her national interests. Much of the old feudal system was swept away, something resembling a representative government was established, universal education was adopted, and an impressive beginning was made in the direction of industrialization. In the great task of modernization, advice and technicians were solicited throughout the world. By the end of the century, in a period of only a few decades, Japan stood forth as the strongest and most modern country in Asia, with an army and navy capable of compelling respect from any would-be aggressor.

In the field of foreign relations the new Government adopted a policy of friendlier and widened contacts with the outside world. Anti-foreignism remained a factor, but discouraged by the Government it progressively declined in significance.

*Mutsuhito is generally known by his reign name, Meiji. In September 1868 Edo was renamed Tokyo, or Eastern Capital, and in March 1869 it became the actual capital and residence of the Emperor.

A new Tariff Convention had been negotiated and signed on June 25, 1866, by officials of the Bakufu and representatives of the United States, Great Britain, France and the Netherlands. However, the convention was not submitted to either the Shōgun or the Emperor, and the Shōgun's officials are alleged to have made it clear that it would remain in force only for a few years. Actually it remained in force until August 1899.[22] It was unilateral in its benefits; that is to say, in favor of the foreign powers and at the expense of Japan. Tariff rates were fixed and the importation of opium was prohibited.[23]

After the Restoration of 1868 the principal Japanese objective in foreign policy was to obtain a revision of the unilateral treaties which were offensive to national pride and injurious to the national interest. These treaties were particularly odious because they deprived Japan of two very important rights of sovereignty: (1) the right to regulate her own tariffs and thereby protect her commercial and industrial interests, and (2) the right to subject aliens to the law of the land. It was rightfully felt by the Japanese that as long as these humiliating and harmful restrictions remained in force, Japan could not hope to be admitted to the comity of nations as an equal member.

By this time most of the foreign powers were no longer uncompromisingly opposed to revision. However, whereas the Japanese wanted revision as a sovereign right, the foreign powers, with the exception of the United States, insisted on revisions on a *quid pro quo* basis. Despite these divergent views, the Japanese Government on several occasions between 1869 and 1871 sounded out the foreign diplomats in Tokyo, but the overtures were in general coldly received and it became apparent to the Japanese that revision was a major problem and likely to require a long time.

Late in 1871 a Japanese mission headed by Prince Tonomi Iwakura, comprising more than a hundred officials and servants, departed for the United States and Europe with the object of studying Western institutions and making soundings on treaty revision. In the United States the mission found President Grant and Secretary of State Hamilton Fish sympathetic to the idea of wholesale treaty revision, but in Europe almost no encouragement was received. In fact, Great Britain was pronouncedly hostile to any revision, and until 1890 was the principal nation opposing it. The mission returned to Japan in September 1873, nearly two years after its departure, wiser for all that it had seen and studied but having failed to achieve anything concrete in the direction of treaty revision.

Since the backwardness of Japan's laws and judicial system was the principal argument advanced by the treaty powers for refusing to surrender extraterritoriality, the Japanese now concentrated on reforming their legal codes and revising the judicial system in conformity with those prevailing in the more advanced countries in Europe. By 1882 the Japanese had succeeded in bringing about substantial reforms in their legal system and they believed that it now compared favorably with those in the West.

The Japanese then contended that no foreign power could any longer conscientiously argue that the legal system of Japan was barbarous and that it therefore precluded the surrender of extraterritoriality. The Western powers, however, still considered the Japanese judicial system unacceptable and refused to surrender their rights, although they did express a willingness to make some concessions. Concerning the obstinacy of the Western powers in this respect, ex-President Grant in 1879 commented, "It seems incredible that rights which Western nations all regard as sacred and inviolable, because absolutely essential to their independence and dignity, should be denied by them to China and Japan."[24]

Public opinion in Japan had become extremely hostile to any concessions on the issue and apparently demanded nothing less than the total abolition of extraterritoriality. So strong was popular feeling on this issue that no Japanese official dared to defy it. The abuses of extraterritoriality on the part of the Western nations further aggravated the problem. As in China, foreign offenders were generally acquitted or let off leniently by the consuls who tried them. It is to be noted, however, that American officials in Japan probably exercised the right of extraterritoriality more conscientiously than did any others.

Between 1873 and 1885 the American diplomatic representative in Japan was John A. Bingham, a man of considerable experience in public affairs, able and of high ideals. He advocated the restoration of full tariff autonomy to Japan and the abolition of extraterritoriality as soon as an acceptable judicial system had been established in Japan. Before the termination of his tour of duty in Japan, he took the position that the Japanese had in fact established such a judicial system and that the continuation of extraterritoriality was no longer justified. During his tour of duty he persistently opposed any interpretation of the treaties which might serve further to weaken the sovereignty of Japan, and he held to the view that even though extraterritoriality remained in force the foreigners should abide by the laws of Japan.[25]

Meanwhile, however, some progress was being made in the direction of treaty revision. In 1878 the United States and Japan had concluded a convention which annulled the existing tariffs and permitted Japan to establish her own tariff schedules. Since American exporters with interests in Japan would be ruined if the provisions of this treaty were not applicable to all nations, especially Great Britain, it was stipulated that the convention would not come into force until the other powers had concluded similar arrangements.

In 1886 the American Minister, Richard B. Hubbard, concluded an Extradition Convention of considerable significance to Japan. In the words of President Cleveland, this convention was concluded not merely to facilitate criminal procedure "but also because of the support which its conclusion would give Japan in her efforts towards judicial autonomy and complete sovereignty." Great Britain refused to conclude a similar convention, and insisted that her extraterritorial privileges required Japan to extradite any British subjects who might be wanted for violations of British law.

Mexico was the first Western nation to conclude a treaty, in February 1887, which recognized the full fiscal and judicial autonomy of Japan. This treaty contained a conventional most-favored-nation clause for the purpose of precluding other nations from enjoying its benefits without having made similar concessions. After the Portuguese Government in 1892 withdrew its consular representatives from Japan as an economy measure, an imperial ordinance issued in July of that year denounced the treaty provisions with Portugal concerning consular jurisdiction over Portuguese nationals. This action elicited no protest from the Portuguese Government.

Important as were these gains, the Japanese Government was primarily concerned with revising the treaties in force with the great powers. Only after these powers had made the necessary treaty revisions could Japan enjoy the full diplomatic equality which was then the major objective in foreign policy. Accordingly the Japanese turned to the nation with the largest interests in Japan, namely Great Britain, believing that if she could be brought to terms the other great powers would promptly fall in line. Ironically, Britain was the nation that had most persistently opposed treaty revision.

Preliminary negotiations were begun in 1893 but without much success. By this time, however, the British were prepared to abandon their anti-revision policy and even to go much further and lay the groundwork for an entente with Japan. The reason for the change of attitude was purely political: the intense imperialistic rivalry with Russia, as well as with Germany and France, made it desirable for Britain to cultivate Japan as a potential ally in the event of far-flung hostilities. The "splendid isolation" that for so long had served Britain so well was no longer adequate in a world bristling with armaments and seething with Anglophobia.

In 1894 negotiations proceeded slowly but smoothly, and on July 16 a new Anglo-Japanese Treaty of Commerce and Navigation was signed. Its major provisions stipulated that: (1) consular jurisdiction, or extraterritoriality, was to be completely abolished by 1899; (2) certain specified articles were to remain subject to a conventional tariff of five to ten percent *ad valorem,* but Japan was to regulate the import duties on all other articles beginning in 1899; and (3) all of Japan was to be opened to the residence of British subjects, although they were not to be granted the right to own land.

In February 1894 the United States, which had been highly in favor of Japan's treaty negotiations with Britain, began discussions with the view of concluding a similar treaty. Such a treaty was negotiated, and signed on November 22. It was promptly ratified by the Senate. Unlike the British treaty, however, it demanded no tariff concessions of any kind and accordingly conceded complete tariff autonomy to the Japanese. Because of its most-favored-nation clause, however, the United States enjoyed the tariff advantages of the British treaty.

By February 1898 Japan had revised her treaties with fifteen other nations, and by June 1899 treaty revisions had been made with an additional four nations. The treaties concluded between

1894 and 1899 technically gave Japan "near-equality"; not until 1911, when tariffs were placed on a *quid pro quo* basis, did Japan actually attain full equality.

The foreigners residing in Japan had been apprehensive of treaty revisions and feared that with the abandonment of extraterritoriality they would be subject to legal inequities and a train of abuses and injustices. These fears proved to be totally unfounded, and subsequent years demonstrated that foreigners and their property rights were as fairly treated in Japan as in any advanced Western country.

By the turn of the century, then, Japan had gone far toward transforming herself from a backward feudal country to a modern nation equipped with the foundations of an industrialized establishment and a relatively formidable army and navy. The last shackles that had fettered her full sovereignty had been shattered. The great powers were now prepared to accept her as an equal in fact as well as in theory. By contrast, China still remained hopelessly backward, pitifully weak, and generally hostile to the modern ideas of the West. Whereas Japan now walked with pride and dignity in the halls of the great powers, China throughout the early part of the twentieth century continued to remain in a state of semi-colonialism, partly enslaved, not by one, but by many great powers.

Beginning at the turn of the century Japan, conscious of her newly found power, set forth on a path of expansion, territorial as well as economic, which brought her into a series of strains and crises with the United States that finally culminated in the great Pacific holocaust of 1941-1945.

With minor and infrequent exceptions the period beginning with the opening of Japan and continuing to the end of the century was one of official and unofficial American friendliness for Japan, just as it was for China. Both nations were regarded by the United States as not fair prey for plunder and the general level of moral rectitude which pervaded American policy and actions is something of which an American cannot fail to be proud.

In Japan the United States asked for no special privileges and it was consistently willing to surrender the unilateral rights it possessed provided the other powers would do likewise. The sympathetic understanding of outstanding American diplomats, notably Harris, Pruyn and Bingham, contributed greatly in helping Japan to weather the storms of her critical years. Unofficially, too, many Americans contributed their talents to the modernization of the country, particularly in the field of education, and in the latter part of the century Americans served as advisers to the Japanese Foreign Office. Nor can the dedicated role of countless American missionaries who labored under almost primitive conditions be overlooked. The Japanese, for their part, were generally deeply appreciative of the help of Americans and the spirit of friendliness and justice which was almost consistently manifested by the United States Government.

CHAPTER SEVEN

Imperialist Fever and the Samoan Adventure

In the second half of the nineteenth century the United States gave visible evidence of rapidly coming of age. The discovery of gold in California in 1848 resulted in the rapid settlement of the west coast, and the completion of the first transcontinental railroad in 1869 stimulated its further economic development. In all sections of the country energetic captains of industry, big and small, were feverishly engrossed in the stupendously profitable task of exploiting the vast resources of the country. Millions of immigrants and a high birth rate combined to supply the manpower needed for the unrestricted economic development of the country. The great industrial development of the United States was clearly borne out by the expansion of its foreign trade which increased from $162,000,000 in 1800 to $1,503,000,000 in 1880. By the end of the century it exceeded two billion dollars.

As in other countries, although to a notably lesser extent, industrial interests began demanding additional sources of raw materials and new markets for the products of their industries, while bankers expected the government to support them in the extension of their investments to backward and politically unstable regions of the world. The Far East, however, played a very minor part in the phenomenal expansion of America's foreign trade. Nine-tenths of this trade was with Europe, and less than one-tenth was with Asia, Africa and South America combined. The trade with China, then the most important in the Far East, amounted to less than three percent of the total.

131

The principal countries of Western Europe underwent a similar industrial development during the latter part of the nineteenth century. Prodded by the demands of industrial and financial interests, many of them resorted to the conquest by force of extensive backward areas in every quarter of the globe. In the last two decades of the nineteenth century a veritable scramble for colonies took place in which the threat of a world war was ever present as a result of the bitter rivalries that developed among the principal imperialist powers. Great Britain, France and Russia took the lead in this mad and immoral scramble, but after 1884 Germany entered the game, if such it may be called, followed by Japan, which after 1895 had risen to the rank of a great power. Since Germany was a late comer in the scramble and most of the choice areas had already been appropriated, her imperialist activities were characterized by a brashness and militancy which consternated Great Britain and to a lesser extent France and Russia.

To many European philosophers and writers it appeared that the Western peoples were endowed by the Creator with superior innate characteristics which accounted for their military and economic power and the ease with which they conquered areas inhabited by various colored peoples, whether in Africa or Asia or the Pacific islands. In the biological theories of Charles Darwin they found the sanctions needed for the development of an imperialistic pattern of thinking and reasoning. Darwinism proclaimed that in the world of nature there were superior and inferior biological specimens engaged in a constant struggle for survival in which the superior survived at the expense of the inferior. Darwinism seemed to justify the assumption that as in the world of nature, so among the nations of the world there were strong or superior and weak or inferior nations, and that the strong had the sacred right, and even duty, to conquer and dominate the weak in the interest of progress.

In the United States the historian John Fiske contributed greatly to the political interpretation of Darwinism, and in a sense he was the father of the imperialistic philosophy that came to obsess a considerable number of politically influential Americans in the last decade of the nineteenth century. Darwin himself inadvertently gave direct inspiration to the development of an American philosophy of imperialism. In *The Descent of Man,* published in 1871, he declared, for example: "There is apparently much truth in the belief that the wonderful progress of the United States, as well as the character of the people, are the results of natural selection; the more energetic, restless, and courageous men from all parts of Europe having emigrated during the last ten or twelve generations to that great country, and having there succeeded best."[1]

The thinking of the new American imperialists of the last two decades of the nineteenth century has been admirably summarized by Julius Pratt in his *Expansionists of 1898*.* The central theme in the thinking of these men was the alleged supremacy of the Nordic race, especially its Anglo-Saxon element. To this central theme politically minded clergymen added the concept of the moral supremacy of Protestantism and its civilizing mission in "heathen lands." It is superfluous, of course, to point out that there was hardly a shred of scientific truth to the new imperialist philosophy. It is certainly equally superfluous to point out that this philosophy flagrantly contradicted the central theme of the Declaration of Independence, which may rightly be considered to be the fundamental charter of American political idealism.

In a notable essay entitled "Manifest Destiny" which appeared in *Harper's Magazine* in 1885, Fiske set the course of the new thinking by revealing the unfolding of the evolutionary theory. "It is enough," he wrote, "to point to the general conclusion that the work which the English race began when it colonized North America is destined to go on until every land on the earth's surface that is not already the seat of an old civilization shall become English in its language, in its religion, in its political habits and traditions, and to a predominant extent in the blood of its people." He further contended, "The day is at hand when four-fifths of the human race will trace its pedigree to English forefathers, as four-fifths of the white people of the United States trace their pedigree to-day."[2]

The theme of the Christian mission was emphatically sounded by the Congregationalist clergyman Josiah Strong. In the same year that Fiske's essay was published, in 1885, he authored a small volume, *Our Country: Its Possible Future and Its Present Crisis*. In this work he represented the Anglo-Saxon as the foremost representative of two great ideas, civil liberty and "a pure spiritual

* Julius W. Pratt, *Expansionists of 1898* (Baltimore: Johns Hopkins Press, 1936).

Christianity," by which he meant Protestantism. The Anglo-Saxon, he wrote, was divinely commissioned, in a peculiar sense, to be his brother's keeper. There was no question of the unique superiority of the Anglo-Saxon race and its ultimate domination of the world. "This powerful race," he prophesied, "will move down upon Mexico, down upon Central and South America, out upon the islands of the sea, over upon Africa and beyond."[3] The impact of this book cannot be minimized, for it had a circulation of some 170,-000 copies in the United States.

Prof. John W. Burgess was another important contributor to the development of the new American imperialist philosophy. Having studied two years in Germany, he returned to the United States deeply infected with German ideas on Teutonic supremacy. In his most outstanding work, *Political Science and Comparative Constitutional Law,* published in 1890, he contended that only the Teutonic race had been capable of developing a true national state and that on this account it was destined to dominate the entire world.[4] In this thinking, of course, the American nation was a part of the virile Teutonic race.

Captain Mahan was still another extremely important contributor to the development of the new philosophy. His distinctive contribution was the theory of the decisive importance of sea power. His reputation as the foremost exponent of this theory was firmly established by his publication, in 1890, of *The Influence of Sea Power upon History.* This book and subsequent articles and speeches caused influential Americans to become keenly aware of the importance of sea power, naval bases and colonies as means for strong nations to assume and maintain dominant positions in the world. He stressed that sea power was not an end in itself but "the handmaid of expansion, its begetter and preserver." He lamented the lack of American colonies which afforded "the surest means of supporting abroad the sea power of a country." It is interesting to note that he contemplated the possibility of the huge Chinese population erupting from its boundaries eastward as well as westward and the United States being compelled to play a primary role in containing it.[5] The young Theodore Roosevelt, who became Assistant Secretary of the Navy during the first administration of McKinley, was deeply impressed by Mahan's ideas and played an important part in building up a first-class American navy in the late 1890's.

Dr. Albert Shaw, a political writer, who was editor of the influential *Review of Reviews* from May 1897 to February 1898, is especially significant because his views carried great weight with a number of men in positions of governmental responsibility. During the period of his editorship, the *Review of Reviews* repeatedly and convincingly editorialized on the annexation of Hawaii, the construction of an isthmian canal, and the need to acquire and control the islands of the Caribbean for the purpose of eventually dominating the Pacific, which was envisioned as the "theater of great events in the coming century."[6]

One important result of the spread of imperialistic feeling in the United States was the rising demand for overseas possessions which could be utilized as advance naval bases for the protection of the commercial interests of the country which were alleged to be world wide. Interest in overseas naval bases at first was expressed only by the small band of imperialists who were considerably in advance of the people in their concept of America as a potential world power with naval bases scattered at strategic points abroad. Not until after the outbreak of the war with Spain in 1898, and particularly after Dewey's dramatic victory over the Spanish fleet in Manila, did the general public warm up to the idea of treading the exciting but perilous path of imperialism.

The United States' first Pacific outposts, a group of desolate guano islands comprising Jarvis Island, Baker's Island and Howland's Island, were obtained in 1857 and 1858, primarily for use as coaling stations necessary for the promotion of commerce in the Pacific. It does not appear that there was any imperialistic motivation connected with their acquisition. In 1867 the farsighted and imperialistically minded Seward secured the Midway Islands. Seward was also interested in acquiring the Hawaiian Islands, and it was he who almost single-handedly was responsible for the purchase of Alaska from Russia.

The decade of the 1850's was one of pronounced Pacific-expansion sentiment on the part of a number of imperialistically minded Americans, whose principal spokesman was William H. Seward, then a member of Congress. To Seward the destiny of America

135

lay in the vast Pacific area. In 1852 when the expedition for the opening of Japan was being prepared, Seward had eloquently proclaimed that the Atlantic interests of the United States would "relatively sink in importance, while the Pacific Ocean, its shores, its islands, and the vast regions beyond" would become "the chief theatre of events in the world's great hereafter." He predicted that the commercial interests of the United States in the Pacific area would become increasingly important, and that the United States, as the leading Pacific power, was destined to play a principal part in the renovation of the governments and institutions of Asia.[7] In Seward's thinking the acquisition of the West Coast was not the fulfillment of America's "Manifest Destiny" but only an intermediate stage in the fulfillment of America's greater destiny to dominate the Pacific.

That the Pacific was not to be categorically excluded from the extension of American power was made clear by President Pierce in March of 1853 when he announced that no "timid forebodings of evil from expansion" would restrain his administration. It was, of course, under the auspices of President Pierce that Japan was opened to Western trade and intercourse, and it was Seward who in later years as Secretary of State acquired Midway Island and Alaska.

It was Commodore Perry, however, who formulated concrete projects for the ambitious planting of the American flag far in the Pacific and for laying the foundations of American imperial power in that vast ocean. Perry's project has often been referred to as the "Grand Design," and justly so. As noted by Tyler Dennett, "No American before his time, and few after it, ever had such an extensive ambition."[8]

In brief, Perry's Grand Design contemplated the acquisition of the Bonins and the Ryūkyūs and the establishment of a protectorate over the big island of Formosa. In Perry's scheme this strategically located island triangle, dominating the approaches to Japan, the Asiatic mainland and the islands of the South Pacific, would not only permit the immediate establishment and control of vitally needed coaling stations but also serve as an advance post for the development of American commerce in that vast area. As a preliminary action to the anticipated and hoped-for approval from the State Department, Perry, while in Asiatic waters in connection with his mission to Japan, utilized Formosa, made use of the port of Naha in Okinawa, and took possession of Peel Island in the Bonin group.

"It is self-evident," Perry informed the Secretary of the Navy in 1853, "that the course of coming events will ere long make it necessary for the United States to extend its territorial jurisdiction beyond the limits of the western continent, and I assume the responsibility of urging the expediency of establishing a foothold in this quarter of the globe, as a measure of positive necessity to the sustainment of our maritime rights in the east."[9] Washington did not at that time share this imperialistic exuberance, however, and Secretary Marcy cautioned Perry that while coaling stations might be established under correct circumstances no protectorate was to be imposed on Formosa and no territory was to be acquired.[10] Perry, of course, had no alternative but to comply with the instructions of his superior.

Perry's burning faith in the Pacific destiny of America remained unquenched, however, and in 1856 in a paper read to the American Geographical and Statistical Society he rhetorically predicted that the American people would continue to expand westward, as well as northward and southward, "until they shall have brought within their mighty embrace multitudes of the islands of the great Pacific, and placed the Saxon race upon the eastern shores of Asia." He also predicted that Russia would likewise expand, eastward and southward, until, as he put it, "the Saxon and the Cossack will meet once more" in strife. The "Saxon and the Cossack" have indeed met "once more" in Asia, but elsewhere too, and they have met in strife, as predicted by Perry, but not as a result of the process which he had envisaged.

Shortly after Perry had completed his Japan mission, Peter Parker, the American commissioner in Peking, picked up a part of the "Grand Design" and suggested to Secretary Marcy the advisability of placing Formosa under American occupation and utilizing it as a naval base and coaling station.[11] He was unable to arouse any enthusiasm in Washington, however, and nothing came of the suggestion. Thereafter dreams of empire in the Pacific area languished until revived by a new crop of imperialists and big-

137

navy men who appeared on the American scene in the late 1890's. These men had an America to listen to their rhetoric that was almost "come of age" and bursting with industrial strength and energy.

American ships had frequented the South Pacific almost as early as they had the North Pacific. Spearheaded by the hardy and enterprising New Englanders, Americans had called at a number of islands in this area, notably the Marquesas, the Fijis, the Carolines, the Friendly Islands, the Admiralty Islands, and Tahiti. The principal motive for calling at these distant islands was to obtain items for the China trade, such as sandalwood, tortoise shell, edible birds' nests and *bêche-de-mer,* which had great value as exchange commodities for Chinese products and precious metals.[12]

One of the first major island groups in the South Pacific to engage the attention of adventurous Americans were the Samoans, originally known as the Navigator Islands. The Samoan archipelago consists of fourteen islands, nine of which are inhabited, and only three of which are of any appreciable size. The total area of the archipelago is only about 1,200 square miles. The largest island, Savaii, is only forty miles long and twenty miles wide.[13] Some 4,160 miles from San Francisco, less than 2,000 miles from Australia, and even closer to New Zealand, these islands command a number of important shipping lanes. Pago Pago, situated on the island of Tutuila, possesses one of the finest natural harbors in the world. Prior to the coming of the Westerners the islands were ruled by native chiefs and the inhabitants were in a stage of development not far removed from savagery.

The Samoan Islands were discovered by the Dutch navigator Jacob Roggeveen (Roggewein) in 1722, and they were visited again in 1768 by Louis de Bougainville, who named them the Navigator Islands because of the large number of native craft that surrounded his vessel when he touched at Manua.[14] Neither of these explorers, however, set foot on any of these islands, and the first Westerner to actually examine any of the islands was La Pérouse in 1787.[15] The first Europeans to settle on the islands were British missionaries, who arrived in the early 1830's and found the friendly natives willing and even eager to be converted to the Christian faith. By this time American whalers were occasionally

138

putting in at the islands, and in 1839 Lieut. Charles Wilkes surveyed the archipelago area and concluded an arrangement with the native chiefs of Tutuila for the regulation of commerce and the treatment of shipwrecked sailors. Apparently a small amount of American trade existed at that time, for Wilkes appointed John Williams a United States consul.[16]

The missionaries were followed by grasping traders, who were also initially welcomed by the hospitable and unsuspecting natives: first, the Germans who came in substantial numbers about the middle of the century, followed by Englishmen and Americans. The Germans became the most numerous and aggressive and developed the largest commercial interests. Concentrated in Apia, they reaped large profits from the copra business and acquired considerable areas of land from the natives in exchange for firearms and liquor. Copra, or dried coconut meat, was then much in demand in Germany as its oil was used in the making of candles and the residue was utilized to feed cattle. Like other Western traders, the Germans were little concerned with the fact that the sale of firearms and liquor was in violation of the law that had been put into effect as a result of the influence of the missionaries. One is reminded of the callous manner in which Britons and other Westerners participated in the opium trade at Canton in the early 1800's, also in violation of the law of China. Although anxious to have Germany take over the islands as a protectorate, the German nationals in Samoa were primarily concerned with the prospering of their commercial activities.

American interest in a Samoan naval station developed as a result of the application to Congress of the entrepreneur William H. Webb for a subsidy to facilitate the operation of a steamship line from San Francisco to Australia and New Zealand, with Pago Pago as a port of call. Undaunted by Congress' lack of interest, Webb turned to the government of New Zealand and received the required financial assistance to permit the inauguration of the line in 1869. The Navy Department subsequently stressed the importance of a naval base in Samoa as a means of contributing to the defense of a contemplated isthmian canal in Panama or Nicaragua and of also safeguarding the navigation routes of the southern Pacific.[17]

In February 1872 Captain Meade, while on a cruise through

the southern Pacific, stopped at Pago Pago and on his own initiative concluded an agreement with a local chief which granted to the United States "the exclusive privilege of establishing in the said harbour of Pago-Pago on the island of Tutuila a naval station for the use and convenience of the vessels of the U.S. Government." In return the treaty provided for the "friendship and protection of the great Government of the United States."[18] Although Meade had acted without authorization, the expansionist-minded President Grant submitted the agreement to the Senate, but that body declined to take any action on it. A petition submitted by Samoan chiefs for annexation of the islands was also rejected.

In the following year, however, Grant commissioned Colonel A. B. Steinberger to investigate conditions and commercial prospects on the islands. Of German ancestry, Steinberger conducted himself on the islands in such a manner as to cast doubt on whether his loyalties lay with the United States or Germany. His conduct was anything but that of an investigator. He intervened ruthlessly in the purely domestic affairs of the islands and proceeded to get Malietoa Laupepa generally recognized as king and himself as prime minister. On learning of what Steinberger was doing, Congress ordered an investigation of its own, and in May 1876 the Senate denounced any pretension of an American protectorate and practically repudiated Steinberger.[19]

As a result of the machinations of the Germans on the islands and the fear that the German Government might take measures to abrogate their independence, the native chiefs appealed to Great Britain, and then to the United States, to take over the islands as a protectorate. Although both nations declined the offer, both were determined not to permit Germany to acquire the islands.

In January 1878 Secretary Evarts concluded a commercial treaty with La Mamea, the representative of the Samoan chiefs, which also granted the United States the use of Pago Pago as a naval base. The United States was not, however, granted the exclusive use of the harbor. The treaty further stipulated that the United States would offer its good offices to adjust any differences which might arise between Samoa and any foreign power.[20] The State Department subsequently exploited this provision to forestall either of its two rivals on the islands, Germany and Great Britain, from gaining exclusive political control. Similar treaties were also concluded by the German Government for the exclusive use of Saluafata, not far from Apia, as a naval base. The British treaty granted the British Government the use of any site as a naval base, except Saluafata and the site which the United States would select at Pago Pago. The British treaty contained the additional provision that Samoa would not grant to any other power any rights or privileges in excess of those enjoyed by Great Britain.

By 1879, then, the Samoan policy of the three rival powers had crystallized: none would permit any of the others to gain exclusive control over the islands. In that year the consuls of the three rival powers concluded a convention which provided for the establishment of a municipal government in Apia, the principal town, under their joint control. The agreement was subsequently broadened, with the adherence of the native government, to provide for the establishment of what amounted to a joint protectorate, with the native chief Malietoa recognized as the nominal king. President Hayes' administration regarded the convention as an executive agreement rather than a treaty because of the fear that it would be rejected if submitted to the Senate.

Up to 1884 Bismarck, the Chancellor of Germany, had been opposed to any acquisitions of territory overseas and contended that colonial possessions were not worth the bones of a single Pomeranian grenadier. In that year, however, Bismarck changed his mind as a result of the pressure and influence of German business and financial interests. At first the new colonial policy of the German Government was somewhat cautious, but after 1888, when Wilhelm II ascended the throne, this policy became bold and even recklessly aggressive.

Acting on his own initiative, the German consul in Samoa in 1884 raised the German flag over Apia and proclaimed the establishment of a German protectorate over the islands. Fearing the Germans more than any of the others, Malietoa and 48 chiefs appealed to Great Britain to forestall Germany by herself establishing a protectorate. The German consul then stirred up a native revolt against Malietoa Laupepa and his supporters. On learning of what had happened, the German Government repudiated the unauthorized actions of its consular representative.

Alarmed by these developments and deeply concerned that either Germany or Great Britain might seize the islands, Secretary Bayard invited the British and German governments to participate in a conference at Washington for the purpose of finding a *modus vivendi* to end the disturbed conditions prevailing on the islands. The invitation was accepted by both governments, but prior to the convening of the conference Great Britain agreed to support Germany in Samoa in return for German support of her aspirations in Egypt and the Near East. The conference convened in 1887, but no agreement was reached, largely because of Germany's demand for a mandate over the islands, which was faithfully supported by Great Britain.

Shortly after the adjournment of the conference, the German consul Brandeis, acting on instructions, intrigued to bring about the dethronement of Malietoa on the trumped-up ground that German rights were being violated. He set up a puppet government under the chieftain Tamasese, with himself as prime minister, and Malietoa was made a prisoner and deported to Germany. Defiant Samoans then took to the jungles and engaged in guerrilla warfare against the Germans. On one occasion a party of German sailors was ambushed, whereupon the enraged Germans declared martial law and even shelled native villages in reprisal. Angered by the high-handed German actions, Congress appropriated $500,-000 for the defense of American interests in Samoa and an additional $100,000 for the development of Pago Pago harbor, which up to that time had been neglected.[21] On orders from the President, a naval squadron steamed to Apia.

The situation at Apia was now explosive. In the harbor were seven war vessels: one British, three American, and three German. Their decks were cleared for action and their crews were literally glaring at each other. Suddenly and unexpectedly, on March 16, 1889, a fierce hurricane arose and lashed the area, wrecking all of the vessels except the British one, which managed to escape from the harbor and ride out the storm. It is very probable that but for this "Act of God" the German and American vessels might have fired on each other and touched off an armed conflict. Commenting on the catastrophe, Robert Louis Stevenson, who knew this Samoa well, declared that the United States and Germany "both paused aghast; both had time to recognize that not the whole Samoan Archipelago was worth the loss in men and costly ships already suffered."[22]

The Apia tragedy had the effect of sobering both Washington and Berlin. Secretary Bayard dispatched a note to the German Government in which he stressed that the policy of the United

States in the Samoan Islands was motivated not by a desire to further American commercial interests but to preserve the independence of the islands. Desirous of remaining on good terms with the United States as well as Great Britain, Bismarck suggested the convening of a tripartite conference in Berlin to negotiate a definitive settlement of the troublesome Samoan problem. Both Britain and the United States accepted the suggestion. The *New York World,* which had engaged in its share of saber rattling, doubtless mirrored a calmed public opinion when it lamented, "Surely the awful devastation wrought in the harbor of Apia makes our recent quarrel with Germany appear petty and unnatural." It went on to express the hope that "the bonds which now join us to Germany as together we mourn the fate of those who perished in their duty will make the coming diplomatic conference at Berlin a council of friends, not a quarrel of restless rivals."[23]

The tripartite Berlin conference convened on April 29, 1889. In the agreement that was reached, the Berlin Act, the three powers recognized "the independence of the Samoan Government, and the free right of the natives to elect their chief or king and choose their form of government." At the same time, however, the three powers agreed on the choice of Malietoa Laupepa as king "in view of the difficulties that surround an election in the present disordered condition of the government."[24] Moreover, the foreign-controlled municipal government at Apia was to be maintained.

Malietoa, who was released from captivity, and the native chiefs accepted the agreement, but it failed to work out satisfactorily because of the intense rivalry that persisted on the islands between Americans and Germans and their continuing intrigues. Strife soon broke out among the native chiefs and Malietoa, the nominal king, was again deposed. Warships of the foreign powers were required to restore order.

In 1893 Grover Cleveland began his second term in the White House. He looked upon the Samoan adventure with considerable disfavor and was particularly displeased by the callous manner in which the sovereign rights of the natives had been violated, even by Americans, in the tripartite intrigue that was in full play on the islands. His Secretary of State, Walter Q. Gresham, described the Samoan adventure as "the first departure from our traditional and well established policy of avoiding entangling alliances with foreign powers in relation to objects remote from this hemisphere." In reviewing the recent events on the islands, Gresham declared that "we well may inquire what we have gained by our new departure from our established policy beyond the expenses, the responsibilities, and the entanglements that have been its only fruits."[25] In his annual message to Congress of December 1894 and also of December 1895 Cleveland recommended the withdrawal of the United States from the tripartite protectorate, but Congress failed to take any action.

American interest in Samoa subsided for a few years, but it was rekindled in 1898 when strife broke out again among rival Samoan chiefs laying claim to the nominal throne. American and British warships were compelled to land marines for the restoration of order. Several Americans were killed and a considerable amount of property was destroyed. The outbreak of the Spanish-American War that year and the subsequent acquisition of Hawaii, Guam and the Philippines fired the spark of imperialism, and the State Department put forth renewed efforts to secure the American foothold on the islands. The State Department was fully aware, however, that Germany would never consent to the abandonment of its own position on the islands. In 1899 the tripartite powers sent a joint mission to make an on-the-spot investigation of the situation on the islands. Upon the completion of its investigation the mission reported that the tripartite protectorate was a failure and that its continuation would not promote order and harmony on the islands.

The State Department then decided to make a "deal" with Germany for the division of the islands. Great Britain agreed to withdraw her claims in return for compensation elsewhere, namely the Gilbert and Solomon islands. In November 1899 the United States and Germany concluded an agreement which provided that Germany would receive the two largest islands, Upolu and Savaii, together with all other islands west of 171° west longitude.* All the remaining islands, including Tutuila, would be taken over by the United States.[26]

The native chiefs formally ceded Tutuila to the United States

*Armed forces of New Zealand seized these German islands after the outbreak of World War I, and the Treaty of Versailles transferred them to New Zealand under the so-called Mandate System.

in July 1900, and Manu in 1904. The absence of any deep American interest in these islands is apparent from the fact that Congress did not get around to taking formal action on the cessions until 1929, when they were accepted as territories of the United States.[27]

Despite the general approval of the American public to the deal made with Germany, there were many outspoken anti-imperialists who bitterly resented our being a party to an agreement allegedly made without any consideration whatsoever for the sovereign rights of the natives concerned. Senator Pettigrew of South Dakota doubtless epitomized the sentiments of the anti-imperialists when he declaimed: "Now, without consulting those people, without their being a party to the agreement, we take a portion of the islands and Germany takes the rest of them. We blot out, then, a sovereign nation, a people with whom we have treaty obligations, and divide the spoils."[28] But these anti-imperialist sentiments, faithful as they may have been to the ideals of the Republic, were drowned out by the trumpetings of the imperialists and big-navy men who, for the moment at least, had captured the imagination of the general public. Moreover, Samoa was remote and "small pickings" compared to Hawaii and the Philippines, which had recently been acquired. The nominal native king of Samoa in vain protested against the deal, and in a letter to the *London Times* sadly lamented that the civilization which the West had introduced into Polynesia had shown itself to be inferior to that which the natives had formerly possessed.

Notwithstanding the misgivings of some of his own countrymen, President McKinley moved rapidly. On February 19, 1900, only three days after he had announced the partition treaty, he placed the islands under the administration of the Navy Department. This was done by an executive order, which stipulated: "The island of Tutuila, of the Samoan group, and all other islands of the group east of longitude 171° West of Greenwich, are hereby placed under the control of the Department of the Navy for a naval station."[29]

It is difficult to see how the outright annexation of islands in the Samoan archipelago was necessary or contributed significantly to the promotion of genuine American interests in the Pacific at that time. Deep in the southern Pacific, they are far-removed from

China, where we believed a fabulous trade was only a matter of time, and from the Philippines, which had been acquired early in 1899. Our trade with Australia and New Zealand, from which they are not distant, was insignificant and therefore the claim that they were valuable for the facilitation of steamship service with those countries is not particularly valid. Moreover, it was not necessary to destroy the independence of the natives to secure a naval station, for a leasehold of Pago Pago would have completely fulfilled the strategic or commercial needs of the country. The Samoan deal with Germany can only be explained as being a desperate maneuver of power-minded officials in the Government to forestall Germany from gaining exclusive possession of all the islands. Manifestly the pressure and influence of the big-navy men was decisive and traditional American diplomacy yielded abjectly to *Realpolitik*.* Commercially the islands are of almost no importance whatsoever. Militarily they would only be of value if Australia and New Zealand were to develop into military threats to American security, and that seems as improbable as an invasion from a distant planet.

Realpolitik is the name given to the diplomacy adopted by Germany late in the nineteenth century. It is best described as "practical amoral politics."

CHAPTER EIGHT

The Acquisition of Hawaii

The Hawaiian Islands, an archipelago comprising 6,407 square miles, occupy a strategic position in relation to the West Coast of the United States and the defense of the Panama Canal area. Oahu, the most prized of these islands, possesses the magnificent port of Honolulu, which is only about 2,100 miles from San Francisco. Blessed with enchanting beauty, a fertile soil, and a delightful climate, the Hawaiian Islands are indeed, as is well known, a veritable tropical paradise.

These islands were discovered in 1778 by Captain James Cook, who named them the Sandwich Islands in honor of his patron, the Earl of Sandwich. They first became significant to Americans through the activities of the New England traders who utilized their friendly ports as way stations in the China trade as early as the winter of 1789-90, when four American vessels stopped at these islands. The first of these vessels to call at the islands was the *Columbia,* commanded by Captain Robert Gray, which was also the first American vessel to circumnavigate the globe.[1] Rounding Cape Horn, the enterprising American traders picked up furs on the Northwest Coast of North America in exchange for inexpensive ironware and trinkets and then utilized the islands as bases for drying peltries and revictualizing before resuming their voyages to Canton, where the furs were sold at high prices. With the proceeds, cargoes of tea, silk, porcelain and other Chinese products were purchased and then transported to America for sale at handsome profits.

Sandalwood, which abounded on the islands, for a time played a significant part in the China trade. This fragrant wood was highly valued by the Chinese for the making of incense and certain types of furniture. The sandalwood trade does not appear to have been of much importance until 1810, but small quantities of sandalwood had been purchased by traders for several years previously. The active exploitation of the sandalwood resources was begun in 1811 by American entrepreneurs engaged in the China trade. The sandalwood trade flourished during the 1820's, but by 1829 practically came to an end because of the depletion of the sandalwood groves.[2] From the standpoint of the development of the Hawaiian economy, the sandalwood trade was significant because it for the first time gave the islands an item to export, whereas up to then they had only been suppliers of provisions and services.[3]

The American whalers, however, first made the islands of considerable economic significance to the United States. From about 1820 to 1860 Americans dominated the whaling industry, and during this period the Hawaiian Islands served as their principal base of operations in the Pacific. The first American whalers to put in at the islands, in September 1819, were the *Equator* of Nantucket and the *Balaena* of New Bedford. By 1822 as many as 24 American whalers were in the ports of the islands at one time. In 1847, when whaling activity was at about its peak in the northern Pacific, the Hawaiian Government reported that 497 whalers manned by 14,905 seamen had utilized the islands. About four-fifths of these vessels were American-owned.[4] Recent research indicates that actually a total of 596 whalers called at the islands in 1846. These intensive whaling operations contributed to a significant phase of the islands' economic development. Considerable sums were spent on the islands for supplies and repairs and a large number of natives were employed as seamen and in other capacities.

The peak years of Hawaiian whaling were from 1843 to 1860, and throughout this period as many as a hundred whaling vessels, mostly American, were lying at anchor off Lahaina and Honolulu on any given day of the spring or autumn seasons.[5] The last banner year of whaling for Hawaii was in 1859, the very year that petroleum was discovered, when 549 whalers called at the islands. With the outbreak of the Civil War, American whaling operations declined greatly, and in 1862, for example, only 73 whalers utilized Hawaiian ports. After the war there was a revival of whaling operations in the Pacific and the Hawaiian Islands recaptured some of their former significance as a whaling base. The whaling fleet disaster of 1871 in the Bering Strait area, however, was a blow from which the American whaling fleet never recovered. Thereafter whaling ceased to be of much importance to the economy of the islands, although whalers continued to call at Hawaiian ports for many more years.[6]

At the time Captain Cook discovered the islands, the natives were in a primitive cultural stage, disunited, and under the rule of petty chiefs who were almost continuously at war with each other. As a result of the efforts of a capable and energetic chieftain, Kamehameha, the various chiefs were subjugated and the islands were unified under a single government. Kamehameha died in 1819 and was succeeded by his son Liholiho, who took the title of Kamehameha II. Before his death Kamehameha had provided that his favorite queen, Kaahumanu, share power with his son as Queen Regent under a unique system of dual government.[7] The strong-willed Kaahumanu was instrumental in forestalling the fragmentation of the islands again under the rule of chieftains and in consolidating the central power of the government. It was during these years that the American missionaries gained a strong foothold on the islands and came to exercise a considerable influence on the policies of the Hawaiian Government.

The first group of New England missionaries of the Congregationalist denomination arrived at Honolulu in 1820. Interest in establishing a mission on the islands had been aroused by the contacts of the New England traders and whalers with the islanders. Prominent religious leaders in New England became deeply concerned about the "immorality" and "paganism" prevailing on the islands and they came to consider it a holy duty to bring enlightenment and the "word of God" to the "benighted" islanders. Hiram Bingham, the leader of the first group which went to the islands, described their motivation as follows: "The object for which the missionaries felt impelled to visit the Hawaiian race, was to honor God, by making known his will, and to benefit these heathen tribes, by making them acquainted with the way of life,—to turn them from their follies and crimes, idolatries and oppression, to the service and enjoyment of the living God, the adorable redeemer,—to give them the Bible in their own tongue, with the ability to read it themselves,—to introduce and extend among them the more useful arts and usages of civilized and Christianized society, and to fill the hospitable parts of these important islands with schools and churches, fruitful fields, and pleasant dwellings."[8] Hence the object of the missionaries was not only to propagate Christianity but also to completely transform the way of life of the islanders, to educate them to a new culture, and to change and improve their standard of living.

Bingham's pioneer group of missionaries sailed from Boston on October 23, 1819 aboard the brig *Thaddeus* for the long voyage to the Hawaiian Islands via Cape Horn. Twenty-two were in the group which consisted of two ordained preachers, two schoolmasters, a physician, a printer and a farmer, their wives, five children, and three Hawaiians. The little band arrived off the coast of Hawaii on March 30 of the following year and debarked at Honolulu five days later.[9]

One of the first accomplishments of the missionaries was to establish schools, and before the end of 1820 about a hundred Hawaiians of all ages were attending classes. By 1822 the missionaries had not only reduced the Hawaiian language to writing but had also produced the first printed work in this language.[10] By 1840 seven companies of missionaries were operating on the islands and no less than twenty thousand Hawaiians had been converted to Protestantism.

The exemplary conduct of the missionaries contrasted sharply with the rough behavior of the whalers and the too-often dishonest conduct of the traders. Practically from the outset the group under the leadership of Bingham gained the confidence of the Queen Regent, the King and other officials of the Hawaiian Government. This was partly a result of the studied policy of the missionaries to convert the highest-ranking people of the islands first and depend on their influence to bring about the speedier conversion of the masses. A proclamation of Queen Kaahumanu in 1824 revealed a strong Puritanical influence even at that early date.[11]

For several decades there was open hostility between the missionaries and the other foreign elements on the islands. To the credit of the missionaries, it is to be noted that whenever the foreign traders and whalemen clashed with the Hawaiian authorities on matters of law and morals, they almost invariably sided with the Hawaiians. There can be no doubting the genuine interest of the missionaries in the welfare and advancement of the Hawaiian people. Even as late as 1851 the American diplomatic agent on the islands reported that there were many Americans who hated the missionaries and were desirous of entirely eliminating their influence.[12]

By the second half of the nineteenth century the missionaries had succeeded in almost completely transforming the "heathen" natives into Christians with at least the veneer of Westerners. In addition to a Christian religion and Western customs, the missionaries gave the islanders an alphabet and a dictionary, schools, new concepts of industry, and a constitution. Although they did so inadvertently, the missionaries actually prepared the ground for the Americanization of the islands and their ultimate absorption by the United States.

Commenting on the achievements of the missionaries, the noted writer Richard H. Dana declared in 1860 that "whereas they found these islanders a nation of half-naked savages, living in the surf and on the sand, eating raw fish, fighting among themselves, tyrannized over by feudal chiefs, and abandoned to sensuality, they now see them decently clothed, recognizing the laws of marriage, knowing something of accounts, going to school and public worship . . . and the more elevated among them taking part in conducting the affairs of the constitutional monarchy under which they live, holding seats on the judicial bench and in the legislative chambers, and filling posts in the local magistracies."[13]

Inevitably the missionaries became the most influential foreigners on the islands, and some of them served as trusted political advisers of the sovereigns. Many of their sons became engaged in commercial pursuits and obsessed with the acquisition of material wealth. It was they who later played important roles in the overthrow of the native monarch and in the movement for the annexation of the islands to the United States.

The first official representative of the American Government to serve in the Hawaiian Islands was John Coffin Jones, who in October 1820 was appointed "Agent of the United States for Commerce and Seamen" in Hawaii. Jones, a resident of Massachusetts, also served as agent for the Bostonian firm of Marshall and Wildes, and it was this firm which obtained the governmental connection for him. Until 1837 Jones was the most influential trader on the islands, and it appears that most of his interest was in his commercial position. Although the U.S. Government had clearly not intended that he should perform the functions of a consul, he practically usurped these functions, as well as some of a genuine diplomatic nature, and illegally designated himself a consul in signing documents.[14]

Jones early clashed with the American missionaries. He particularly resented the efforts of the Hawaiian Government, under the prodding of the missionaries, to enforce puritanical codes of morality and conduct. In 1823 Jones bitterly but unjustly accused the missionaries of "living like lords in this luxurious land" while at the same time being engaged "in fruitless and hypocritical labors."[15] Again in 1826 he accused them of being determined "to oppose every thing like enterprise and exertion."[16] In November 1837 the piqued Hawaiian Government memorialized President Van Buren with a request for Jones' removal. Two weeks later the President complied with the request and replaced Jones with Peter A. Brinsmade, a graduate of Yale Divinity School who had abandoned the ministry for a commercial career, as the new commercial agent for the United States. Although Brinsmade, like Jones, served as the agent of a commercial company as well as of the United States, he established rapport with the missionaries and seems to have gotten along very well with them.[17]

Early American relations with the islanders were not regulated by treaty until 1826 when Captain Thomas ap Catesby Jones of the U.S. Navy negotiated a commercial treaty with King Liholiho. In command of the warship *Peacock,* Jones arrived at Honolulu on October 10, 1826, with instructions to investigate conditions on the islands and seek a settlement of the claims of American citizens against the Hawaiian King. Exceeding his instructions, Jones on November 13 submitted to the King the draft of a proposed treaty and informed him that the United States desired "equal privileges with the most favoured in time of peace, and strict neutrality in case of war." On December 23 the Hawaiian Government signed the first treaty in its history with Jones, and at the same time took action for the settlement of the American claims. Jones later claimed that he had brought about the settlement of more than half a million dollars of debts owed Americans, but this seems to be a gross exaggeration.[18]

Jones' treaty contained no extraterritorial provisions and recognized that American citizens were under the legal jurisdiction of the Hawaiian Government. Although the treaty was never submitted by the President to the Senate for ratification, its provisions were respected by both Hawaii and the United States until superseded by a treaty of amity, commerce and extradition in 1849.[19] Treaties similar to the one negotiated by Jones were concluded by France in 1836 and by Great Britain in 1839.

In 1843 the United States strengthened its diplomatic bonds with the islands. Congress appropriated funds for the stationing of a paid agent in Honolulu with the title of "Commissioner," who was to enjoy diplomatic status. The first appointee to this post was George Brown of Massachusetts in March 1843. Brown arrived on the islands in October of that year. It cannot be said that he enhanced the true interests of the United States. He manifested very little respect for the dignity or rights of Hawaiian officials and was obsessed, to use his own words, with the determination not "to allow the interests or the honor of the U. States, or any of its citizens, to be interfered with, or trampled upon." The Hawaiian Government finally refused to have dealings with him and succeeded in bringing about his recall in March 1845.[20]

Brown was replaced by Anthony Ten Eyck, who sailed for the islands in October 1845 and arrived at his post in June of the following year. Like his predecessor, he had little respect for the sovereignty of the Hawaiian Government. In one of his dispatches to the State Department he complained that the King and his ministers were "reckless and overbearing" and suggested that "nothing but brute force can induce them to administer the government with honesty and justice toward foreign residents." After Britain and France had forced the King to conclude extremely one-sided treaties, Ten Eyck was instructed to negotiate an agreement to facilitate American commercial relations with the islands. He proposed a treaty to the King which provided for trial of Americans in both criminal and civil cases by all-white juries. This proposal greatly antagonized the Hawaiian Government, and even Secretary Buchanan was indignant about it. Buchanan in fact roundly rebuked Ten Eyck and reminded him that the Tyler Doctrine* required complete respect for the sovereignty of Hawaii. Ten Eyck was recalled early in 1849. In his final communication to the State Department, Ten Eyck denounced Secretary Buchanan for "sacrificing" his agent "in the vain hope of advancing his own political interests." Ten Eyck's deficiency, like that of Brown, was an almost complete inability to comprehend the rising tide of Hawaiian nationalism at that time.[21]

Charles Eames, who succeeded Ten Eyck as Commissioner in Hawaii, was instructed by Secretary Buchanan in February 1849 to bring to conclusion a "Treaty of Commerce and Navigation" similar to the ones the United States had in force with the principal powers. Buchanan emphasized that the recent acquisition of the Pacific Coast made such a treaty imperative. The desired treaty was signed late in 1849, and ratified in the following year. The negotiations for a treaty had actually been initiated several years before, in 1845.[22] The 1849 treaty provided for "reciprocal liberty of commerce and navigation," mutual non-discriminatory tariff arrangements, and special rights for American whaling vessels and American citizens residing on the islands.

Up to 1851 several attempts had been made by Europeans to destroy the sovereignty of the native rulers. Two of these attempts were by the British, two by the French, and one by the Russians. The first attempt was made by Captain George Vancouver in 1794, but the British Government declined to support him. The second attempt was made in 1815 by Baranov, the Russian governor of Alaska, who forced the king of the island of Kauai to conclude a treaty which placed his domain under the protection of the Tsar. The Tsar however refused to ratify the treaty. The third threat to the islands came in 1839 when the commander of a French gunboat demanded freedom of worship for Roman Catholics. The King was absent from Oahu at the time, and his Prime Minister, fearing that the French might resort to warlike actions, concluded a treaty whose provisions complied with the French demands. Prior to this incident, a British naval commander had also obtained under duress a one-sided commercial treaty.

* See below, p. 155.

154

Alarmed by the possibility of a French or British seizure of the islands, the King in 1842 dispatched abroad a commission for the purpose of securing formal recognition of Hawaii's independence on the part of the United States, Great Britain and France. The commission was gone two years, and returned to Hawaii in 1844.

In Washington the commissioners held discussions with Secretary Webster, ex-President Adams, Caleb Cushing, Lewis Cass, and other influential men. Acting on Webster's suggestion, the commissioners on December 14, 1842, presented a formal note which called attention to the commercial significance of the islands to the United States, the extent of the whale fisheries, and the investment of some five or seven million dollars by Americans on the islands.[23] Webster then in turn drew up a formal note in which he pledged American recognition of Hawaii's independence as follows: "that the Government of the Sandwich Islands ought to be respected; that no power ought either to take possession of the islands as a conquest, or for the purpose of colonization, and that no power ought to seek for any undue control over the existing Government, or any exclusive privileges or preferences in matters of commerce."[24]

Largely as a direct result of pressure from New England interests, such as the traders, whalers and missionaries, President Tyler was in a sense compelled to make the position of the United States clear and explicit concerning the status of the islands. This he did on December 30, 1842, on the advice of Secretary Webster, when he informed Congress that the commercial and other interests of the United States in Hawaii were of such importance that although the United States Government had no territorial ambitions in the islands it could not consent to any other power possessing them or subverting the native government.[25] Webster went even further than this position and indicated that the United States might not hesitate to employ force to prevent Hawaii from being seized by a foreign power. Said Webster: "We might even feel justified, consistently with our own principles, in interferring by force to prevent its falling into the hands of one of the great powers of Europe."[26] These statements of Tyler and Webster became the substance of the American policy for Hawaii, which was subsequently restated on several occasions by succeeding secretaries of state.

To return to the Hawaiian commissioners mentioned above. Following their arrival in Europe in 1843, Great Britain and France each concluded agreements with them pledging to respect the independence of the islands. Great Britain and France then made a joint declaration to the effect that they engaged reciprocally to respect the Hawaiian Islands as an independent state and never to take possession of them either directly or indirectly under the guise of a protectorate. The United States was invited to subscribe to this declaration, but the State Department declined to do so on the ground that the historic policy of the United States precluded entangling alliances with foreign powers. The State Department was undoubtedly motivated by the desire not to become a party to an agreement in which the United States would forever renounce any intention of ultimately acquiring the islands.

Meanwhile in February 1843 Lord Paulet, commanding the British warship *Carysfort,* had demanded reparations from the King of Hawaii for alleged indignities which had been imposed on British subjects. Frightened by the threatening attitude of the British officer, the King temporarily ceded the islands to the protective custody of Great Britain and then appealed to both the British and American governments for the restoration of his powers. Before the British Government in London learned of what had happened, Admiral Richard Thomas proceeded to Hawaii and in July repudiated the action of Lord Paulet and disavowed the cession.[27]

In 1849 a French admiral, supported by two warships, temporarily seized Honolulu, primarily as a reprisal against restrictions which had been imposed by the Hawaiian Government on the importation of French wines. The admiral then presented the king with ten demands, the most extreme of which asked for a fifty percent reduction in duties on French brandy and a pledge to use the French language in diplomatic intercourse. Secretary Clayton seized upon this incident to restate the Hawaiian policy which had been clearly established by President Tyler. He reiterated that the United States did not covet the islands, but at the same time it could not permit them to pass "under the domination or exclusive control of any foreign power." No further American action was called for, however, as the Hawaiian controversy with France was settled amicably by the conclusion of a Franco-Hawaiian agreement which granted the Catholic clergy complete religious privileges and also provided for a significant reduction in the duties on French brandy.

Meanwhile, aware that Hawaii was unable to defend itself militarily, the King in 1851 had offered to place all the islands under the protection of the United States until a mutually satisfactory agreement could be reached with France. His offer went even further: if an agreement with France was not possible, then the United States should permanently annex the islands. The draft of such a treaty of annexation was actually drawn up in 1854, but it was rejected by President Pierce because of its stipulation that the islands would ultimately become a state of the Union and that the royal family would be paid an annuity.

While the opportunity to annex the islands was allowed to pass, largely because of domestic political considerations in the United States, the groundwork was laid for a policy looking toward their ultimate annexation at the opportune moment. In January 1855 Secretary Marcy, in instructions to the American diplomatic agent in Honolulu, stated that if the Hawaiian Government "should become so far enfeebled that it can not be continued, and the sovereignty of the islands must be transferred to another power, then a state of things will exist in which it will be proper for the United States to have a regard to the future condition of that country." He further stated that if the Hawaiian Government and people became convinced of the necessity for change, "it is probable that they will, if left to their free choice, look to the United States as the country to which they would wish to be united." He affirmed that "To a proper arrangement of this kind this Government certainly has no objection."[28]

During the decade preceding the American Civil War, the rapid development of the Pacific Coast had given a fresh impetus to the increasing prosperity of the islands. Whaling operations had ceased to be the principal basis of Hawaiian prosperity and a significant agricultural development was under way. The cultivation of sugar, potatoes and other crops was begun, and the islands came to depend primarily on the sale of agricultural products to the American West Coast. Sugar cane was indigenous to the islands, but its systematic cultivation had been initiated in 1835 by Ladd,

157

Hooper and Brinsmade, all New Englanders. Although this firm failed in 1845, the cultivation and processing of sugar became the mainstay of the island's economy within two decades.[29] By the end of the Civil War the product of the sugar plantations alone was valued at more than five times the total revenue received from the whaling fleets.[30] A broad commercial treaty was concluded in 1855 for the purpose of favoring the admittance of Hawaiian agricultural products to the United States, but it was rejected by the Senate because of the hostility of sugar interests in Louisiana who feared they could not compete with the Hawaiian product if it entered the country on a favored basis.

During the Civil War, Hawaii was for the time practically forgotten by the United States. In 1867, however, another commercial treaty was concluded, but it too was rejected by the Senate, partly because the wording of the treaty seemed to preclude ultimate annexation, and partly because of the continued hostility of southern sugar interests. That the United States now looked forward to the inevitable annexation was apparent from the instructions of Secretary Seward to the American diplomatic representative in Honolulu. These instructions, dated September 12, 1867, stated that "a lawful and peaceful annexation of the islands to the United States, with the consent of the people of the Sandwich Islands, is deemed desirable by this Government."[31] Despite Seward's lively interest in the annexation of the islands, the American nation was not then sufficiently interested in Pacific affairs or in overseas acquisitions to support him in such an unprecedented move as the acquisition of territory outside the continental limits of North America.

But the dream of annexation could not be resisted by zealous, and admittedly far-sighted, American diplomats. Early in the 1870's the American minister in Honolulu, Henry A. Pierce, revived the annexation issue in the State Department with a dispatch to Secretary Fish which pointed out that "Annexation of these islands to the United States and a reciprocity treaty between the two countries are the two important topics of conversation and warm discussion among Government officials and foreign residents."[32] Although Congress continued to manifest very little enthusiasm for annexation, Fish was more than warm to the idea. In a dispatch to Pierce he stressed that the position of the

Hawaiian Islands "as an outpost fronting and commanding the whole of our possessions on the Pacific Ocean" made their future of "peculiar interest to the Government and people of the United States." Their transfer to "any powerful and maritime or commercial nation" could not be tolerated. While many in the United States opposed the acquisition of insular possessions, argued Fish, "there are also those of influence and of wise foresight who see a future that must extend jurisdiction and the limits of this nation, and that will require a resting spot in the mid-ocean, between the Pacific coast and the vast domains of Asia, which are now opening to commerce and Christian civilization."[33] With these words Fish not only restated the established Hawaiian policy but made a firm advancement of the "enlarged Hawaiian policy," namely, that we would not permit any other power to possess the islands, that they were essential to our security, and that hence it was inevitable that they would some day come into our possession.

A comprehensive commercial treaty was again concluded in 1875, and this time it was ratified by the Senate in the following year. The treaty provided for commercial reciprocity, including the duty-free entrance of Hawaiian sugar to the United States, and a pledge on the part of the Hawaiian King never to cede any of his territory to a third power. In 1884 the treaty was renewed with the added provision that Pearl Harbor was to be placed at the disposal of the United States for exclusive use as a naval base. The British minister in Honolulu protested the Pearl Harbor clause, but his protest was ignored by the Hawaiian King. This treaty was not ratified by the Senate until 1887 because of the stubborn opposition of American sugar and rice interests.

Greatly concerned that the United States might completely dominate the islands, the British minister in Washington suggested that the United States join Britain and France in restating the old compact of 1843 in which Britain and France had pledged to respect the neutrality and sovereignty of Hawaii. Secretary Bayard declined this invitation to abnegation and explained that the islands occupied a different position with respect to the United States than with other countries.[34]

The commercial treaties of 1875 and 1884 stimulated the rapid expansion of the sugar industry, and the islands entered upon a period of unprecedented prosperity in which Americans came to have the largest stake. By 1887 the islands had become completely transformed into an American economic outpost, in which sugar was the real king. More than two thirds of all taxable real estate was owned by Americans. Exports of Hawaiian sugar to the United States, which had averaged less than 20 million pounds annually, increased by 1887 to about 200 million pounds.[35]

Partly because of the rapid decrease of the native population and partly because of its reluctance to labor on the plantations, the planters began importing large numbers of low-wage laborers. The first immigrant laborers were imported from the Azores, but they subsequently came almost exclusively from China, India and Japan. Japanese immigrant laborers arrived in large numbers in the latter part of the century. The native Hawaiians, who had numbered 130,313 in 1832, declined to 69,800 by 1860, and by 1900 had further declined to only 29,799.[36] The census of 1900 gave the total population of Hawaii as 154,000, of whom nearly 40 percent were Japanese, nearly 19 percent were Caucasians, and about 16 percent were Chinese. The native Hawaiians had dwindled to about 19 percent of the total population.

Kalakaua became King of Hawaii in 1874, and reigned until his death in 1890. During his reign the white element, mostly comprised of Americans, came to play an increasingly dominant role in the political as well as economic life of the islands. This element was composed of merchants, sugar planters, and the proprietors of "missionary stores." It actually came to constitute a political grouping, known as the "down-town" party, and apparently had as its objective the subversion of the King's prerogatives. It practically controlled the government by dominating the cabinet members appointed by Kalakaua, the most important of whom were whites. In 1887, restive under Kalakaua's pretensions to sovereignty based on his divine rights, the whites organized a mass meeting and drew up a constitution which they compelled the King to sign and proclaim. This instrument, known as the "Bayonet Constitution," in effect turned the islands and its people over to complete white domination. It deprived the King of all vestiges of power, made him a mere puppet, and practically disfranchised the native Hawaiian people.[37]

Meanwhile, Secretary Blaine had anticipated the imminent annexation of the islands by the United States. In December 1881

160

he had informed the American minister in Honolulu that the United States had acquired a "largely dominant influence in the North Pacific," and that since the Hawaiian Islands were "the key to the maritime domination of the Pacific states" it was necessary to make them "practically a part of the American system without derogation of their absolute independence." He pointed out that while the native population was dying out and Orientals were migrating to the islands in large numbers, the islands "cannot be joined to the Asiatic system." He indicated the possibility of the islands drifting from their independent status but insisted that such a drift "must be toward assimilation and identification with the American system, to which they belong." He further maintained that the islands were the key to the domination of the "American Pacific" and hence it was desirable that they should preserve a position of neutrality, but if this neutrality could not be preserved then the United States would "unhesitatingly meet the altered situation by seeking an avowedly American solution for the grave issues presented."[38]

In 1890 the uninterrupted prosperity of the islands came to a sudden end when the American Congress placed all foreign sugar on the free list and paid American producers of the commodity a bounty of two cents per pound. Thus Hawaiian sugar was forced to compete with Cuban and other foreign sugar and the bounty-supported sugar of the southern states. The prosperity of the islands was consequently dealt a staggering blow. The value of raw sugar and sugar lands dropped precipitately. The loss to owners of sugar plantations as well as the depreciation of other properties probably amounted to as much as $12,000,000.[39] Needless to say, the economic hardship stimulated the desire of an increasing number of Americans on the islands for annexation to the United States. In 1894 the Wilson-Gorman Tariff reimposed a duty on foreign sugar but permitted Hawaiian sugar to enter the country duty free. The Hawaiian "sugar depression" that had begun in 1890 ended almost immediately and the islands entered upon a period of renewed prosperity.

In 1891 King Kalakaua, who had been a puppet in the hands of the whites, died, and was succeeded by his sister Liliuokalani who became queen of the islands. Able and talented but vindictive by nature, the Queen chafed under the white domination and looked forward to the full recovery of the royal powers. By the fall of 1892 it was apparent that she was planning some drastic action. On November 20 the American minister in Hawaii, John L. Stevens, informed Secretary Foster that conditions on the islands might soon require "the adoption of decisive measures" to defend our interests and supremacy. He recommended annexation of the islands, and if that was not possible, at least an implied protectorate based on a perpetual customs union and the permanent acquisition of Pearl Harbor. "The golden hour is near at hand," he said, and annexation would preclude the possibility of either England or the Canadian Dominion securing a Hawaiian harbor for use as a coaling station.[40] Foster, an annexationist at heart, sympathized with the ideas of Stevens and complied with his request for the dispatch of a warship ostensibly to protect American lives and property in case of disturbances on the islands.

The anticipated disturbances broke out in the following year. On January 14, 1893, Queen Liliuokalani announced her intention of abrogating the "Bayonet Constitution" and promulgating a new one which would restore effective control of the islands to the native Hawaiians. In the afternoon of that same day a so-called committee of public safety, consisting of thirteen whites, was organized "to consider the situation and devise ways and means for the maintenance of the public peace and the protection of life and property." The committee convened again on the following day and resolved, among other things, to establish a provisional government "to exist until terms of union with the United States of America have been negotiated and agreed upon." At a mass meeting of Americans and other whites held in the afternoon, the Queen was condemned and the acts of the committee were approved. Alarmed and perhaps frightened that the Queen might employ force, the committee later that afternoon notified the American Minister Stevens that the lives and property of the people were in peril and that "we are unable to protect ourselves without aid, and therefore hope for the protection of the United States forces."[41]

The request for assistance was doubtless precisely what Stevens had anticipated and hoped for, and on the following day, January 16, he requested the commander of the warship *Boston* to land marines "to protect American lives and property." A force of 150 marines was promptly landed, which immediately occupied positions to threaten the Queen and her supporters rather than to protect American lives and property. Believing that the force of the United States was for the moment behind the revolutionists, the Queen on the following day surrendered her authority under protest until such time as the United States Government could investigate the incident and restore her authority. Two days later, on January 18, Stevens hastily recognized the new provisional government of the Americans as the *de facto* government of Hawaii. As historians have well noted, this was a curious *de facto* recognition, for only three days previously the Americans had cried for military assistance to maintain themselves.

On February 1 Stevens high-handedly raised the American flag over Honolulu and proclaimed Hawaii an American protectorate. He then informed Secretary Foster that "The Hawaiian pear is now fully ripe, and this is the golden hour for the United States to pluck it." He warned that if the islands were not promptly annexed by the United States the white element "might be forced towards becoming a British colony."[42]

A commission of the provisional government, consisting of four Americans and one British national, had meanwhile rushed to the United States immediately after the coup d'état for the purpose of concluding a treaty of annexation. Such a treaty was concluded on February 14 in Washington with eager Secretary Foster, and it was submitted to the Senate for ratification on the following day. But before the reluctant Senate could act on it, the anti-expansionist Grover Cleveland moved into the White House, on March 4. He promptly replaced Foster with Walter Q. Gresham as Secretary of State, and on March 9 withdrew the treaty from the Senate.

No man was ever more devoted to the right than Grover Cleveland. Suspecting that there had been foul play, he dispatched a personal representative, ex-Congressman James H. Blount of Georgia, to make an on-the-spot investigation of the facts in Honolulu. Blount arrived at Honolulu on March 29, 1893. One of his first official acts was to take down the American flag and order the marines back to their ship. These actions were symbolic of the withdrawal of American military support from the Provisional

Government. In the report which he submitted to Washington, Blount contended that the new government represented only the white, propertied class, that the Americans had acted illegally, and that Stevens had callously violated his responsibilities as minister to a friendly country. He also contended that "The undoubted sentiment of the people is for the Queen against the Provisional Government, and against annexation."[43]

Convinced that a great wrong had been perpetrated and that the honor of the United States had been sullied, Cleveland was determined to see that justice was done. In September 1893 Albert S. Willis was appointed the new minister to Hawaii, and accredited to the Provisional Government. He was instructed to convey to Liliuokalani the President's regret for the "flagrant wrong" that had been committed because of the "reprehensible conduct of the American minister and the unauthorized presence on land of a military force of the United States." He was also instructed to inform the ex-Queen that she would be restored to authority provided she would grant an amnesty to all Americans and others who had participated in the revolution and at the same time maintain the provisions of the 1887 Constitution.[44]

Willis arrived at Honolulu on November 4, 1893, and was formally received by the Provisional Government. The embittered ex-Queen at first refused to consent to an amnesty and insisted that she would have the head of every conspirator, but she finally accepted Willis' terms. Willis then requested President Dole and his associates to transfer the government to Liliuokalani. Dole, who was also the foreign minister, protested against Cleveland's interference in the internal affairs of Hawaii and denied the validity of the charges made in Blount's report. "I am instructed to inform you, Mr. Minister," he categorically declared, "that the Provisional Government of the Hawaiian Islands respectfully and unhesitatingly declines to entertain the proposition of the President of the United States that it should surrender its authority to the ex-Queen."[45]

It was apparent that Liliuokalani could be restored to the throne only by ordering American troops to employ force against American citizens in Hawaii. Insistent as he was on justice, Cleveland manifestly could not be a party to the shedding of American blood. He accordingly turned the problem over to the "extended powers and wide discretion of the Congress." In his final report to Congress on the matter, the intensely moral Cleveland reiterated that the Queen had been wronged and that the revolution would never have succeeded but for the unlawful and reprehensible conduct of the American minister in Honolulu. In explaining why he refused to submit the treaty of annexation to the Senate, he reminded that body of the obligation to respect what he called "international morality." "It has been the boast of our Government that it seeks to do justice in all things without regard to the strength or weakness of those with whom it deals," he declared. "I mistake the American people if they favor the odious doctrine that there is no such thing as international morality, that there is one law for the strong nation and another for a weak one, and that even by indirection a strong power may with impunity despoil a weak one of its territory." He spoke, too, with equally imperishable words of his conception of the American mission: "If national honesty is to be disregarded and a desire for territorial extension, or dissatisfaction with a form of government not our own, ought to regulate our conduct, I have entirely misapprehended the mission and the character of our Government and the behavior which the conscience of our people demands of their public servants."[46]

In 1895 a counter-revolution, instigated by Liliuokalani and her chief supporters, broke out in several localities, but it was easily crushed by the alerted Government in minor actions that resulted in a few dead and some wounded. About two hundred of the counter-revolutionists, including Liliuokalani and some twenty or thirty foreigners, were rounded up and placed under arrest. They were all released, however, within a few months. The foreigners were compelled to leave the islands. Liliuokalani, while in prison, wrote a letter to Judge Dole in which she renounced all claims to the throne and pledged to live peaceably on the islands.[47]

With the hope of annexation by the United States temporarily abandoned, the Americans residing in Hawaii on July 4, 1894, established an independent Republic of Hawaii under the presidency of Judge Dole. The new republic was promptly recognized by most of the principal nations, including the United States, which did so by Congressional resolution. The lonely and feeble island republic persisted in courting annexation by the United States, however, and looked forward to the inauguration of a president who would be favorably disposed toward annexation. Such a man became president in March 1897, when William McKinley took office. Though imbued with a high sense of righteousness, he was unable to resist the pressure of the influential imperialists who surrounded him, and he gave his support to annexation.

Meanwhile, the Hawaiian Government had become involved in a controversy with Japan which played into the hands of the imperialists who were pressuring for prompt annexation of the islands. In 1896 the Hawaiian Government, upon the urging of the sugar growers, negotiated a cheap-labor treaty with Japan for the purpose of facilitating the influx of Japanese laborers to work on the plantations. As a result of this treaty, the Japanese on the islands increased rapidly. Whereas in 1883 there was a mere handful of 116 Japanese in Hawaii and by 1896 there were still only 24,407, by 1900 their numbers soared to 61,111, comprising about 40 percent of the islands' total population. This increase of the Japanese greatly alarmed the white elements which had no stakes in the plantations. Yielding to their pressure, the Hawaiian Government in March 1897 inadvertently precipitated an international crisis by barring entrance to 1,174 Japanese immigrants in violation of the 1896 treaty. The Japanese Government made a strong protest and even dispatched a warship to Honolulu. The American Government countered by ordering three warships to keep the vessel under surveillance. As a result of the mediation of the United States, however, the Hawaiian Government made satisfactions to Japan and the incident was liquidated.[48]

The above development may have greatly influenced President McKinley to speed up the process of annexation. In any event, a Treaty of Annexation was signed in Washington on June 16, 1897, by Secretary John Sherman and three representatives of the Hawaiian Republic, namely Francis March Hatch, Lorrin A. Thursten, and William A. Kinney. President McKinley submitted the treaty to the Senate for ratification on the very day that it was signed. By the terms of the treaty the Republic "ceded absolutely and without reserve to the United States of America all rights of sovereignty of whatsoever kind." The treaty provided that "all territory of and land appertaining to the republic of Hawaii is hereby annexed to the United States of America under the name

166

of the Territory of Hawaii." Existing treaties of Hawaii with other nations were to "cease" and to be replaced "by such treaties as may exist, or as may be hereafter concluded between the United States and such foreign nations." The public debt of the islands was to be taken over by the United States, but the liability of the United States was not to exceed $4,000,000. One provision of the treaty was directed against the Chinese residents on the islands. This provision stated that "There shall be no further immigration of Chinese into the Hawaiian Islands, except under such conditions as are now or may hereafter be allowed by the laws of the United States, and no Chinese, by reason of anything herein contained, shall be allowed to enter the United States from the Hawaiian Islands."[49]

Queen Liliuokalani, who was in Washington at the time the treaty was concluded, even at this late hour clung to the hope that a Christian nation would see that justice was done to her. The day after the treaty was signed, she dispatched a formal protest to the State Department. "I, Liliuokalani of Hawaii," she pleaded, "do hereby call upon the President of that nation, to whom I alone yielded my property and my authority, to withdraw said treaty (ceding said islands) from further consideration." She concluded her protest with the pathetic words: "I ask the honorable Senate of the United States to decline to ratify said treaty, and I implore the people of this great and good nation, from whom my ancestors learned the Christian religion, to sustain their representatives in such acts of justice and equity as may be in accord with the principles of their fathers, and to the Almighty Ruler of the universe, to him who judgeth righteously, I commit my cause."[50]

Impervious to the entreaties of the dethroned Queen, McKinley refused to withdraw the treaty from the Senate. In that body, however, it encountered strong opposition from the combined forces of the anti-imperialists and the representatives of the American sugar interests. Its supporters were unable to muster the necessary two-thirds majority, and the treaty languished.

Meanwhile the Japanese Government, having learned of the conclusion of the treaty of annexation, protested that the continuation of good relations between Japan and the United States depended on the maintenance of an independent Hawaii. Japan especially feared that annexation would prejudice the rights of the

167

Japanese nationals who had emigrated to Hawaii in considerable numbers. Japan withdrew her protest, however, after being reassured that the rights of Japanese nationals in Hawaii would be safeguarded. The "legitimate interests of other powers" could not be injured by "the more perfect union of Hawaii to the United States," explained Washington.[51] With this assurance, the Japanese Government took a friendlier attitude toward the inevitable annexation.

Following the outbreak of the war with Spain in April 1898 and Admiral Dewey's spectacular victory over the Spanish fleet in Manila Bay on May 1, a widespread feeling arose among the American people that the country would be letting Dewey down if the Hawaiian Islands were not annexed and utilized as a base to support him. McKinley then resorted to the stratagem of annexation by means of a joint resolution of Congress, which required only a majority vote in each House. Such a resolution, embodying the provisions of the languishing treaty of annexation, was passed by both Houses by considerable margins. The joint resolution was signed by President McKinley on July 7, and in affixing his signature he pronounced that "Annexation is not change: it is consummation." On August 12 the islands formally became a possession of the United States and the American flag was symbolically raised over the executive building in Honolulu. The conscience of ex-President Cleveland could not remain silent. "Hawaii is ours," he wrote to a friend. "As I look back upon the first steps in this miserable business and as I contemplate the means used to complete this outrage, I am ashamed of the whole affair."[52]

An act of Congress in April 1900 contained organic provisions which organized the islands into a Territory of the United States, conferred rights of American citizenship on all Hawaiian citizens, as stipulated in the treaty of annexation, and provided that the constitution and laws of the United States would have the same force on the islands as in the United States. Judge Dole was appointed the first governor of the Territory and took office on June 19. On February 20 of the following year, 1901, the first territorial legislature was convened. Thus Hawaii began its new life as a Territory of the United States.

CHAPTER NINE

The Korean Problem and the Rise of Japan

At the turn of the century Japan became the dominant power in the Far East. That position was greatly enhanced as a result of the opportunities presented by World War I which were fully exploited by Japan and a decade of ruthless territorial expansionism that began in 1931 and culminated in the great Pacific holocaust. During this period the most serious problems of American foreign policy concerned Japan.

The most momentous development of Far Eastern history from the middle of the nineteenth century was, without question, the rise of Japan to vast power and dominance in East Asia and then her total defeat and reduction to the ranks of a minor power after 1945. Even in the wake of Japan's defeat, far-reaching developments were set in motion, partly as a consequence of Japan's actions, notably the collapse of colonialism and the rise of a number of newly independent Asian states that were to greatly alter the configuration of world power. It seems pertinent therefore to examine in some detail the rise of Japan to the status of a great power between the period of her resumption of intercourse with the West and the turn of the century.

During the early years of the Meiji period Japan was confronted with the aggressive imperialism of the West which had already clawed China and was threatening the territorial integrity of the Japanese Empire. The most feared of the imperialistic nations was Tsarist Russia, which since 1858 had resumed her insatiable territorial expansion in the Far East. In 1860 Russia had obtained the immense Maritime province, which stretches east and south of the Amur River, and on its coast Vladivostok was immediately founded as a Far Eastern outpost of the Russian Empire. Russia had also laid claim to all of Sakhalin and the Kurile Islands, thereby encroaching toward Japan from the north. Some Japanese for a time feared the possibility of an agreement among Russia, France and Great Britain for the partitioning of the Japanese islands. One of Japan's main concerns therefore was to protect herself from the fate that had already befallen China and the perhaps even worse fate that seemed to lie in store for her. From this critical need for self-defense there consequently arose the urge to obtain advance outposts to keep the imperialistic nations at as great a distance as possible.

On the other hand, there were historic forces within Japan which encouraged territorial aggrandizement *per se* as a symbol of imperial greatness. Expansionism and aggrandizement of the Empire had been urged by imperial supporters even before the Imperial Restoration, and a Chōshū patriot had predicted that the restoration of the Emperor to his powers would result in the acquisition of an extensive domain that would include Formosa, the Kurile Islands, Sakhalin, Kamchatka, Korea and a large part of Manchuria and Siberia.[1] In March 1858 when Lord Hotta had argued for imperial approval of the Harris Convention, he predicted that after Japan had become a member of the family of nations "Our national prestige and position thus assured, the nations of the world will come to look up to our Emperor as the Great Ruler of all nations, and they will come to follow our policy and submit themselves to our judgment."[2] This expansionist heritage was fanned by the imperialism of the West which the Japanese eagerly adopted and considered a concomitant of a great and virile power.

To some degree the unofficial basis of Japanese policy with regard to the Western powers and their imperialism may be considered to have been laid down by Viscount Tani in 1886. In that year he had sagely urged his countrymen to depend on military preparedness for the defense of Japan. "Encourage and protect the people at home," he admonished, "and then wait for the time of the confusion of Europe which must come eventually sooner or later" and "we may become the chief nation of the Orient."[3] In other words, the rivalries and jealousies of the European powers would create situations which Japan could exploit to enhance her power. As the years unfolded, this was substantially what happened and what Japan did, particularly during World War I, the period of the great world depression, and the years of Hitler's aggressions.

The urge for expansionism was further stimulated by the industrial revolution which was having its beginnings in Japan. Whereas agrarian Tokugawa Japan had been practically self-sufficient, the new Japan that was rapidly becoming industrialized required increasing sources of raw materials and expanding markets for the products of her factories. As Japan became more industrialized, this economic impetus to imperialism became increasingly more intensified.

Expansionism requires an adequate military force. Such a force was lacking in Japan when the Imperial Restoration took place, but it was quickly established as a result of the government purchase of war equipment abroad and the government support of incipient war industries. During the early part of the Meiji period the need for a strong military establishment was dictated largely by defensive and security considerations, but after the turn of the century armed power became the tool of expansionism.

The first threat to the territorial integrity of Japan took place in 1861 when a Russian naval commander occupied the island of Tsushima for use as a naval base and constructed barracks there for a small military force. Several protests were made by Japan, but she was powerless at that time to expel the Russians with force and consequently turned to Great Britain for support. Secretary Seward offered to serve as mediator; and betraying his ignorance of the real nature of Russian imperialism he somewhat naïvely informed Minister Harris that "I will, in the name of this government, as the friend of Japan, as well as of Russia, seek from the latter explanations which I should hope would be satisfactory to Japan."[4] Before Japan could act on Seward's offer, the British Admiral Sir James Hope realistically led a powerful squadron to Tsushima and induced the Russians to withdraw from the island.

Meanwhile, Japan was in the midst of other territorial problems with Russia concerning claims of ownership over Sakhalin and the Kurile Islands.* A Japanese mission was dispatched to St. Petersburg in 1866 to settle this problem, but it met with no success. Acting on a suggestion made by Seward when he had stopped in Japan on his world tour, the Japanese in 1872 offered to purchase the Russian claim to Sakhalin for 2,000,000 yen, but after the Russians had consented to sell and negotiations were well underway they withdrew the offer on the assumption that the island was worthless.[5] Not until 1875 did Japan reach an agreement with Russia concerning the status of Sakhalin and the Kuriles. By the terms of an agreement concluded in St. Petersburg that year, Japan renounced all claims to Sakhalin in return for Russian renunciation of all claims to the Kurile Islands. The Japanese however reserved certain economic rights on Sakhalin. This treaty was also of significance as it marked the first time that Japan had negotiated as an equal with a European power in the nineteenth century.[6] The Japanese diplomatic success was doubtless largely due to Russia's preoccupation at that time with the Russo-Turkish War which was being fought in the distant Balkans.

Late in 1861 the Japanese Government had notified Minister Harris that Japan intended to "reoccupy" the Bonin Islands and promised that the rights of Americans there would be respected. Commander Kelly had formally taken possession of one of these islands in 1853 on instructions from Commodore Perry, but the State Department had never sanctioned the seizure. Japan's claims to these islands were practically indisputable, for in 1592 Sadayori Ogasawara, a Japanese national, had founded a settlement on the islands.[7] In 1873 Secretary Fish formally renounced all American claims to any part of the islands. Great Britain similarly surrendered her claims, and hence the islands came into the exclusive and undisputed possession of Japan.[8]

In September 1871 a crisis arose between Japan and China as the result of the murder of 66 Ryūkyū islanders by a savage tribe, the Boutans, on the island of Formosa. A short time previously, the United States had been forced to send a punitive expedition to Formosa because of the wreck of the bark *Rover* and the murder of its

*Sakhalin had first been explored by the Japanese, and some Japanese nationals had passed a winter there as early as 1620, long before the Russians had reached the Pacific coast. Russian claims to Sakhalin only extended as far back as 1804. A Russo-Japanese Treaty of 1855 had provided for joint occupation of the island of Sakhalin and division of the Kurile Islands at a line between Urup and Iturup.

172

crew by the aborigines. The expedition was a small one, and Secretary Seward assured the Chinese Government that the United States had no intention of seizing or retaining any part of the island. After inflicting minor punishment on the aborigines, the small expedition of 181 men promptly withdrew from the island. In this punitive expedition the Japanese found a precedent for their more ambitious attack on the island as a reprisal for the murdered Ryūkyūans.[9]

On the ground that she was responsible for the foreign relations of the Ryūkyūans, Japan promptly dispatched an expedition of considerable strength to Formosa and thoroughly chastised the savages responsible for the murder of the Ryūkyūans. Since China claimed Formosa as an integral part of her Empire, Japan sent a special diplomatic agent to China for the purpose of obtaining indemnification for the outrage. After considerable haggling over the status of the Ryūkyū Islands and the precise responsibility of China for affairs in Formosa, an agreement was finally concluded in October 1874, known as the Peking Convention, whereby China promised to pay an indemnity to the families of the murdered Ryūkyūans and a further sum of 400,000 taels to defray the costs of the Japanese expedition. The British Minister in Peking, Thomas Wade, was greatly instrumental in bringing the disputants together to reach this agreement.[10]

By the terms of the above convention, China had indirectly admitted the existence of Japanese sovereignty over the Ryūkyū Islands. Japan then proceeded to accelerate the complete integration of these islands in the Empire, to the great displeasure of China which insisted that they were tributary to her. For a time the dispute over the status of these islands threatened to involve the two nations in war. During his sojourns in Tokyo and Peking while on his world tour, ex-President Grant had suggested the division of the islands between China and Japan. The Japanese initially thought well of the suggestion, but they later changed their mind and insisted on all of the islands. China soon lost interest in the islands, however, because of more pressing problems at home, and Japan proceeded to make them an integral part of the Empire without any further complications resulting.

The scene of the rise of Japan as a great power now shifts to Korea, where Chinese and Japanese interests soon clashed. Before engaging in a discussion of this phase of Sino-Japanese rivalry, however, it seems desirable to examine briefly Korea's background

173

of isolation and the efforts of the powers to open her doors to international intercourse.

A mountainous peninsula jutting southward from Manchuria, and separated by only 125 miles of sea from Japan, Korea points like a dagger at the Japanese islands. Geographically it is therefore of great importance, serving as a springboard to either the heart of East Asia or the Japanese islands. Comprising only about 85,000 square miles and today containing less than 30,000,000 people, Korea is not and will not become a power in the Far East. Her role today and tomorrow is precisely what it has been in the past century, namely a pawn in the struggle for security and power in East Asia.

Korea is an ancient country with a written history extending back to the pre-Christian era. Culturally the Koreans were strongly influenced by the Chinese, whose written language and arts and sciences became the foundations of Korean culture. It was from the Koreans in the early centuries of the Christian era that the Japanese first became acquainted with the brilliant culture of China.

Korea's earliest political and economic relations were with China, which occasionally invaded the land but never remained for long as a conqueror. Most of the time Korea was ruled by native kings who recognized a tributary allegiance to the Emperor of China. Occasionally tribute was also paid to Japan. In the sixteenth century the Japanese general Hideyoshi attempted to conquer Korea as a prelude to the subjugation of China, but the effort was abandoned after his premature death.* The cruel excesses of the Japanese troops in Korea are alleged to have left an indelible hatred of Japan in the hearts of the Koreans. After the withdrawal of the Japanese troops, the Korean kingdom settled down to a period of relative stability and clung to a policy of rigid seclusion.

At the time the great powers became interested in opening

*The Japanese had established a trading settlement at Pusan in the middle of the fifteenth century. After this settlement was abolished the Lord of Tsushima was allowed to send eight junks annually to Pusan. The Japanese had had relations with the Koreans long before this period, but these relations are beyond the province of this discussion. Tribute was paid by the Koreans irregularly at various times after the invasion of Hideyoshi. The last tribute was paid in 1832. (*Cf.* Hishida, *The International Position of Japan as a Great Power,* p. 163.)

Korea to commerce the rulers of the country were arrogantly anti-foreign, deeply convinced of the superiority of their culture, and blindly reactionary. Internally the country had become blighted by political intrigue, corruption and oppression which stifled progress. It could be said that there were but two classes of people in Korea: the oppressors and the oppressed. In foreign relations the King of Korea recognized the suzerainty of the Emperor of China and some commercial contacts were maintained with the Chinese. Lesser commercial contacts were maintained with the Japanese, who were permitted to send eight junks annually to Pusan for the exchange of goods. As in China, all Westerners were regarded as "barbarians." Hatred of the Japanese became particularly intense after Japan opened her doors to the West and began Westernizing many of her institutions. To the minds of the ultraconservative Koreans these actions of the Japanese were a betrayal of the East. It might be noted that as a vassal of China it was the practice of the Korean Government to return shipwrecked sailors through the good offices of Chinese officials in Korea. A short time after, however, a serious incident occurred when the *General Sherman* was stranded in a Korean river and some of its crew became involved in a brawl ashore that resulted in the death of eight crewmen and the imprisonment of several others. The gravity of the incident was increased when some enraged Koreans destroyed the ship. The actual details of this incident were not known to the American Government until about twenty years later.[11]

Since France was also involved in difficulties with Korea at this time, Secretary Seward proposed the sending of a joint Franco-American punitive expedition, but the proposal was turned down by France because of her preoccupation with more pressing international problems. Meanwhile, the Shōgun's government had offered to "tender friendly advice to Corea" and to serve as a mediator. It made reference to Korea "being the neighbor of Japan" and "the sincere friendship subsisting between Japan and the United States."[12] Nothing came of the Shōgunate's offer, however, as it became preoccupied with a revolt in Japan which shortly afterward resulted in its overthrow.

There was no alternative for Seward but to take unilateral measures against the stubborn and recalcitrant Koreans. In 1867 American Far Eastern naval forces made two futile attempts to ascertain the details concerning the *General Sherman* incident.[13] Four years later, in 1871, another expedition, modelled after that of Commodore Perry to Japan, was dispatched to make an on-the-spot investigation and also to explore the possibility of a treaty. The expedition, consisting of five warships under the joint command of the Minister to China, Frederick F. Low, and Rear Admiral Rogers, arrived off the coast below Seoul in May of that year. As the result of a skirmish which took place when a Korean fort fired on the surveying party, two Americans were killed and a number of Koreans were killed and wounded. Low's demand for an apology was scorned, and in retaliation five Korean forts were destroyed and some 350 Koreans were killed and wounded. Despite this demonstration of force, the Korean Government refused to deal with the American officials. Lacking authority to engage in further hostilities, Rogers and Low withdrew from Korea on July 3, 1871.[14] Once more the jubilant Korean Government foolishly believed that a great victory had been won over the "barbarians" and that its ability to enforce the seclusion policy had again been demonstrated. Since there were no active American interests in Korea to be protected, and since Far Eastern affairs in general evoked but slight concern, the American Government dropped the matter.

It remained for the Japanese to break the hard shell of Korean seclusion, partly as a consequence of their concern over Russian expansionism. The Japanese fear of Russian expansionism had been intensive since a very early date. Practically from the outset of the Meiji period the Japanese adhered to a policy of favoring the independence of Korea and her establishment of diplomatic relations with the great powers as a possible means of forestalling any Russian ambitions to annex or occupy the peninsula. In 1868 a special Japanese envoy had been dispatched to Korea to inform its Government of the Imperial Restoration that had taken place in Japan and to discuss the establishment of diplomatic relations, but the Korean Court had refused to deal with him.[15] In the following year two more Japanese missions were rebuffed, and in 1872 Yoshikata Hanabusa accompanied by two warships also failed in his attempt to discuss a commercial treaty. These incivil rebuffs suffered at the hands of the Korean Government greatly inflamed Japanese public opinion and loud demands arose for war.

176

As the result of a cabinet crisis on the issue of war or peace, Taneomi Soejima was dispatched to Peking to sound out the Chinese Government on its attitude and policy concerning Korea. In Peking the officials of the Tsungli Yamen informed him that while Korea was a vassal state, China was not responsible for her internal administration and the problems of peace or war. On his return to Japan Soejima urged his government to invade and conquer Korea. On this issue the cabinet crisis became grave, and the "war party" might have carried the day but for the personal decision of the Emperor Meiji to settle the Korean problem by peaceful means since Japan was not yet strong enough to embark on expensive overseas wars.[16]

In 1875 the "war party" in Japan again clamored for military action when a small Japanese ship engaged in soundings off the Korean coast was fired on by a Korean fort. In retaliation the fort was destroyed and heavy casualties were inflicted on its garrison. Once again the Japanese Government ignored the clamor for war, and again a commission was dispatched to Korea to attempt the negotiation of a treaty of amity and commerce. This commission, headed by General Kuroda and Count Inoue, was instructed to use the firm methods that had been so successfully employed by Perry and Harris against Japan some years before. At the same time, Japan obtained assurances from China that no objection would be raised to diplomatic discussions provided they were restricted to the commercial opening of Korea.[17] The Japanese mission arrived in Korea in December 1875. The ultraconservative elements in Korea bitterly opposed any discussions with Japan, but a rival faction with more enlightened views finally won out and it was decided to conclude a treaty since it appeared that the opening of the country was inevitable.

The treaty, known as the Treaty of Kianghwa, was at length signed on February 27, 1876. It provided for the establishment of diplomatic relations, the opening of three ports, and extraterritorial jurisdiction over Japanese nationals. One of its most significant provisions was Article 1, which stipulated that "Chosen, being an independent state, enjoys the same sovereign rights as does Nippon."[18] This provision was the first step in Japan's plan to detach Korea from the feeble and equivocating suzerainty of China. A supplementary treaty concluded in August contained a clause, inserted on Japanese prompting, which prohibited the importation of opium.

In the following year the first Japanese chargé d'affaires arrived in Seoul. In 1880 the Japanese diplomatic post in Seoul was elevated to the status of a ministry. Despite the conclusion of the above treaty, relations between the Japanese and the Koreans remained unfriendly. The Koreans as a whole remained bitterly antiforeign, and the country had actually been opened begrudgingly and largely because of expediency and the fear of possible Japanese retaliation. In subsequent years attacks on Japanese and other foreign nationals residing in Korea became frequent occurrences.

In November 1878 Commodore R. W. Shufeldt was authorized by Secretary Evarts to investigate the possibility of concluding a treaty "similar in spirit and purpose to those already in existence with other oriental countries."[19] Actually neither Evarts nor President Hayes had any interest in Korea, and the initiative for treaty negotiations with that country came entirely from Shufeldt, who was motivated by his own ambition for fame and the sincere belief that the treaty would redound to the advantage of the United States. Since the Korean-Japanese treaty of 1876 had created the impression of a close relationship between Japan and Korea, Shufeldt initially attempted to establish communication with the Korean Government through the Japanese consul in Pusan. The attempt failed, doubtless because of the bad faith of the Japanese official and his suspicions concerning Shufeldt's ulterior motives.

Concerned by Shufeldt's dealings with the Japanese, Li Hungchang, the Chinese official with primary responsibility for Korean affairs, invited him to visit Tientsin for discussions and promised to use his influence to persuade the Koreans to conclude the treaty he desired. Li also held out to Shufeldt the hope of an important position in the Chinese navy. Li obviously resented the wedge Japan had driven between Korea and China and hoped to strengthen the weakened Chinese claim to suzerainty. Shufeldt arrived in Tientsin in 1881, and was nominally assigned to the American legation in Peking. Efforts of the American Minister, James B. Angell, to assist Shufeldt in getting the position with the Chinese navy were frowned upon by the other diplomatic representatives, who believed that such a position would enable the

United States to enjoy a privileged status. To put an end to the intrigue of the representatives against him, Shufeldt renounced all interest in the naval position and concentrated on the Korean treaty.[20]

By the spring of 1882 Li and Shufeldt finally got around to the actual discussions concerning an American treaty with Korea. Li had assured Shufeldt that the Korean Government favored his acting as a middle man. Meanwhile, in November 1881 Secretary Blaine had given explicit instructions to Shufeldt and had informed him that "While no political or commercial interest renders such a treaty urgent, it is desirable that the ports of a country so near Japan and China should be opened to our trade and the convenience of such vessels of our Navy as may be in those waters." Blaine further stipulated that a treaty was to be concluded only if the Korean Government desired one. "We will with pleasure establish such friendly relations," he stated, "but we do not propose to use force or to entreat such action."[21]

During the discussions Li informed Shufeldt that he desired a clause inserted in the treaty which would recognize Korea as a dependent state of China. Shufeldt resolutely opposed such a clause and wired the Secretary of State for instructions, but no reply came.* Acting on his own initiative Shufeldt compromised by promising Li he would write him a letter stating that the assistance of China had been requested since Korea was her dependency. He also promised to dispatch to the President of the United States a letter which the King of Korea would write, stating that the treaty had been made with the consent of China. As is apparent, Li was exploiting his role as a middle man to counteract the Japanese who in their treaty had recognized Korea as an independent country. Li by this time had become determined to check the Japanese encroachment in Korea and to retain for China as much of its old influence as possible.

As agreed by Li and Shufeldt, the treaty, which had already been

*Shufeldt, exasperated by the "deception" of Li, had written Senator Sargent of California a letter in which he depicted the Chinese as a contemptible people. The letter was published in the United States, but its contents were not known in the Far East until after Shufeldt had concluded his treaty. It is very likely that this indiscretion on the part of Shufeldt was the reason for the State Department taking no action on his request for further instructions.

negotiated, was carried to the King of Korea by Chinese officials aboard a Chinese vessel. Shufeldt then proceeded to Seoul, where the treaty was signed on May 22, 1882. In accordance with the agreement made by Li and Shufeldt, the King of Korea wrote a letter to President Arthur, which however was given to Shufeldt two days before the signing of the treaty, rather than after its signing, as had been agreed. The letter stated that although Korea had been a tributary state of China since ancient times, the King of Korea had always exercised full sovereignty over internal administration and foreign relations and that the provisions of the treaty would be fully carried out in accordance with international law.[22]

The terms of the Shufeldt Treaty were similar to those of the convention which Harris had concluded with Japan in 1858, and it contained two provisions expressive of America's friendly and sympathetic attitude toward Korea, as toward all oriental nations. One of these provisions stipulated that the United States would surrender its extraterritorial privileges as soon as Korea had reformed its legal system so as "to conform to the laws and course of justice in the United States." The other provision was a pledge by the United States to offer its friendly offices in case Korea became a victim of injustice or aggression. One of the most significant features of the treaty, of course, was its recognition of Korea as a sovereign and independent state. Treaties similar to the American one were concluded by Great Britain and Germany in 1883, by Italy and Russia in 1884, and by France in 1886. Recognition of the independence of Korea was also inherent in each of these treaties.

One very important result of these treaties was to divide Korea into two bitterly hostile groups over the question of foreign intercourse, one group favoring the treaties, and the other group being opposed to them. These treaties, with their implication that the foreigners had forced themselves on Korea, were a principal cause of the intensified outbursts of anti-foreign feeling which followed.

From 1876 to 1894 China and Japan became engaged in a bitter rivalry over the status of Korea and the control of its affairs. China persisted in maintaining that Korea was a "vassal" state of China, with the implication that Korea was sovereign in all internal matters but that China was responsible for protecting her in her relations with foreign powers. Japan was equally persistent in maintaining that Korea was fully sovereign and independent. This rivalry on several occasions threatened to break out into open warfare and finally culminated in a short but decisive conflict which resulted in Japan emerging completely victorious and China being totally eliminated from influence in Korean affairs. During the period of Sino-Japanese rivalry over Korea, the country was ruled by a weak government and bitter factionalism which seriously compromised the internal stability and security of the country. The continuous internal disorders, the widespread corruption and inefficiency, and the backwardness of the country invited intervention of some kind from strong foreign powers. As for the Japanese and the Chinese, the Koreans generally favored the latter because of their cultural and historic ties with them.

China was unable to pursue a strong policy in Korea, for at this time she was threatened by Russian and French encroachment from the north and south respectively. Moreover, Russia had also become interested in Korea and looked forward to the possession of warm-water ports on the peninsula and its possible annexation as a springboard for further expansion on the East Asia mainland. Britain consequently became desirous of Korea remaining within the Chinese orbit, and for a time actually acted as an unofficial ally of China in her struggle against Russian, French, and even Japanese encroachment.[23]

The United States had no clearly defined policy or program with which to confront the rivalries of the powers in Korea other than the somewhat nebulous tradition of favoring the development of strong and independent states everywhere in the Orient. There were no American commercial or other tangible interests of any significance to be protected at that time in Korea. The State Department was primarily concerned with remaining on good terms with the rival powers, but it persistently upheld the premise that Korea was sovereign and independent.[24] To a great degree this premise played into the hands of the Japanese, who felt that their interests could be promoted more effectively in a Korea with an independent status. In 1883 the United States established a diplomatic post in Seoul with the rank of Minister, the same rank as the posts in Tokyo and Peking, but in the following year it was reduced to Resident Minister. A request by the Chinese Government to make the Seoul post an appendage of the Peking Legation was turned down by the State Department.

One result of the treaties that had been concluded by Korea with the powers was to imbue the Korean Government with a feeling of its importance in international affairs, and for a time it pursued a policy that actually was as opposed to Chinese as to Japanese domination. In an attempt to counteract the encroachment of China and Japan, the Korean Government turned to the United States and requested an adviser for the Foreign Office, school teachers, and instructors for the army. The adviser never arrived, only a few teachers reached Korea, and three military instructors arrived several years after the request.[25] Nevertheless, for a brief period American influence was in the ascendancy, and it might have been rather successfully exploited for the purpose of safeguarding and strengthening Korean independence had the United States Government not been so completely uninterested in the Korean problem.

In 1886 the Korean Government made a belated attempt to assert its independent status by dispatching abroad diplomatic representatives, as had been provided for by the treaties with the powers. China looked with extreme displeasure upon this project and did everything possible to prevent the departure of the diplomats. The attitude of China evoked a strong protest from Secretary Bayard, who expressed "surprise and regret." Despite the opposition of China, a Korean minister departed for the United States in February 1887 aboard the American warship *Ossipee,* but a Korean envoy to Europe was unable to get beyond Hongkong. The minister to Washington was received by President Cleveland as the "representative of an independent state,"[26] much to the annoyance of Li Hung-chang. On the minister's return to Seoul in 1889 Yüan Shih-K'ai, the representative of Li Hung-chang in Korea, attempted to have him punished for having acted contrary to the wishes of China.[27]

As the culmination of a long period of intense rivalry, in which acts of violence broke out on several occasions, China and Japan in April 1885 had concluded an agreement in which the two countries agreed to withdraw troops which they had stationed in Korea and in the future not to dispatch troops there without first notifying the other.[28] While the agreement was a diplomatic victory for

Japan in that China recognized equal rights of intervention, it nevertheless failed to solve the real basic problems involved in the long Sino-Japanese controversy.[29] It was a *modus vivendi* rather than a definitive solution of basic problems.

By 1890 it had become apparent that Sino-Japanese rivalry in Korea would ultimately lead to war. Actually, the economic interests of China were very limited, and she was mainly concerned with maintaining Korea's status as a dependency. The essence of China's Korean policy was quite clear: while China did not want to annex Korea or even to assume responsibility for its actions as an alleged vassal state, at the same time she did not want any other nation, particularly Japan, to annex it.[30]

Japan, on the other hand, took the position that geographical propinquity made the status and the internal condition of Korea matters of critical importance to the security of Japan. She did not want to see any powerful Western nation, such as Russia, become entrenched on the peninsula. Japan believed that the weakness and corruption of the Korean Government invited foreign intervention, and possibly permanent occupation. Her aim therefore was to favor a Korea totally independent of China so that the necessary reforms could be carried out to introduce efficiency in government, execute the necessary fiscal changes, modernize the army, and promote material progress and internal stability. China was regarded as the inveterate foe of reform. Once the baneful Chinese influence was eradicated, however, the Japanese apparently believed that they should have a position of primary influence over the Korean Government because of the geographical proximity of Japan to the peninsula.* In addition to being concerned about her security, Japan was also interested in promoting Japanese economic penetration of the peninsula, which by this time had become more extensive than that of any other nation.

In 1893 a serious crisis arose as the result of a revolt by the so-called Tong Hak Society (Society of Eastern Learning) against the maladministration of the Korean Government. The Tong Hak Society had been organized by a Korean scholar in 1859. Originally it had been semi-religious in nature, anti-Christian and anti-foreign. Although its founder had been executed as a heretic and

---

*The attitude of Japan toward Korea at this time bears comparison with that of the United States toward Cuba when the chronic disorders on that island finally led to an American declaration of war against Spain in 1898.

its followers had been severely persecuted, the society had managed to survive.

In March 1894 the Tong Haks began advancing on Seoul, and the frightened Korean King on June 2 asked for Chinese military assistance. China dispatched a large number of troops from Tientsin on June 6, and on the following day Japan was given due notification as required by the Sino-Japanese agreement of 1885. In the notification it was explained that the dispatch of the Chinese troops was "in harmony with our constant practice to protect our tributary states."[31] The Japanese had been following the developments in Korea closely, however, and they also dispatched troops. In notifying China of her action, Japan reiterated that Korea was recognized as an independent state and that the Chinese claim of suzerainty had never been recognized.[32]

Meanwhile, the Tong Hak uprising had been brought under control by troops of the Korean Government, and the Korean King no longer needed the assistance of either Chinese or Japanese troops. The King therefore requested their withdrawal, but both China and Japan refused to do so until the troops of the other had first been withdrawn.[33] Actually Japan was now determined to obtain a definitive solution of the vexing Korean problem, and she took the position that her troops could not be withdrawn until the necessary fiscal and other reforms had been carried out. On June 17 Japan invited China to collaborate in bringing about the desired reforms, but China declined to cooperate on the traditional ground that while Korea was a tributary state there could be no interference in her purely internal affairs.

The Japanese Government then instructed its minister in Seoul to carry out the reforms single-handedly and to employ force if necessary. Efforts by China to get the big powers to mediate failed, partly because of Britain's suspicions of the motives of the powers and her hesitancy to cooperate with them. On June 30 the Japanese Minister obtained a statement from the Korean Government to the effect that Korea was a sovereign and independent state. Under further Japanese pressure the King on July 24 abrogated the treaty with China and authorized Japan to expel Chinese troops who were then occupying Ansan. The King became a virtual prisoner of the Japanese, and all actions of the Korean Government after June 1894 were actually Japanese inspired and directed.

Formal declarations of war were made by both China and Japan on August 1, after actual hostilities had already broken out more than a week before on July 25. On August 20 a formal treaty of alliance was concluded between Korea and Japan which exempted Korea from supplying troops and authorized Japan to expel the Chinese and establish the complete independence of Korea.[34] In the brief struggle which ended early in 1895, the Chinese were no match for the better trained, better equipped, and better disciplined Japanese who opposed them. On land and sea the Japanese were completely victorious. The Chinese were driven from Korea and Japanese forces were landed in southern Manchuria and on the Shantung peninsula. When it became apparent that further resistance was useless and that a prolongation of the conflict might culminate in a Japanese attack on Peking, China consented to negotiate peace. A treaty was negotiated and signed at Shimonoseki on April 17, 1895. This treaty required China to pay a huge indemnity of $133,000,000 in gold and to cede Formosa, the Pescadores Islands and the Liaotung peninsula. China also recognized Korea as a sovereign and independent state.

Prior to the declaration of war by China and Japan in August 1894, the great powers had been contemplating some form of intervention against Japan. The United States, however, refused to become a party to any multi-power action against Japan. Efforts of the Korean Government in June to enlist American assistance were rebuffed. In early June 1894 Secretary Gresham made it clear to the Korean Minister in Washington that the United States intended to view the Korean question with "impartial neutrality" and that it would deal with Japan only in a "friendly way" and under no circumstances "intervene jointly with other powers."[35] At the same time, Gresham conscientiously informed the Japanese Minister that he hoped Japan would deal "kindly and fairly with her feeble neighbor."[36]

After the outbreak of actual hostilities between China and Japan, the United States continued to maintain an effective neutrality and impartiality toward the belligerents and refused to became embroiled in any European machinations at the expense of either China or Japan. Firmly rejected was a proposal by the British Minister of October 8 that the United States, Russia, Germany, France and Great Britain intervene to terminate the war on the basis of an indemnity to be paid by China and a multi-power guarantee of Korea's independence.

In November China appealed to President Cleveland for the good offices of the United States. Cleveland replied that the United States would mediate only if both belligerents requested its good offices. Meanwhile, Secretary Gresham instructed the American Minister in Tokyo to inquire if the Japanese Government desired American mediation. Gresham's instructions stated that while "Our attitude toward both belligerents is that of an impartial and friendly neutral, desiring the welfare of both," it was not unlikely that the great powers might intervene and force a settlement that would be disadvantageous to Japan. Gresham clearly saw through the guise of the European powers; he knew that they were not concerned with the welfare of either Korea or China, but rather that they wanted Japan expelled from all influence on the continent so that the partitioning of China might be resumed.[37] Japan, however, courteously rejected the American offer of mediation, and made it clear to China that peace could be obtained only by direct negotiations between China and Japan.*

Indicative of the esteem in which both China and Japan held the United States were their requests for American diplomats to handle the interests of their nationals in the respective enemy countries for the duration of the war. After the conclusion of peace the Emperor of Japan personally wrote President Cleveland thanking him for his humanitarian attitude during the war and the efforts of American diplomatic representatives in Tokyo and Peking to bring the Chinese and Japanese together for peace discussions. The actions of the United States during the war, he noted, "served to draw still closer the bonds of friendship and good brotherhood which happily unite our two countries."[38]

The decisiveness of the Japanese victory and the provision of the Shimonoseki treaty which gave Japan a foothold on the Asiatic mainland greatly disturbed Russia, which at this time was resuming its aggressive expansion in the Far East, particularly with the object of obtaining "warm water" ports. To the Russians, Japanese entrenchment in southern Manchuria would represent an obstacle

*It is to be noted that Great Britain, while not friendly to Japan at the beginning of the conflict, later shifted to a policy of benevolent neutrality toward Japan. (Tyler Dennett, *Americans in Eastern Asia,* p. 500.)

to their aggressive designs. Consequently Russia took the lead in organizing a tripower intervention, supported by France and Germany, in which the three powers individually "advised" Japan on April 23, one week after the conclusion of the Shimonoseki treaty, to restore the Liaotung peninsula to China.* The Russian note pointed out that the Japanese retention of the Liaotung peninsula would be a constant manace to Peking, render illusory the independence of Korea, and therefore be a "perpetual obstacle to the permanent peace of the Far East." In the note the Tsar professed to give proof of his friendship for the Japanese Government by "advising them to renounce the definitive possession of the peninsula."[39] Great Britain refused to be a party to the diplomatic intervention.

Without an ally, and aware that refusal to accept the "advice" might lead to grave complications with all three intervening powers, Japan had no alternative but to return the peninsula to China. Although Japan was partly compensated by a small increase in the indemnity which China was to pay, this was small consolation to the Japanese, who, flushed with the exultation of victory, held Russia strictly accountable for depriving them of the full fruits of victory.

Despite the restoration of the Liaotung peninsula, Japan emerged from the war with important gains and rose to the stature of a great power. The acquisition of Formosa added an agriculturally rich region to the Empire and gave it a strategic position flanking the southeastern coast of China. The huge indemnity, paid in gold, made it possible for Japan to go on the gold standard and to pump-prime a remarkable industrial expansion without parallel in the Orient. Japan's enhanced position and strength now paved the way for her acceptance as a full equal by the other great powers. Moreover, she still had a foothold on the Asiatic mainland, for the victory had left her in a position of paramount influence on the Korean peninsula.

The Treaty of Shimonoseki had recognized Korea as a sovereign and independent state. The Japanese interpreted this to mean that

---

* France, of course, supported Russia because she had been allied with her since 1894. Germany, on the other hand, apparently participated in the intervention in the hope of getting Russia embroiled in Far Eastern complications, thereby hoping to lessen the Russian threat to her eastern flank.

while China was to abstain from all political activity in Korea, Japan was to have a free hand. With China eliminated, however, Russia stepped into the vacuum and seized the opportunity to extend her influence on the peninsula. In characteristic fashion, Russia posed as the friend of the Korean people in their struggle against Japan and at the same time laid the groundwork for concrete concessions. In February 1896 the Korean King fled to the Russian legation for security, and from then on Russians displaced Japanese as leading advisers to the Korean Government. Of some significance was a concession granted the Russians for the cutting of timber along the Yalu and Tumen rivers. Russian influence contributed very little to Korea's welfare, however, and actually the chronic corruption in the government increased.

The Russian determination not to allow Japan a free hand in Korea induced the Japanese to attempt the conclusion of a *modus vivendi* with their powerful and feared rival. In a series of diplomatic agreements concluded between 1896 and 1898,* Japan recognized the political *status quo* in Korea in return for a free hand in the commercial and industrial development of the country.[40] With these agreements Japan was actually marking time, for she believed that it would ultimately be necessary either to withdraw from the peninsula or fight the Russians.

During this period both Russia and Japan attempted to enlist the support of the United States. Although the American Government at this time had only a lukewarm interest in the Far East, and almost no interest at all in Korea, most Americans sympathized with Japan. Russia was generally regarded as the most aggressive and dangerous element threatening the peace of the nations in the Far East, the territorial integrity of China, and the principle of equal commercial opportunity. Of great value to Japan was the change in British policy which now aimed at a more positive support of Japanese aspirations as a check on Russian expansionism.

Notwithstanding the American Government's policy of neutrality and impartiality concerning the Korean problem, many Americans in Seoul, especially Minister Sill, engaged in considerable

*Namely, the Lobanov-Yamagata agreement of June 9, 1896; the Waeber-Komura agreement of May 14, 1897; and the Rosen-Nishii agreement of April 25, 1898.

political meddling. The meddling activities of Sill finally drew a sharp rebuke from Secretary Olney late in 1895, when he informed him that "intervention in the political concerns of Korea is not among your functions."[41] Sill was replaced in July 1897 by Dr. H. N. Allyn, who was instructed "to say or do nothing that can in any way be construed as taking sides with or against any of the interested powers." He was further instructed that unneutral conduct was not only improper for a minister but "might have the unfortunate effect of leading the Koreans themselves to regard the United States as their natural and only ally for any and all such purposes of domestic policy as Korea's rulers may adopt."[42]

By the end of the century it was apparent that despite the diplomatic agreements concluded by Russia and Japan concerning Korea, each of these powers was marking time and hoping ultimately to eliminate the other entirely in the struggle for domination of Korea. Russian influence remained strong, for many Korean nationalists had come to regard Russia as the only possible source of support against the growing ambitions of Japan. Japanese influence, on the other hand, was on the rise again, largely because of the support being received from Great Britain, which was rapidly moving toward an alliance with Japan.

The clash of interests in Korea between Japan and Russia in a few years culminated in the decisive Russo-Japanese War of 1904-05, from which Japan to the astonishment of the world emerged victorious. By the terms of the Treaty of Portsmouth, signed on September 5, 1905, Russia transferred to Japan the southern half of the island of Sakhalin, her leasehold on the Liaotung peninsula, and her railroad and mining concessions in southern Manchuria. In addition the treaty conferred on Japan a "free hand" in Korea, which in 1910 was made an integral part of the Japanese Empire by imperial decree. Firmly entrenched on the Asian mainland, in possession of a vast arc of territory which extended from the Aleutians to the southeast coast of China and commanded the approaches to that country, in possession of an increasingly powerful navy, and in the process of a remarkable industrial and commercial expansion—Japan now firmly took her place among the great powers of the world.

CHAPTER TEN

America Becomes a Far Eastern and World Power

In the meantime the United States had also become a Far Eastern and world power. This was directly occasioned by the victory over the decadent Spanish Empire in 1898 which resulted in the distant Philippine Islands, located less than 500 miles from the Chinese mainland, coming under American control. Undoubtedly the United States would have achieved the status of a world power even if this war had never been fought, for its industrial power had come to equal that of any nation in the world and its navy, then the true measure of world power, was rapidly increasing to dimensions that challenged those of England.

The origins of the Spanish-American War seemed to have no connection whatsoever with the possible extension of American power and influence to the Far East, for they lay in the troubled conditions prevailing on the nearby island of Cuba. Because of its strategic position athwart the Caribbean Sea this island was of vital interest to the United States for security reasons. The chronic disturbances persisting on this island appeared to have nothing whatsoever to do with the distant Pacific, yet they were ultimately to result in the United States acquiring a foothold in a distant area of the Pacific, close to Japan and the Chinese mainland. This foothold was to bring about an almost revolutionary reorientation of American foreign policy in general and Far Eastern policy in particular.

From 1868 to 1878 the Cubans had carried out a protracted

rebellion against the oppression and misrule of the hard-headed Spanish officials who governed the island. The Cuban insurrection of this period collapsed largely because of the exhaustion of the insurrectionists, who were unable to recoup their strength and rise again against the Spanish administration until 1895.

On February 24, 1895, the oppressed Cubans once more broke out in open rebellion against the intolerable rule of Spain. In the decade prior to this recrudescence of the rebellion in Cuba, public interest in foreign affairs had all but vanished in the United States, largely as a result of the feverish economic expansion of the country which had absorbed the interest and energy of every segment of the population. Threatened in no way by any foreign nation, the American people seemed to feel that the world beyond the continental limits of the country was far-removed and relatively unimportant. Writing in 1889 the then youthful Henry Cabot Lodge noted: "Our relations with foreign nations today fill but a slight place in American politics, and excite generally only a languid interest. We have separated ourselves so completely from the affairs of other people that it is difficult to realize how large a place they occupied when the government was founded." The renewal of civil strife in Cuba, however, was to rekindle the interest of Americans in foreign affairs and plunge the United States into new and dangerous adventures far-removed from the continental limits of the country.

The renewal of the civil war in Cuba was not wholly the result of Spanish misgovernment and oppression. An equally important factor was the economic hardship on the island that resulted from the passage of the Wilson-Gorman high tariff of 1894 which terminated the tariff concessions that had been granted Spain on Cuban sugar. Sugar had been the foundation of Cuban prosperity, and the tariff sharply reduced its earnings in the United States.

The policy of Grover Cleveland, then president, was to honor the country's obligations under international law as a power friendly to Spain, to protect the treaty rights of Americans in Cuba, and to exert pressure on Spain to accept the mediation of the United States. It was difficult, however, to enforce this official neutrality. The property of Americans in Cuba was valued at about $50,000,000 and much of it was destroyed or heavily damaged in the course of the insurrection. The Cubans deliberately carried on a scorched earth policy with the object of making the island unprofitable for Spain and also of possibly embroiling the United States in the conflict because of the damage to property of its citizens. Reports also reached the United States of the ruthlessness and cruelty of the Spaniards, particularly with regard to the filthy concentration camps in which thousands of women and children died as a result of crowded and unsanitary conditions. The Cubans waged war fully as savagely as the Spaniards, but newspaper accounts of their cruelties did not circulate in America as freely as did those of the Spaniards. This was partly because of the propaganda activities carried on by Cuban exiles and revolutionists in America, and partly because of the deliberate anti-Spanish propaganda conducted by the "yellow journals" of the time, particularly those owned by William Randolph Hearst and Joseph Pulitzer, who found inflammatory and sensational atrocity stories an excellent medium for building up the circulations of their newspapers. The sympathies of most Americans were consequently with the Cuban insurrectionists whom they considered to be underdogs fighting a sacred war of liberation against Spanish despotism and oppression.

In the national elections of 1896 the Republican Party under the inspiration of Henry Cabot Lodge campaigned on a platform designed to appeal to the rising imperialistic sentiments of the American people. The platform explicitly advocated the independence of Cuba, the acquisition of Hawaii, and the construction of an American-owned canal in Nicaragua. In the election returns the Republicans captured the presidency and increased their majorities in both houses of Congress. Just prior to retiring from the presidency, Cleveland in his last annual message of December 7, 1896, deplored the continuation of the "useless sacrifice of human life" in Cuba and indicated that American intervention might become necessary as the result of a situation "in which our obligations to the sovereignty of Spain will be superseded by higher obligations, which we can hardly hesitate to recognize and discharge."

McKinley entered office in March 1897, but not until September did he intervene in the Cuban struggle and then only to the extent of offering the mediation of the United States to Spain, which was rejected. In October a liberal government came into power in Spain and attempted to pacify the rebellious Cubans with concessions. For a short time it seemed as though the disturbances in Cuba might be terminated, but by the end of 1897 it became apparent that the open struggle would be resumed. It was patent that neither the Spaniards in Cuba with vested interests nor the Cubans themselves were content with what the liberal Spanish Government had done or was prepared to do.

On January 24, 1898, on the request of the American Consul-General, Fitzhugh Lee, the battleship *Maine* was ordered to Havana on a "friendly visit." The jingoist papers blatantly applauded the action, and many of them expressed the hope that it presaged military action by the United States. Senator Lodge was elated, and in a letter to Henry White he indicated that "There may be an explosion any day in Cuba which would settle a great many things." He noted that "We have a battleship in the harbor of Havana, and our fleet, which overmatches anything the Spaniards have, is masked at Dry Tortugas."[1] On February 15 the warship mysteriously blew up in the harbor of Havana with the loss of 266 officers and seamen. Spain immediately offered her condolences for the loss of life. She also suggested a joint investigation to determine the cause of the explosion, but this was rejected.

Meanwhile, the yellow journals screamed with inflammatory headlines that aroused widespread demands for war with Spain. On March 9 Congress appropriated $50,000,000 for the armed forces, but the conscientious and deeply religious McKinley hesitated to take the fatal step that would mean war. Shortly afterward, an American Court of Inquiry composed of U.S. naval officers reported that the *Maine* explosion had been caused by a submarine mine. The jingo American press insisted that the mine had been planted by Spanish agents and the cry was raised, "Remember the *Maine,* to hell with Spain." The *New York Journal,* in an outburst of circulation-building patriotism, offered a reward of $50,000 for the identification of the perpetrators of the cowardly deed. It also launched a fund drive for a national monument to be erected in memory of those who had lost their lives on the *Maine* and sought to enlist the support of a committee of prominent persons. Among those it sought for the committee was ex-President Cleveland, but he would have no part of the project. In a candid letter to William Randolph Hearst he made it clear that he would not permit his sorrow "for those who died on the *Maine* to be perverted to an advertising scheme for the *New York Jour-*

nal." The *Evening Post,* a New York paper whose editors had not imbibed at the bar of imperialism, perhaps called the Hearst war memorial project by its right name, a scheme "to produce more credence for its lies and perversions."[2]

Unable to resist the clamorous and swelling demand for positive action, President McKinley reluctantly moved toward war. Efforts to persuade the Spanish Government to liquidate the strife in Cuba on a basis that would satisfy the expressed aspirations of the Cuban people failed. Added to the pressure of the press and public opinion was the pressure being exerted by prominent imperialists of great influence such as Captain Mahan, Theodore Roosevelt, Senator Henry Cabot Lodge, and Senator Albert J. Beveridge. These men regarded a war with Spain as an opportunity to embark on the so-called "large policy" of Senator Lodge, a policy which envisioned a foothold in the far Pacific and possibly the annexation of the Philippines.

In Spain, however, Minister Stewart L. Woodford was valiantly striving to save the peace, and apparently doing quite well. On April 9 he was summoned by the Spanish Foreign Minister and informed that the Queen "at the request of the Pope and in deference to the wishes and advice of the representatives of the six great European powers" had decided to grant an armistice in Cuba. Elated, Woodford believed that war could now be avoided with honor to all, and early the following morning, a Sunday, he dispatched an urgent telegram to President McKinley. "I hope that nothing will be done to humiliate Spain, as I am satisfied that the present Government is going, and is loyally ready to go, as fast and as far as it can," it stated. "With your power of action sufficiently free, you will win the fight on your own lines."[3] But it was too late. Unknown to Woodford, the President's power of action was no longer really free. He had yielded to the mounting pressures about him and had satisfied his conscience that war with Spain was morally right. As Julius Pratt puts it, "McKinley was clay in the hands of the little group of men who knew all too well what use to make of the war."[4]

On April 11, despite Spain's belated offer to comply with any American demands which would not dishonor her, President McKinley asked Congress for authority to employ, if necessary, the armed forces to restore peace and order to the island of Cuba. In a

194

message to Congress he stressed the necessity of protecting American lives and property in Cuba and putting an end to a conflict which, because of its proximity, menaced the peace and security of the United States. He mentioned the losses and cruelties of the civil war in Cuba, the inhuman concentration decrees, the damage suffered by American commercial interests, and the inability of Spanish arms to restore order. He reviewed his own efforts to ameliorate the state of affairs and his efforts for peace through diplomatic negotiations. "In the name of humanity," he perorated, "in the name of civilization, in behalf of endangered American interests which give us the right and the duty to speak and to act, the war in Cuba must stop."[5]

Authorization to employ the armed forces was granted by the House and Senate on April 13. Six days later, on April 19, the Senate passed a war resolution by a vote of 42-35. The House concurred that same day, 310-6. The resolution was promptly signed the next morning by the President. The war that was wanted was now at hand. Throughout the land the war drums began to beat as the press aroused the nation with the call to honor and greatness in the name of destiny, humanity, and even God's will.

On April 20 McKinley issued a formal ultimatum to Spain which gave her until April 23 to withdraw from Cuba. As a self-respecting nation, Spain had no alternative but to reject the ultimatum. On the following day, April 22, she severed diplomatic relations with the United States. Promptly that same day, McKinley ordered Admiral Sampson, who was in readiness at Key West, to steam for Cuba and initiate a blockade of the island. Orders were also cabled to Admiral Dewey, who was likewise in readiness at Hongkong, to proceed to the Philippines and "commence operations at once, particularly against the Spanish fleet."[6] That same day Congress authorized the President to issue a call for volunteers. The war had actually begun. On April 25 Congress declared that a state of war had existed with Spain since April 21. Lodge spoke for his fellow imperialists when he wrote, in 1899: "The pretenses were over, the wrongs which had lived on for three-quarters of a century were now to be redressed, the restless question was to get its true and right answer."[7]

The intoxication of the imperialists was epitomized by Senator

Albert J. Beveridge in a speech made at Boston on April 27, two days after Congress had passed its war resolution. In this speech he disclosed a blueprint for world domination that relegates even the wild dreams of a Hitler to modesty. After proclaiming that American land and industry were producing more than the people could consume, he declaimed:

> Fate has written our policy for us; the trade of the world must and shall be ours. And we will get it as our mother [England] has told us how. We will establish trading-posts throughout the world as distributing points for American products. We will build a navy to the measure of our greatness. Great colonies governing themselves, flying our flag and trading with us, will grow about our posts of trade. Our institutions will follow our flag on the wings of commerce. And American law, American order, American civilization, and the American flag will plant themselves on shores hitherto bloody and benighted, but by those agencies of God henceforth to be made beautiful and bright.

In the process of fulfilling this destiny, he declared, "The Philippines are logically our first target."[8]

It is now generally recognized that the President and Congress were more or less maneuvered into the war with Spain by an influential part of the press, big-navy advocates, and outright imperialists. It is highly significant that the series of crises with Spain which preceded the outbreak of the war came at a time when a new form of journalism, called the "new journalism" by the *New York Journal,* was becoming popular. The distinguishing characteristic of this new journalism was its exploitation of unusual and sensational incidents with the object of building up circulations. In so doing there was little attempt to be unbiased or factual in the reporting. This type of journalism has since earned the appellation "yellow journalism." The principal protagonists in the battle for circulations were William Randolph Hearst of the *Journal* and Joseph Pulitzer of the *New York World.* Both Hearst and Pulitzer found the Cuban situation a fruitful source of headline stories for increasing circulations. Both favored the cause of the Cuban insurrectionists. Pultizer's bias toward the Cubans was based on his belief that the great issue of liberty was at stake, but like Hearst he "rather liked the idea of war, not a big one, but one that would arouse interest and give him a chance to gauge the reflex in his circulation figures." The Hearst and Pulitzer papers were perhaps the most influential in generating popular enthusiasm for war, but there were many others of significance in this respect, among which were Dana's *Sun,* Bennett's *Herald,* and Medill's *Tribune.*[9]

Even organized religion, through its organ publications, played a notable part in arousing war enthusiasm. A large part of American Protestantism in the decade of the 1890's had become deeply imbued with the belief that the Anglo-Saxon race had a conquering destiny because it possessed, as Dr. Strong had written, a pure "spiritual Christianity" (Protestantism). The missionary-minded among the Protestants had in fact become as eager for new foreign fields of activity as had the commercial elements. The Philippines naturally enticed them as an area for extensive Protestant missionary work. One could fill a volume with quotations from various Protestant organ publications which supported war and the fulfillment of the alleged Anglo-Saxon mission to dominate the world.* Here only a few quotations should suffice to indicate their general nature. The *Religious Telescope* of February 16, 1898, for example, advocated strong measures even if they led to war, for "there are some things worse than war." The *Christian and Missionary Alliance* (March 2, 1898) insisted that the Spanish Government had plotted the blowing up of the *Maine* and that war was the proper remedy. The *Evangelist* (March 31, 1898) cried out: "And if it be the will of Almighty God, that by war the last trace of this inhumanity of man to man shall be swept away from this Western hemisphere, let it come!" The *Northern Christian Advocate* (April 13, 1898) declared: "Should we go to war our cause will be just, and Methodism will be ready to do its full duty. Every Methodist preacher will be a recruiting officer." And the *Church Standard* (May 14, 1898) contended that the only way to back up the President's humane and righteous determination was by force of arms "and that means war."[10]

Not all Protestant sects, by any means, caught the war spirit or preached the doctrine of the new imperialism. The most notable

---

* Julius W. Pratt in his *Expansionists of 1898* (Baltimore: Johns Hopkins Press, 1936) has devoted a full chapter to this subject, which he picturesquely entitles "The Imperialism of Righteousness."

exceptions, of course, were the Friends and the Unitarians. Early in April 1898, when the issue of peace or war was still in the balance, the Society of Friends went to the extent of submitting a memorial to Congress and the President which declared, "We hold there can be no difference between nations that cannot be more advantageously settled by peaceful negotiations."[11]

The Catholic Press was overwhelmingly against the use of force in seeking a solution to the crisis with Spain. Typical of the comments in Catholic organs were those of the *Ave Maria* (May 7, 1898) which caustically declared: "The pulpits of the country resound with war-cries and calumnies against our foes. Many of the pious men who occupy them preferred war to peace, and war at any cost rather than peace as a result of the Holy Father's arbitration." The Catholic press, of course, was not unmindful that Spain was a Catholic nation and that most of the Filipinos had been converted to the Catholic faith. After the United States had become involved in the war, however, the Catholic press supported it and its objectives as enthusiastically as the Protestant press. On May 28, 1898, for example, the *Catholic Herald* jubilantly declared: "In a few weeks the chains forged by Spain will be loosed by American bravery, and the world will wonder why the United States tolerated them so long."[12]

Much has been written about the role of American business interests in bringing on the war with Spain. A few decades ago it was fashionable to believe that these interests were major culprits in forcing the country into the war. Actually American business in general was initially opposed, and somewhat strongly, to involvement in hostilities with Spain. A notable exception, of course, were the sugar interests with actual stakes in Cuba. After hostilities had commenced, however, the sentiment of business began to shift, doubtless as a result of conversion to the "large policy" and the belief that territorial expansion would be beneficial, especially as a means toward acquiring a larger share of the China trade.[13]

Most of the European nations except Great Britain sympathized with Spain and regarded the United States as a callous aggressor. While the official attitude of the German government was one of correct neutrality, public opinion in that country was highly sympathetic to Spain and hostile to the United States. Despite the "correct" neutrality of the German Government, it was acutely suspicious of American motives and moreover feared that the war would spread to the Pacific area and that American military action in that area might create conditions which would obstruct its own imperialistic ambitions. There is no evidence that Germany was planning to obtain the Philippines, although later in 1898, when the war was over, she did purchase for $5,000,000 several islands from Spain, including the Carolines, the Pelews (Palaus) and the Ladrones (Marianas), excluding Guam.

Great Britain was the only friendly European power, not because of any particular enthusiasm for American aspirations but primarily because of her isolated position in a world of powerful rivals which made it expedient for her to cultivate the friendship of some important power, especially a naval power. The United States was a logical ally. Germany was a rapidly rising naval and industrial power which was threatening Great Britain in almost every quarter of the globe. Her feverish quest for colonies was an ever-present potential source of conflict between the two countries. France was also a menace, threatening to enter the Nile Valley and challenge Britain's control of that region, and Russian imperialism was threatening the frontiers of India. Some influential British leaders, particularly Joseph Chamberlain, the Colonial Secretary, considered the moment opportune to bring about an Anglo-American entente, but they received no encouragement from either the President or the State Department, for neither was prepared to flout the public and depart from the traditional policy laid down by Washington which shunned alliances with any foreign power. At the outset of the Cuban insurrection, however, Great Britain's friendliness had been doubtful. She was then still involved in a dispute with the United States over the Venezuelan-British Guiana boundary and discussions concerning American control over an isthmian canal were in progress. Moreover, Queen Victoria personally sympathized with her dynastic relatives in Spain.[14]

The war with Spain lasted less than five months. Decrepit Spain was no match for the might of the vigorous American republic which had now become one of the great industrial nations of the world and one of the leading sea powers. In the Caribbean area, however, the American army failed to cover itself with glory, largely because of inefficiency and unpreparedness, but it accomplished its objectives, chiefly because of the weakness of the Spanish forces. An army of 10,000 under General Shafter landed on the island of Cuba and advanced toward Santiago. By July 3 the fall of that city was assured, and the Spanish fleet under the command of Admiral Cervera was ordered to make a dash for freedom in broad daylight. In a running sea fight that lasted four hours every ship of Cervera's fleet was destroyed by a powerful American squadron under the command of Admiral Sampson. On July 17 Santiago fell and resistance in Cuba came to an end. Four days later General Miles landed on the island of Puerto Rico and easily overcame all opposition. The war in the Caribbean was over.

As Assistant Secretary of the Navy, Theodore Roosevelt in the fall of 1897 had been urging the President and Secretary of the Navy Long to attack the Philippines the moment war broke out with Spain. He was instrumental in getting Admiral Dewey placed in charge of the Asiatic squadron located in Far Eastern waters. On February 25, 1898, when war with Spain seemed likely, Roosevelt on his own initiative cabled Dewey that in the event of war with Spain it would be his duty to prevent the Spanish squadron from leaving the Asiatic coast and then to begin offensive operations in the Philippine Islands.

With the outbreak of the war on April 25, Dewey consequently was prepared for swift action against Spain in the Far East. His squadron immediately steamed to Philippine waters, and on May 1 he annihilated the dilapidated Spanish fleet in the harbor of Manila and then began a blockade of the harbor while Filipino insurrectionists under Aguinaldo and American troops under General Merritt attacked the city. Meanwhile, British and German fleets hovered in the harbor, ostensibly in the role of "observers." On August 13, when Dewey's fleet maneuvered to shell the Spanish forts while the troops under Aguinaldo and Merritt launched land attacks, the German fleet under Admiral von Diederichs allegedly steamed between Dewey's fleet and the line of fire, to be dislodged however by a maneuver of the British fleet under Captain Chichester. There is no evidence to indicate the truth of this allegation, but at the time it was widely exploited for propaganda purposes by both Britons and American Anglophiles to stir up anti-German feeling in the United States.

Meanwhile, as indicated in a previous chapter, the Hawaiian

Islands had been formally annexed by the United States on August 12. In addition, Wake Island had been occupied in July by American troops en route to Manila. It was formally annexed on January 17 of the following year.

Realizing the futility of continuing the hopeless struggle, the Spanish Government put forth peace feelers through the good offices of the French Ambassador in Washington, Jules Cambon. In a note dated July 22, 1898, signed by the Spanish Minister of State and addressed to the President, which was transmitted through Cambon, Spain proposed that the two nations should seek the termination of the war and offered to negotiate on the political status of Cuba. Puerto Rico and the Philippines were not mentioned. This apparently indicated that Spain clung to the hope they might still be retained.

This note was answered by Secretary Day on July 30. Day's note declared: "The President witnessed with profound disappointment the frustration of his peaceful efforts by events which forced upon the people of the United States the unalterable conviction that nothing short of the relinquishment by Spain of a claim of sovereignty over Cuba which she was unable to enforce would relieve a situation that had become unendurable." The note recognized the uneven nature of the war and stated that the President was inclined "to offer a brave adversary generous terms of peace." The terms proposed, however, were far from generous. First, Spain was to relinquish sovereignty over Cuba and evacuate it immediately. Secondly, the President, "desirous of exhibiting signal generosity," would not demand an indemnity, but he could not be insensible to the losses suffered by American citizens in Cuba and hence he would have to demand the cession of Puerto Rico and other islands under Spanish sovereignty in the West Indies, together with an island in the Ladrone (Mariana) group, which would be selected by the United States. Thirdly, as compensation for losses suffered by Americans, the United States insisted on holding the city, bay and harbor of Manila "pending the conclusion of a treaty of peace which shall determine the control, disposition and government of the Philippines."[15]

Spain, of course, had no alternative but to accept the terms offered by Day, and on August 12 she subscribed to a protocol which embodied the above terms. The protocol moreover provided that Spain would immediately evacuate Puerto Rico and other islands in the Caribbean as well as Cuba, and that Spain and the United States would send commissioners to Paris, not later than October 1, to negotiate a treaty of peace. The final article of the protocol stipulated that hostilities between the two nations would be suspended and the military commanders of the two countries would be so notified.[16] On the following day, ignorant of the conclusion of the armistice, troops under the command of General Merritt attacked and occupied the city of Manila.

The peace conference convened in Paris on October 1. Of the five members of the American delegation, three were ardent expansionists: Whitelaw Reid of the *Tribune,* Senator Cushman K. Davis of Minnesota, and Senator William P. Frye of Maine. Day, who had resigned as Secretary of State to become a member of the American delegation, stood in a middle position between imperialism and anti-imperialism. The fifth member, Senator George Gray, was the only Democrat and violently anti-imperialist. Regardless of their personal orientations, however, the crucial decisions were not theirs but McKinley's to make.

The thorniest problem to be settled at the peace conference was the disposition of the Philippine Islands, which were then practically unknown to most Americans. Even President McKinley confessed that at the time he did not know their location within two thousand miles. A considerable segment of the American public was opposed to the acquisition of overseas territories with large alien populations and considered that such a step would be a negation of the hallowed republican traditions of the nation. On the other hand, the increasing number of imperialists and big-navy men, rallying around persuasive enthusiasts like Lodge and Mahan, considered the acquisition of the entire Philippine archipelago an inevitable necessity if the United States was to fulfill its destiny as a great world power. American big-business interests, which hitherto had not been enthusiastic about the war, now suddenly became interested in the fancied commercial potentialities of the Philippines and their value as a base for the development of what was believed to be a potentially lucrative and limitless trade with China. Added to these influences was the pressure of the missionaries who believed that an American foothold in the Far East would facilitate religious propagation among the peoples of the Orient, particularly in China and Japan.

Prior to the convocation of the peace conference, President McKinley could not make up his mind as to what disposition should be made of the Philippine archipelago. Dewey's dramatic victory at Manila and the occupation of part of the island of Luzon, however, had suddenly fired public interest in the Far East and a widespread demand arose for a foothold there. Between the time of Dewey's victory at Manila on May 1 and September 16, the President swung around to the position that we should retain at least part of the Philippine archipelago. He may have been influenced in this decision to some extent by expressions on the part of Great Britain and Japan that they would look with favor upon the United States taking over the Philippines. A Japanese note of September 8, for example, stated that Spain was incapable of maintaining order on the islands, that the establishment of a native government would be an invitation to seizure by some foreign power, and that accordingly Japan would desire to see the islands taken over by the United States or administered conjointly by the United States, Japan and some third power.[17]

In his instructions of September 16 to the American peace commissioners, McKinley declared that "the march of events rules and overrules human action" and that "without any original thought of complete or even partial acquisition, the presence and success of our arms at Manila imposes upon us obligations which we can not disregard." "We can not be unmindful," he said, "that without any desire or design on our part, the war has brought us new duties and responsibilities which we must meet and discharge as becomes a great nation on whose growth and career from the beginning the Ruler of Nations has plainly written the high command and the pledge of civilization." After indicating the new commercial opportunities that would arise through obtaining a foothold in the Far East, he stipulated that "the United States cannot accept less than the cession in full right and sovereignty of the island of Luzon."[18] By October 26 the President had cast all restraint and hesitation aside, and on that date his Secretary of State, John Hay, wired the commissioners that "The cession must be of the whole archipelago or none." Information received by the President, stated Hay, had convinced him that the cession of Luzon alone was not enough and that "leaving the rest of the islands subject to Spanish rule, or to be the subject of future contention can not be justified on political, commercial or humanitarian grounds."[19]

A year or two later McKinley told a group of visiting clergymen how and why he had finally arrived at the fateful decision of demanding the entire archipelago. He confided that after many anxious nights pacing the floor of the White House and going down on his knees to "Almighty God" for guidance, the right decision came to him as if inspired. We could not return the islands to Spain, as that would be cowardly and dishonorable; we could not permit commercial rivals such as Germany or France to acquire them, as that would be bad business; and we could not set the Filipinos free, as they were not ready for self-government. "There was nothing left for us to do," he explained, "but to take them all, and to educate the Filipinos, and uplift and civilize and Christianize them, and by God's grace do the very best we could by them, as our fellowmen for whom Christ also died."[20] In this remarkable confession, as is obvious, there are some noteworthy misrepresentations. There is absolutely no evidence that France had any desire for these islands, and it is equally apparent that Germany, although feverishly desirous of acquiring overseas possessions, was not willing to alienate the United States by meddling in the islands in any way. McKinley also overlooked, or was ignorant of, the fact that under Spanish rule most of the islanders had already been "civilized" and converted to Roman Catholic Christianity.

At the peace conference the Spanish commissioners stubbornly resisted the American demand for the cession of the entire archipelago, but they finally yielded, somewhat under duress, when the American commissioners offered $20,000,000 as compensation. The finalized treaty was signed on December 10, 1898. In addition to the Philippine settlement, it also provided for Spain's relinquishment of Cuba and her cession of Puerto Rico and Guam to the United States. Commenting on the treaty, Thomas B. Reed, the Speaker of the House, caustically declared that we had bought ten million Filipinos, "yellow-bellies," as he called them, at a price of two dollars per head.[21]

During the negotiations the American commissioners had incidentally made an effort to do something for American Protestant groups with missionary interests in the Caroline Islands, which were then under Spanish sovereignty. The effort consisted largely of an offer to purchase the island of Kussaie and of a request for the establishment of religious toleration in all the Carolines. Germany opposed any concessions on these islands to the United States and obtained a pledge from Spain that she would not sell Kussaie to the United States. Actually Germany, in September, had obtained a secret commitment from Spain to sell her Kussaie, Ponape and Yap with the understanding that no concrete action would be taken until after the fate of the Philippines had been determined. It was doubtless as a result of German pressure that Spain took the position the Caroline Islands were beyond the purview of the peace discussions because the war had not been carried to these islands. The American commissioners did not contest this position.[22]

The treaty was presented to the Senate for approval on January 4, 1899. It was the subject of bitter controversy because of strong opposition to the annexation of the heavily-populated Philippines. It was debated in executive sessions behind closed doors, although there was discussion of some resolutions that were presented concerning the acquisition of overseas territory. Senator Lodge justified the closed sessions of the Senate. "The discussion of the treaty is being conducted," he said on January 24, 1899, "and to my mind properly conducted, behind closed doors, for there is much that must be said affecting other nations and other people which could not with propriety be said in public."[23]

The anti-imperialists rallied around the slogan, "the flag of the Republic forever, the flag of an empire never." Senator George F. Hoar of Massachusetts was the leader of the opposition. He indignantly declared it not to be his belief that "America is to begin the twentieth century where Spain began the sixteenth."[24] He argued with righteous eloquence that the annexation of a foreign country and governing it without the consent of its people was a violation of the Declaration of Independence and the Constitution. He bitterly declaimed that the fathers of the Republic had never dreamed that their descendants "would be beguiled from these sacred and awful verities that they might strut about in the cast-off clothing of pinchbeck emperors and pewter kings; that their descendants would be excited by the smell of gunpowder and the sound of the guns of a single victory as a small boy by a firecracker on some Fourth of July morning."[25] The real motive of the annexationists, charged Senator Caffery of Louisiana, was "lust for power and greed for land, veneered with the tawdriness of false humanity."[26] He derided the inflated claims made about the commercial potentialities of an outpost in the distant Far East. "The statistics show that not one-tenth of the exports of the United States go to Asia, Africa, and South America combined," he argued. "Nine-tenths of our exports go to our neighbors in Western Europe."[27] Senator Mason of Illinois deplored the crass commercial motives of the annexationists. He sarcastically declared that a "distinguished friend" had suggested that "we ought to rake those islands with our guns and compel their people to wear shirts—not that they need the shirts, but to increase the demand for calico."[28] Senator Daniel of Virginia pleaded for America to resist temptation: "Let no glittering temptation of trade, let no gold from the gorgeous East tempt her eye or head."[29] Senators Hoar, Spooner and Chilton all cogently warned of the perils of political entanglements that would surely result from the retention of the Philippines.

The supporters of the treaty were no less rhetorical. "The opposition tells us we ought not to rule a people without their consent," chided Senator Beveridge in a speech to an audience of several thousands. "I answer, the rule of liberty, that all just governments derive their authority from the consent of the governed, applies only to those who are capable of self-government." Thunderous applause greeted these words. "The Philippines not contiguous?" he challenged, in answer to those who feared the problems that would arise from possessing populous islands so distant. "Our navy will make them contiguous!" His oratorical description of the possibilities of marketing industrial and financial surpluses at great profits in the Philippines was impressive.[30] The fact was, however, that extensive trade in the Philippines was a vision of the future, and subsequent developments were to show that the vision had actually been a mirage.[31] Senator Lodge eloquently strove to allay the fears of the anti-imperialists in the Senate. "To the American people and their Government I am ready to intrust my life, my liberty, my honor; and, what is far dearer to me than anything personal to myself, the lives and liberty of my children and my children's children," he declared. "If I am ready thus to trust my children to the Government which the American people create and sustain, am I to shrink from intrusting to that same people the fate and fortune of the inhabitants of the Philippine Islands?"[32]

The approval of the treaty was assured when William Jennings Bryan, the leader and presidential aspirant of the Democratic Party, advocated its immediate ratification. Looking forward to the presidential election of 1900, and apparently aware that the treaty could not be defeated, he doubtless wished to liquidate the issue of imperialism, temporarily at least, to concentrate on the issue of "free silver." Bryan nevertheless remained an anti-imperialist at heart, and his maneuver was essentially tactical. Recalcitrant senators made a desperate attempt to push through a resolution pledging immediate independence to the Filipinos, but it was defeated, although only as a result of the Vice-President casting the deciding vote. On February 6, 1899, the treaty was finally approved, but only by the barest two-thirds majority of 57-27.

With the acquisition of the Philippines, the United States completed its process of the spoliation of Spain which had begun with the obtaining of the Florida territory in 1819. To the imperialists of the last decade of the nineteenth century this was but a just and natural process, and there was no reason for regrets or pity for Spain, the once proud mistress of the world's greatest empire. Writing in 1899 on the war with Spain, Senator Lodge doubtless epitomized this thinking when he declared: "Spain has ceased to rule; her once vast empire has gone, because she proved herself unfit to govern, and for the unfit among nations there is no pity in the relentless world-forces which shape the destinies of mankind."[33]

Meanwhile, peace had not come to the islands. An inspired Philippine nationalist movement had long been seeking to destroy Spanish sovereignty on the islands. Among the leaders of the movement was Emilio Aguinaldo, who was in Singapore when Admiral Dewey steamed into Manila Bay. With the assistance of Dewey, Aguinaldo had returned to the Philippines on May 19, 1898. Five days later he organized a revolutionary movement, with himself as the titular head, and on June 23 promulgated a provisional constitution which embodied the aim of independence. In August Aguinaldo's Government petitioned the powers for recognition, but without success. These actions were taken, of course, without the encouragement or approval of any American officials.

Aguinaldo had naïvely believed that the American victory over Spain meant immediate independence for the Filipinos. When he discovered that the United States intended to remain in occupation of the islands and carry out a prolonged program of tutelage, he organized a savage guerrilla campaign against his former American allies.* In the fighting that took place with Aguinaldo's guerrillas the United States was compelled to employ larger forces and to expend larger sums of money than had been required to defeat the Spanish land forces. At a cost of $170 million an American force of some 70,000 men took two years to crush the Filipino struggle for independence. In the course of this bitter struggle American arms were sullied by resort to brutalities which shocked the conscience of many Americans back home. Aguinaldo was finally captured on March 23, 1901, and the guerrilla opposition shortly thereafter crumbled. Beaten on the field of battle, the Filipino nationalists sadly reconciled themselves to the realization that America had not fought the war with Spain to liberate them, but for other reasons.

In June, 1901, the American civil administration of the islands was separated from the military and William Howard Taft, then a judge, became the first civil governor.[34] Thus began the long period of tutelage which forty-four years later resulted in the Filipinos finally obtaining full independence. It was not until 1916, however, when the Jones Bill was passed by Congress, that the United States had made a clear formal commitment of ultimate independence to the Filipinos.

As a result of the Spanish-American War, caused by a seemingly inconsequential insurrection on the island of Cuba lying at its backdoor, so to speak, the United States acquired extensive territorial possessions thousands of miles distant in the Pacific and hence became a power with an important stake in the peace and

*The first clashes between Filipinos and Americans broke out on February 4, 1899.

status quo of the Far East. For better or worse, events on the Asian mainland were henceforth to be of great and increasing concern to the United States. Whether we liked it or not (and most Americans apparently liked it), the United States was now a world power with new and vastly enlarged responsibilities. With the victory over Spain, the United States in effect emerged from its self-containment in the Western Hemisphere and became an active participant in "world politics, naval rivalry, and imperial dominion."[35] To a small minority of fully inebriated imperialists, the United States now possessed the key to world domination. Senator Beveridge, for example, spoke of the Pacific as "our ocean" and of the power that rules the Pacific ruling the world. "With the Philippines," he said to outbursts of enthusiastic applause, "that Power is and will forever be the American Republic."[36]

To American commercial and financial interests the acquisition of the Philippines was a guarantee that they would share in the profits to be made from increasing trade with the Far East. As Senator William Sulzer of New York had put it: "The booming guns of Dewey's battleships sounded a new note on the Pacific shores, a note that has echoed and reechoed around the world, and that note is that we are on the Pacific, that we are there to stay, and that we are there to protect our rights, promote our interests, and get our share of the trade and commerce of the opulent Orient."[37]

Coming events were to disclose that the Filipinos and the islands were not an unmixed blessing. Certainly the glowing claims of forthcoming great expansion of trade and huge profits never materialized. One of the most ardent advocates of the Philippine annexation had been Theodore Roosevelt. Within eight years of their acquisition he was wishing, as President, that it would be possible to get rid of them. He became obsessed with the fear that Japan coveted them and that we could not defend them if attacked by that country.[38] "The Philippines form our heel of Achilles," he wrote to his Secretary of War. "I think that to have some pretty clear avowal of our intention not to permanently keep them and to give them independence would remove a temptation from Japan's way and render our task easier." Roosevelt had actually been greatly concerned about Japan's alleged coveting of the Philippines as early as 1904, and in 1906 he even confided to an intimate friend, Sternberg, that he would like to get rid of them.[39]

The victory of Japan over Russia in the war of 1904-05 marked a sharp turning point in the history of Japanese-American relations. Up to the outbreak of that conflict the United States had pursued a rather consistent policy of friendliness to Japan. Actually President Roosevelt was even pleased to see Japan go to war with Russia, whom he considered the most serious disturber of the peace in the Far East, and he even confided that Japan in going to war with Russia was "playing our game." When the consequences of the Japanese victory became clear to him, however, he began to see Japan in an entirely different light as the dominant power in the Far East whose ambitions and policies on the Asian mainland would conflict with American commitments.

Preoccupied with concern for the security of the Philippine Islands, Roosevelt in the summer of 1905, shortly before the Treaty of Portsmouth was concluded by Japan and Russia, promoted an executive agreement with Japan in the best tradition of *Realpolitik*. On July 29 of that year William Howard Taft, his Secretary of War, negotiated a secret agreement with the Japanese Foreign Minister, Kogorō Katsura, in which the United States recognized Japan's "sovereignty over Korea" in return for a Japanese disclaimer of any aggressive designs on the Philippines. In entering upon this agreement Roosevelt had manifestly concluded that the defense of the Philippines against an attack by Japan had become seriously compromised because of her vastly enhanced power. He therefore apparently considered it wise and expedient to "barter" Korea, which was already in the physical possession of Japan, for a Japanese guarantee not to attack the Philippines. Notwithstanding, as Japan's naval and military power continued to expand, the Philippines became increasingly more vulnerable to a Japanese attack and in effect became hostages which might easily be seized in the event of a war with the United States.

CHAPTER ELEVEN

Epilogue

The turn of the century, distinguished by the rise of the United States to the status of a major Far Eastern power, terminates the chronological scope of this volume.* In the history of American foreign relations the year 1898 is clearly a decisive year, for it marked the acquisition of the Hawaiian Islands, some 2,000 miles distant from San Francisco, and the Philippine Islands, another 3,000 miles from the Hawaiians. Contemporaneously with the acquisition of these strategically and commercially significant outposts, the United States Government began to espouse energetically the aspirations of certain interests in the country with regard to the potential trade in China, which was imagined to be limitless. In 1898, moreover, the United States simultaneously became a Pacific and Far Eastern power within the context of a world power-configuration. The implication of this was that the national power had to be dispersed and rationed for the various areas in which commitments had been undertaken. Another implication was that the United States was swept into the vortex of European power politics, for all the principal European nations had important stakes in China and other areas of the Far East.

Almost sooner than even the most astute students of foreign relations had foreseen, the United States became deeply involved in the international politics having ramifications in East Asia. Confronted with the developments in China from 1895 to 1899 which at the time seemed to herald her possible disappearance as a

*For a somewhat detailed discussion of American relations with the Far East after 1898, the author suggests his *The United States and Asia* (New York: Praeger, 1955).

sovereign and integral state, Secretary Hay in September 1899 committed the United States to the support of a policy calling for the maintenance of equal commercial opportunity in that area. The principles of this commitment, known as the Open Door policy, were actually as old as the American trade in China. The significance of Hay's commitment was that it was now a policy vigorously advocated and supported by the United States Government. Within a few years this policy was expanded to include the principle of the preservation of the territorial and administrative entity of China. Within a few more years the rigid insistence on respect for these principles clashed with the special and vital interests of Japan.

Japan's hegemony in East Asia was buttressed by an agreement with Great Britain that was concluded in January 1902. This agreement provided for the maintenance of the status quo in East Asia. The status quo in this area then served the temporary interests of Japan, faced as she was with the possibility of Russia taking over Korea. The agreement was clearly aimed against Russia. It specifically provided that if either signatory became involved in war the other would remain neutral, but in case a third power joined the enemy nation the other signatory would enter the war as an ally. It was the support of this agreement that encouraged Japan to settle her differences with Russia by resort to arms.

In 1905 the Anglo-Japanese understanding was broadened, and provided that in case either signatory became involved in a war with a third power the other signatory would come to its assistance even if the third power were without an ally. Britain's immediate objective at this time was to obtain the military support of Japan in case Russia moved on India. In return for this support, Britain gave Japan a free hand in Korea. An underlying significance of the Anglo-Japanese alliance, however, was that Britain in effect abdicated her primary position in East Asia to Japan. This was occasioned, of course, by the limitations of Britain's power, confronted with the responsibility of preserving the far-flung empire which encompassed one fourth of the entire world, parts of which were threatened by powerful and hostile European states. In a very real sense, then, it was Britain's abdication of her once dominant role in East Asia that resulted in the United States taking on dangerous commitments which in effect went far beyond what its actual interests justified or required.

The almost simultaneous rise of the United States and Japan to the status of great powers and the United States taking upon itself the role of China's protector against Japanese encroachment clearly foreshadowed the course of future events. With Japan's small and predominantly mountainous islands becoming overcrowded and her industries expanding beyond the capacity of her meager resources to support, Japan's leaders could not resist the example of Western aggrandizement through the process of imperialism. It required no sage to foresee that Japan's leaders, impelled by a flaming nationalism, would in due time seek to dominate the economies of China and other Far Eastern areas to assure her survival as an advanced industrial nation and a power of the first rank. In more ways than one, the underlying course of events that culminated in the Pacific War of 1941-45 had its origins in the developments set in motion by American actions of 1898.

Notes to the Text

(Full facts of publication are given only for those sources not listed in the "Selected Bibliography.")

I. THE LURE OF ASIA AND THE PACIFIC

1. Foster Rhea Dulles, *The Old China Trade,* p. 1.
2. Foster Rhea Dulles, *Forty Years of American-Japanese Relations,* p. 23.
3. Tyler Dennett, *Americans in Eastern Asia,* p. 4.
4. Bernard de Voto, *The Course of Empire,* p. 298.
5. Dennett, *op. cit.,* pp. 26-28.
6. Edouard A. Stackpole, *The Sea-Hunters,* p. 471.
7. *Cf.* Dennett, *op. cit.,* pp. 30-33.
8. *Ibid.,* pp. 30-38.
9. Dulles, *The Old China Trade,* p. 51.
10. Harold W. Bradley, *The American Frontier in Hawaii,* p. 15.
11. Dulles, *The Old China Trade,* p. 55.
12. *Ibid.,* p. 81.
13. *Ibid.,* p. 93.
14. Stackpole, *op. cit.,* p. 356.
15. Dulles, *The Old China Trade,* p. 84.
16. *Ibid.,* pp. 94-97.
17. Clifford W. Ashley, *The Yankee Whaler,* p. 11.
18. *Ibid.,* p. 38.
19. Alexander Starbuck, *History of American Whale Fishery,* p. 96.
20. Stackpole, *op. cit.,* p. 268.
21. *Ibid.,* p. 393.

22. Bradley, *op. cit.*, pp. 98, 215.
23. Clarence C. Hulley, *Alaska, 1741-1953*, p. 187.
24. Henry W. Clark, *History of Alaska*, p. 62.
25. Stackpole, *op. cit.*, p. 473.
26. Ashley, *op. cit.*, pp. 42-43.
27. Carl C. Cutler, *Greyhounds of the Sea*, pp. 43-44.
28. Dulles, *The Old China Trade*, pp. 119-121.
29. Cutler, *op. cit.*, p. 169.
30. Arthur H. Clark, *The Clipper Ship Era*, pp. 96-98.
31. *Ibid.*, p. 196.
32. Cutler, *op. cit.*, pp. 307-308.

II. THE ESTABLISHMENT OF TREATY RELATIONS WITH CHINA

1. Mingchien Joshua Bau, *The Foreign Relations of China*, p. 3.
2. Basil Lubbock, *The Opium Clippers*, pp. 30-31.
3. Carl C. Cutler, *Greyhounds of the Sea*, pp. 16-17.
4. Samuel Shaw, *The Journal of Major Samuel Shaw*, p. 218.
5. Foster Rhea Dulles, *China and America*, p. 30.
6. John W. Foster, *American Diplomacy in the Orient*, p. 36.
7. Tyler Dennett, *Americans in Eastern Asia*, p. 57.
8. Foster Rhea Dulles, *The Old China Trade*, pp. 113-114.
9. Dennett, *op. cit.*, p. 70.
10. *Ibid.*, pp. 73-75.
11. *Ibid.*, p. 75.
12. Hosea Ballou Morse, *The International Relations of the Chinese Empire*, Vol. I, pp. 551-552.
13. Dennett, *op. cit.*, p. 122.
14. *Ibid.*, p. 62.
15. Dulles, *The Old China Trade*, p. 126.
16. Dennett, *op. cit.*, p. 53.
17. *Ibid.*, p. 61.
18. Chinese opinions of Englishmen, cited by Earl Swisher, *China's Management of the American Barbarians*, p. 46.
19. *Cf. ibid.*, pp. 17-22.
20. Claude M. Fuess, *The Life of Caleb Cushing*, Vol. I, p. 441.
21. Dennett, *op. cit.*, p. 93.
22. Foster, *op. cit.*, p. 68.
23. Bau, *op. cit.*, p. 7.
24. Foster, *op. cit.*, p. 69.
25. Bau, *op. cit.*, p. 8.

26. *Ibid.*, p. 9.
27. For details of the Treaty of Nanking and the Treaty of the Bogue, *see* Morse, *op. cit.*, Vol. I, pp. 298-322.
28. *House Ex. Doc.*, No. 40, 26th Congress, 1st Session, pp. 1-4.
29. Dulles, *The Old China Trade*, pp. 179-180.
30. *Ibid.*, p. 181.
31. *Ibid.*, pp. 169-170.
32. *Senate Ex. Doc.*, No. 139, 29th Congress, 1st Session, p. 21.
33. *Ibid.*, pp. 21-22.
34. Dennett, *op. cit.*, p. 128.
35. *Ibid.*, pp. 133-134.
36. Fuess, *op. cit.*, Vol. I, pp. 413-415.
37. Paul Hibbert Clyde, *United States Policy Toward China*, p. 12.
38. Fuess, *op. cit.*, Vol. I, pp. 415-416.
39. Copy of letter in *ibid.*, Vol. I, pp. 419-420.
40. Foster, *op. cit.*, p. 88.
41. Dennett, *op. cit.*, pp. 180-181.
42. *House Ex. Doc.*, No. 123, 33d Congress, 1st Session, p. 204.
43. Dennett, *op. cit.*, p. 280.
44. Foster, *op. cit.*, p. 225.
45. *Ibid.*, pp. 229-230.
46. Clyde, *op. cit.*, p. 57.
47. Paul Hibbert Clyde, *The Far East*, p. 154.
48. *Ibid.*, pp. 155-156.
49. Foster, *op. cit.*, pp. 247-249.
50. Juliet Bredon, *Peking, a Historical and Intimate Description of Chief Places of Interest* (Shanghai: Kelly and Walsh, 1931), pp. 293-294.
51. Eliza R. Scidmore, *China, the Long-Lived Empire* (London: Macmillan, 1900), pp. 221-222.

III. THE REOPENING OF JAPAN TO WESTERN INTERCOURSE

1. Edward E. Hale, "The American Expedition to Japan," *North American Review* (No. CLXXII, July 1856), Vol. LXXXIII, p. 258. (The quotation is from Hale's article, not of John Quincy Adams directly.)
2. Shunzo Sakamaki, *Japan and the United States, 1790-1853*, p. 4.
3. Tyler Dennett, *Americans in Eastern Asia*, p. 242.
4. Sakamaki, *op. cit.*, pp. 150-151.
5. John W. Foster, *American Diplomacy in the Orient*, p. 141.
6. *Cf.* Dennett, *op. cit.*, p. 248.
7. *The Chinese Repository*, Vol. XV, pp. 122-180.

5. *Ibid.*, pp. 12-16.
6. *Ibid.*, p. 223.
7. Cited by Tyler Dennett, *Americans in Eastern Asia,* p. 408.
8. *Ibid.*, pp. 270-272.
9. *Senate Ex. Doc.,* No. 34, 33d Congress, 2d Session, p. 81.
10. Foster Rhea Dulles, *America in the Pacific,* p. 74.
11. Paul Hibbert Clyde, *United States Policy Toward China,* pp. 57-58.
12. Dulles, *op. cit.,* pp. 98-99.
13. George Herbert Ryden, *The Foreign Policy of the United States in Relation to Samoa,* pp. 1-3.
14. Sylvia Masterman, *The Origins of International Rivalry in Samoa, 1845-1884,* p. 24.
15. Ryden, *op. cit.,* pp. 5-9.
16. Masterman, *op. cit.,* pp. 109-110; Ryden, *op. cit.,* pp. 13-23.
17. Samuel Flagg Bemis, *A Diplomatic History of the United States* (New York: Henry Holt, 1955), pp. 454-455.
18. Masterman, *op. cit.,* p. 113.
19. Willis Fletcher Johnson, *America's Foreign Relations* (New York: Century, 1916), Vol. II, pp. 137-138.
20. *Senate Ex. Doc.,* No. 2, 46th Congress, 1st Session, pp. 6-7.
21. Dulles, *op. cit.,* p. 118.
22. Robert Louis Stevenson, *A Footnote to History,* p. 267.
23. Thomas A. Bailey, *A Diplomatic History of the American People* (New York: Appleton-Century-Crofts, 1958), p. 425.
24. Stevenson, *op. cit.,* pp. 277-278.
25. *U. S. Foreign Relations, 1894,* Appendix I, pp. 504-513.
26. Ryden, *op. cit.,* pp. 558-572.
27. Dulles, *op cit.,* pp. 136-137.
28. *Congressional Record,* 56th Congress, 1st Session, p. 1295.
29. Ryden, *op cit.,* p. 575.

VIII. THE ACQUISITION OF HAWAII

1. Ralph S. Kuykendall and Herbert E. Gregory, *A History of Hawaii,* pp. 72-73.
2. Ralph S. Kuykendall, *The Hawaiian Kingdom, 1778-1854, Foundation and Transformation,* pp. 85-92.
3. Harold W. Bradley, *The American Frontier in Hawaii, the Pioneers, 1789-1843,* p. 54.
4. John W. Foster, *A Century of American Diplomacy,* pp. 104-105.

221

5. Theodore Morgan, *Hawaii, a Century of Economic Change, 1778-1876*, p. 140.

6. Kuykendall and Gregory, *op. cit.*, p. 197.

7. *Cf.* Kuykendall, *op. cit.*, pp. 62-64.

8. Hiram Bingham, *A Residence of Twenty-One Years in the Sandwich Islands*, pp. 60-61.

9. *Ibid.*, pp. 61, 69-70.

10. Kuykendall and Gregory, *op. cit.*, pp. 103-107.

11. Morgan, *op. cit.*, p. 87.

12. Sylvester K. Stevens, *American Expansion in Hawaii, 1842-1898*, p. 57.

13. Cited by Foster, *op. cit.*, p. 108.

14. Bradley, *op. cit.*, pp. 89-90.

15. *Ibid.*, p. 93.

16. *Ibid.*, p. 170.

17. *Ibid.*, pp. 93, 303-304.

18. *Ibid.*, pp. 108-109.

19. *Cf.* Kuykendall, *op. cit.*, p. 99.

20. Stevens, *op. cit.*, pp. 12-13; Kuykendall, *op. cit.*, pp. 234-237, 247-251.

21. Stevens, *op. cit.*, pp. 20-22.

22. *Ibid.*, pp. 48-49.

23. *Senate Ex. Doc.*, No. 77, 52d Congress, 2d Session, pp. 37-40.

24. *Ibid.*, pp. 40-41.

25. *Cf. U. S. Foreign Relations, 1894*, Appendix II, pp. 39-41.

26. Cited by Foster Rhea Dulles, *Forty Years of American-Japanese Relations*, p. 2.

27. Kuykendall, *op. cit.*, pp. 213-221.

28. *U. S. Foreign Relations, 1894*, Appendix II, p. 133.

29. Morgan, *op. cit.*, p. 175.

30. Ralph S. Kuykendall, *The Hawaiian Kingdom, 1854-1874, Twenty Critical Years*, p. 143.

31. *U. S. Foreign Relations, 1894*, Appendix II, p. 143.

32. *Ibid.*, p. 153.

33. *Ibid.*, p. 154.

34. *Ibid.*, p. 25.

35. F. W. Taussig, *Some Aspects of the Tariff Question*, p. 59.

36. *Cf.* Foster, *op. cit.*, p. 366.

37. Queen Liliuokalani, *Hawaii's Story by Hawaii's Queen*, pp. 177-184.

38. *U. S. Foreign Relations, 1881*, pp. 635-639.

39. *U. S. Foreign Relations, 1894*, Appendix II, p. 194.

40. *Cf. ibid.*, pp. 188-196.

41. *Cf. ibid.*, pp. 459-463.
42. *Ibid.*, p. 244.
43. Stevens, *op. cit.*, pp. 247-248.
44. *U. S. Foreign Relations, 1894*, Appendix II, pp. 463-464.
45. *Ibid.*, pp. 1276-1282.
46. *Ibid.*, pp. 445-458.
47. Kuykendall and Gregory, *op. cit.*, p. 283.
48. *Cf.* Thomas A. Bailey, "Japan's Protest Against the Annexation of Hawaii," *Journal of Modern History* (Vol. III, 1931), pp. 46-61.
49. Liliuokalani, *op. cit.*, pp. 396-398.
50. *Ibid.*, p. 356.
51. Cited by Willis Fletcher Johnson, *America's Foreign Relations* (New York: Century, 1916), Vol. II, p. 183.
52. Cited by Foster Rhea Dulles, *America in the Pacific*, p. 197.

IX. THE KOREAN PROBLEM AND THE RISE OF JAPAN

1. W. W. McLaren, *A Political History of Japan* (New York: Scribners, 1916), p. 35.
2. Henry Satoh, *Lord Hotta, the Pioneer Diplomat of Japan*, p. 70.
3. Cited by Foster Rhea Dulles, *Forty Years of American-Japanese Relations*, pp. 13-14.
4. Cited by Tyler Dennett, *Americans in Eastern Asia*, p. 430.
5. *Cf.* Shigenobu Okuma, *Fifty Years of Modern Japan*, Vol. I, p. 99.
6. Dennett, *op. cit.*, p. 432.
7. Okuma, *op. cit.*, Vol. I, p. 100.
8. *Cf.* Dennett, *op. cit.*, pp. 432-433.
9. *Ibid.*, p. 411.
10. Okuma, *op. cit.*, Vol. I, p. 101.
11. Dennett, *op. cit.*, p. 417.
12. *U.S. Diplomatic Correspondence, 1867*, Part II, p. 36.
13. Dennett, *op. cit.*, p. 419.
14. *Cf.* Reports of the Low-Rogers Expedition in *U.S. Foreign Relations, 1871*, pp. 111-142.
15. Roy Hidemachi Akagi, *Japan's Foreign Relations, 1542-1936*, p. 114.
16. *Ibid.*, pp. 115-116.
17. *Ibid.*, p. 117.
18. Alfred Stead (ed.), *Japan and the Japanese*, p. 177; cited by Dennett, *op. cit.*, p. 477.
19. Cited by Dennett, *op. cit.*, p. 456.

20. *Cf. ibid.*, pp. 457-458.
21. *U.S. China Instructions*, Vol. 3, November 14, 1881; cited by Dennett, *op. cit.*, p. 461.
22. *Cf.* Dennett, *op. cit.*, pp. 461-462.
23. *Cf. ibid.*, pp. 471-473.
24. *Cf. ibid.*, p. 473.
25. *Ibid.*, pp. 477-478.
26. Seiji Hishida, *The International Position of Japan as a Great Power*, p. 169.
27. *Cf.* Dennett, *op. cit.*, p. 484.
28. Akagi, *op. cit.*, p. 131.
29. *Ibid.*, p. 131; Hishida, *op. cit.*, p. 164.
30. *Cf.* Dennett, *op. cit.*, p. 451.
31. Vladimir (Zenone Volpicelli), *The China-Japan War* (London: Sampson, Low, Marston, 1896), Appendix B, No. 1.
32. *Ibid.*, Appendix B, No. 5.
33. *Cf. U.S. Foreign Relations, 1894*, pp. 20-21.
34. For text of treaty, see *U.S. Foreign Relations, 1894*, Appendix I, pp. 93-94.
35. *Ibid.*, p. 37.
36. *Loc. cit.*
37. *Cf.* Dennett, *op. cit.*, p. 499.
38. Payson J. Treat, *Japan and the United States, 1853-1928*, pp. 158-160.
39. From text of Russian note cited by Okuma, *op. cit.*, Vol. I, p. 112.
40. Dennett, *op. cit.*, p. 504.
41. *U.S. Foreign Relations, 1895*, Part II, p. 972.
42. Dennett, *op. cit.*, p. 506.

X. AMERICA BECOMES A FAR EASTERN AND WORLD POWER

1. Marcus M. Wilkerson, *Public Opinion and the Spanish-American War: A Study in War Propaganda*, p. 100.
2. *Ibid.*, p. 103.
3. Walter Millis, *The Martial Spirit: A Study of Our War with Spain*, p. 137.
4. Julius W. Pratt, *Expansionists of 1898: The Acquisition of Hawaii and the Spanish Islands*, p. 327.
5. Millis, *op. cit.*, pp. 138-139.
6. *Ibid.*, p. 149.
7. Henry Cabot Lodge, *The War with Spain*, p. 44.

8. Claude G. Bowers, *Beveridge and the Progressive Era* (New York: Houghton Mifflin, 1932), pp. 69-70.

9. Wilkerson, *op. cit.,* pp. 131-132.

10. Pratt, *op. cit.,* pp. 283-285.

11. *Ibid.,* p. 289.

12. *Ibid.,* pp. 282, 288.

13. *Ibid.,* pp. 232-252.

14. A. Whitney Griswold, *The Far Eastern Policy of the United States,* pp. 15-16.

15. *U.S. Foreign Relations, 1898,* pp. 820-821.

16. *Ibid.,* pp. 828-830.

17. Pratt, *op. cit.,* p. 333.

18. *U.S. Foreign Relations, 1898,* pp. 904-908.

19. *Senate Ex. Doc.,* No. 148, 56th Congress, 2d Session, p. 35.

20. C. S. Olcott, *The Life of William McKinley* (Boston and New York: Houghton Mifflin, 1916), Vol. II, p. 111.

21. Marion Mills Miller, *Great Debates in American History* (New York: Currrent Literature Publishing Co., 1913), Vol. III, p. 247.

22. Pratt, *op. cit.,* pp. 340-344.

23. *Congressional Record,* 55th Congress, 3d Session, pp. 958-959.

24. Miller, *op. cit.,* p. 269.

25. Pratt, *op. cit.,* p. 347; for full text of Hoar's classic speech, *see Congressional Record,* 55th Congress, 3d Session, pp. 493-502 or Miller, *op. cit.,* pp. 255-270.

26. Pratt, *op. cit.,* p. 351; *cf.* also *Congressional Record,* 55th Congress, 3d Session, pp. 437-438.

27. *Congressional Record,* 55th Congress, 3d Session, p. 438.

28. Miller, *op. cit.,* p. 272.

29. *Ibid.,* p. 320.

30. Bowers, *op. cit.,* pp. 74-76.

31. *Cf.* Griswold, *op. cit.,* pp. 33-34.

32. Miller, *op. cit.,* p. 306.

33. Lodge, *op. cit.,* p. 2.

34. Miller, *op. cit.,* p. 323.

35. Griswold, *op. cit.,* p. 4.

36. *Congressional Record,* 56th Congress, 1st Session, p. 704.

37. Miller, *op. cit.,* p. 211.

38. Griswold, *op. cit.,* p. 35.

39. *Ibid.,* p. 123.

225

Selected Bibliography

Abeel, David, *Journal of a Residence in China and the Neighboring Countries* (New York: J. A. Williamson, 1836), second edition.

Akagi, Roy Hidemachi, *Japan's Foreign Relations, 1542-1936* (Tokyo: Hokuseido Press, 1937).

Ashley, Clifford W., *The Yankee Whaler* (Boston: Houghton Mifflin, 1938).

Augur, Helen, *Passage to Glory* (New York, 1946), a life of John Ledyard.

Bancroft, Hubert Howe, *History of Alaska, 1730-1885* (San Francisco: A. L. Bancroft, 1886).

————, *The New Pacific* (New York: Bancroft, 1915).

Barrows, Edward M., *The Great Commodore, The Exploits of Matthew Calbraith Perry* (Indianapolis and New York: Bobbs-Merrill, 1935).

Battistini, Lawrence H., *Japan and America, from Earliest Times to the Present* (New York: John Day, 1954).

Bau, Mingchien Joshua, *The Foreign Relations of China* (New York: Revell, 1922).

————, *The Open Door Doctrine* (New York: Macmillan, 1923).

Bingham, Hiram, *A Residence of Twenty-One Years in the Sandwich Islands, or The Civil, Religious and Political History of These Islands Comprising a Particular View of the Missionary Operations Connected with the Introduction of Civilization Among the Hawaiian People* (Hartford: Hezekiah Huntington, 1848).

Callahan, James Morton, *American Relations in the Pacific and the Far East, 1784-1900* (Baltimore: Johns Hopkins Press, 1901).

Carpenter, Edmund James, *America in Hawaii* (Boston: Small, Maynard and Co., 1899).

Clark, Arthur H., *The Clipper Ship Era: An Epitome of Famous*

American and British Clipper Ships, Their Owners, Builders, Commanders, and Crews (New York and London: G. P. Putnam's Sons, 1910).

Clark, Henry W., *History of Alaska* (New York: Macmillan, 1930).

Clyde, Paul Hibbert, *International Relations in Manchuria, 1689-1922* (Columbus: Ohio State University Press, 1926).

————, *United States Policy Toward China: Diplomatic and Public Documents, 1839-1939* (Durham: Duke University Press, 1940).

Cole, Allan B., *With Perry in Japan, the Diary Of Edward Yorke McCauley* (Princeton: Princeton University Press, 1942).

————, (ed.), *Yankee Surveyors in the Shogun's Seas* (Princeton: Princeton University Press, 1947).

Cook, James, *A Voyage to the Pacific Ocean* (London, 1784).

Corney, Peter, *Voyages in the Northern Pacific, 1813-18* (Honolulu: Thrum, 1836).

Cosenza, Mario Emilio, *The Complete Journal of Townsend Harris, First American Consul General and Minister to Japan* (Garden City: Doubleday, Doran, 1930).

Crevecoeur (J. Hector St. John, pseud.), *Letters of an American Farmer* (London, 1782).

Crow, Carl, *He Opened the Door of Japan: Townsend Harris and the Story of His Amazing Adventures in Establishing American Relations with the Far East* (New York and London: Harper and Brothers, 1939).

Cutler, Carl C., *Greyhounds of the Sea* (New York: Halcyon House, 1939).

Dennett, Tyler, *Americans in Eastern Asia* (New York: Macmillan, 1922).

————, *John Hay* (New York: Macmillan, 1933).

————, *Roosevelt and the Russo-Japanese War* (Garden City: Doubleday, Page, 1925).

Dennis, Alfred L. P., *Adventures in American Diplomacy, 1896-1906* (New York: Dutton, 1928).

DeVoto, Bernard, *The Course of Empire* (Boston: Houghton Mifflin, 1952).

Dole, Sanford B. (edited by Andrew Farrell), *Memoirs of the Hawaiian Revolution* (Honolulu: 1936).

Dulles, Foster Rhea, *America in the Pacific: A Century of Expansion* (Boston and New York: Houghton Mifflin, 1932).

————, *China and America* (Princeton: Princeton University Press, 1946).

————, *Forty Years of American-Japanese Relations* (New York and London: Appleton-Century, 1937).

227

————, *The Old China Trade* (Boston and New York: Houghton Mifflin, 1930).

Fairbank, John King, *Trade and Diplomacy on the China Coast: The Opening of the Treaty Ports, 1842-1854* (Cambridge: Harvard University Press, 1954), 2 volumes.

————, *The United States and China* (Cambridge: Harvard University Press, 1948).

Fanning, Edmund, *Voyages and Discoveries in the South Seas, 1792-1832* (Salem, Mass.: Marine Research Society, 1924).

————, *Voyages Around the World* (New York: Collins and Hannay, 1833).

————, *Voyages to the South Seas, Indian and Pacific Oceans, China Sea, North-west Coast, Fiji Islands, South Shetlands, etc.* (New York: W. H. Vermilye, 1838), third edition.

Farrar, Victor J., *The Annexation of Russian America to the United States* (Washington: W. F. Roberts, 1937).

Forbes, Robert B., *Remarks on China and the China Trade* (Boston: S. H. Dickinson, 1844).

Foster, John W., *American Diplomacy in the Orient* (Boston: Houghton Mifflin, 1903).

————, *The Annexation of Hawaii* (Washington: Gibson Bros., March 26, 1897).

————, *Diplomatic Memoirs* (Boston and New York: 1909), two volumes.

Fuess, Claude, *The Life of Caleb Cushing* (New York: Harcourt, Brace, 1923), two volumes.

Gillis, J. A., *The Hawaiian Incident* (New York: Lee and Shepard, 1897).

Griffis, William Elliot, *Matthew Calbraith Perry* (Boston: Cupples and Hurd, 1887).

————, *Townsend Harris, First American Envoy to Japan* (Boston and New York: Houghton Mifflin, 1895).

Griswold, A. Whitney, *The Far Eastern Policy of the United States* (New York: Harcourt, 1938).

Griswold, Frank G., *Clipper Ships and Yachts* (New York: Dutton, 1929).

Gruening, Ernest, *The State of Alaska* (New York: Random House, 1954).

Hawks, Francis L., *Narrative of the Expedition of an American Squadron to the China Seas and Japan under the Command of Commodore M. C. Perry, United States Navy, Compiled at His Request and under His Supervision, by Francis L. Hawks* (New York: D. Appleton, 1856).

Hishida, Seiji, *The International Position of Japan as a Great Power* (New York: Columbia University Press, 1905).

Howay, Frederic W., (ed.), *Voyages of the "Columbia" to the Northwest Coast* (Boston, 1941).

Hughes, E. R., *The Invasion of China by the Western World* (New York: Macmillan, 1938).

Hulley, Clarence C., *Alaska, 1741-1953* (Portland, Ore.: Binfords and Mort, 1953).

Jewitt, John R., *A Narrative of the Adventures and Sufferings of John R. Jewitt* (Middletown, Conn.: Loomis I. Richards, 1815).

Joseph, Philip, *Foreign Diplomacy in China, 1894-1900* (London: Allen and Unwin, 1928).

Kimball, Gertrude Selwyn, *The East India Trade of Providence from 1787 to 1807* (Providence: Preston and Rounds, 1846).

Kuykendall, Ralph S., *The Hawaiian Kingdom, 1778-1854, Foundations and Transformation* (Honolulu: University of Hawaii Press, 1947).

————, *The Hawaiian Kingdom, 1854-1874, Twenty Critical Years* (Honolulu: University of Hawaii Press, 1953).

Kuykendall, Ralph S., and Herbert E. Gregory, *A History of Hawaii* (New York: Macmillan, 1927).

Latourette, Kenneth Scott, *A History of Christian Missions in China* (New York: Macmillan, 1929).

————, *The History of Early Relations Between the United States and China, 1784-1844* (New Haven: Yale University Press, 1917).

————, *The United States Moves Across the Pacific* (New York: Harper, 1926).

Ledyard, John, *A Journal of Captain Cook's Last Voyage* (Hartford, 1783).

Liliuokalani, Queen, *Hawaii's Story by Hawaii's Queen* (Boston: Lee and Shepard, 1898).

Lodge, Henry Cabot, *The War with Spain* (New York and London: Harper and Brothers, 1899).

Lubbock, Basil, *The China Clippers* (Glasgow: James Brown & Son, 1916).

————, *The Opium Clippers* (Glasgow: Brown, Son and Ferguson, 1933).

Macdonald, Alexander, *Revolt in Paradise* (New York: Stephen Dayne, 1944).

Macy, Obed, *History of Nantucket* (Boston, 1835).

Mahan, Alfred Thayer, *The Influence of Sea Power Upon History, 1660-1783* (Boston: Little, Brown, 1894).

229

————, *The Problem of Asia and Its Effect Upon International Policies* (Boston: Little, Brown, 1900).

Masterman, Sylvia, *The Origins of International Rivalry in Samoa, 1845-1884* (Stanford: Stanford University Press, 1934).

Melville, Herman, *Moby Dick or the White Whale* (New York: Dodd, Mead, 1923).

Millis, Walter, *The Martial Spirit: A Study of Our War with Spain* (Boston and New York: Houghton Mifflin, 1931).

Morgan, Theodore, *Hawaii, a Century of Economic Change, 1778-1876* (Cambridge: Harvard University Press, 1948).

Morison, Samuel Eliot, *Maritime History of Massachusetts* (Boston and New York: Houghton Mifflin, 1921).

Morse, Hosea Ballou, *The International Relations of the Chinese Empire* (London: Longmans, 1918), three volumes.

Newcombe, C. F., (ed.), *Menzie's Journal of Vancouver's Voyage* (Victoria, 1923).

Nitobe, Inazo Ota, *Intercourse between the United States and Japan* (Baltimore: Johns Hopkins Press, 1891).

Nye, Gideon, Jr., *Tea and the Tea Trade* (New York: G. W. Wood, 1850), third edition.

Okuma, Shigenobu, *Forty Years of Modern Japan* (London: Smith, Elder, 1909), two volumes.

Okun, S. B., (Transl. from the Russian by Carl Ginsburg, Dept. of State), *The Russian-American Company* (Cambridge: Harvard University Press, 1951).

Oliphant, Lawrence, *Lord Elgin's Mission to China and Japan* (New York: Harpers, 1860).

Paine, Ralph D., *The Old Merchant Marine: A Chronicle of American Ships and Sailors* (New Haven: Yale University Press, 1921).

Palmer, Aaron H., *Documents and Facts Illustrating the Origin of the Mission to Japan* (Washington: H. Polkinron, 1857).

Paullin, Charles Oscar, *Diplomatic Negotiations of American Naval Officers, 1778-1883* (Baltimore: Johns Hopkins Press, 1912).

Peabody, Robert Ephraim, *The Log of the Grand Turks* (Boston and New York: Houghton Mifflin, 1926).

Pratt, Julius W., *Expansionists of 1898: The Acquisition of Hawaii and the Spanish Islands* (Baltimore: Johns Hopkins Press, 1936).

Reischauer, Edwin O., *The United States and Japan* (Cambridge: Harvard University Press, 1950).

Ricketson, Daniel, *History of New Bedford* (New Bedford, 1858).

Rowbotham, A. H., *Missionary and Mandarin* (Berkeley: University of California Press, 1942).

230

Ryden, George Herbert, *The Foreign Policy of the United States in Relation to Samoa* (New Haven: Yale University Press, 1933).

Sakamaki, Shunzo, *Japan and the United States, 1790-1853*, printed in "Transactions of the Asiatic Society of Japan" (Tokyo: Asiatic Society of Japan, 1939), second series, Volume XVIII.

Sakanaski, Shio (ed.), *Some Unpublished Letters of Townsend Harris* (New York: Japan Reference Library, 1941).

Sandmeyer, Elmer Clarence, *The Anti-Chinese Movement in California* (Urbana, Ill.: University of Illinois Press, 1939).

Sansom, Sir George, *The Western World and Japan* (New York: Knopf, 1950).

Satoh, Henry, *Lord Hotta, the Pioneer Diplomat of Japan* (Tokyo: Hakubunkan, 1908).

Seward, Frederick W., *Reminiscences of a War-time Statesman and Diplomat, 1830-1915* (New York: Putnam's Sons, 1916).

Spalding, J. W., *Japan and Around the World* (New York, 1855).

Sparks, Jared, *The Life of John Ledyard, the American Traveller* (Cambridge, Mass.: Hilliard and Brown, 1828).

Spears, John R., *The Story of the New England Whalers* (New York, 1910).

Stackpole, Edouard A., *The Sea-Hunters, The New England Whalemen During Two Centuries, 1635-1835* (New York, Philadelphia: Lippincott, 1953).

Starbuck, Alexander, *History of the American Whale-Fishery* (Waltham, Mass., 1878).

Stevens, Sylvester K., *American Expansion in Hawaii, 1842-1898* (Harrisburg: Archives Publishing Co. of Pennsylvania, 1945).

Stevenson, Robert Louis, *A Footnote to History: Eight Years of Trouble in Samoa* (New York: Scribner's Sons, 1892).

Swisher, Earl, *China's Management of the American Barbarians: A Study of Sino-American Relations, 1841-1861, with Documents* (New Haven: Far Eastern Publications, Yale University, 1953).

Taussig, F. W., *Some Aspects of the Tariff Question* (Cambridge: Harvard University Press, 1915).

Taylor, Bayard, *A Visit to India, China and Japan* (New York: G. P. Putnam's Sons, 1853).

Thomes, William H., *The Whaleman's Adventures in the Sandwich Islands and California* (Chicago, 1886).

Thrum's Hawaiian Annual (Honolulu: Honolulu Star-Bulletin, annually).

Tompkins, Pauline, *American-Russian Relations in the Far East* (New York: Macmillan, 1950).

Tompkins, Stuart Ramsay, *Alaska, Promyshlennik and Sourdough* (Norman, Okla.: University of Oklahoma Press, 1945).

Tower, Walter S., *A History of the American Whale Fishery* (Philadelphia, 1907).

Treat, Payson J., *Japan and the United States, 1853-1928* (Stanford: Stanford University Press, 1928).

Tyler, Alice Felt, *The Foreign Policy of James G. Blaine* (Minneapolis: University of Minnesota Press, 1927).

Vancouver, George, *A Voyage of Discovery to the North Pacific Ocean* (London, 1798).

Villiers, A. J., *Whaling in the Frozen South* (Indianapolis: Bobbs-Merrill, 1925).

Wada, Teijuhn, *American Foreign Policy Towards Japan in the Nineteenth Century* (Tokyo: Toyo Bunko, 1928).

Wallach, Sidney (ed.), *Narrative of the Expedition of an American Squadron to the China Seas and Japan under the Command of Commodore M. C. Perry, United States Navy, Compiled at His Request and under His Supervision, by Francis L. Hawks* (New York: Coward-McCann, 1952).

Walworth, Arthur, *Black Ships off Japan: The Story of Commodore Perry's Expedition* (New York: Knopf, 1946).

Wildes, Harry Emerson, *Aliens in the East* (Philadelphia: University of Pennsylvania Press, 1937).

Whipple, A. B. C., *Yankee Whalers in the South Seas* (Garden City: Doubleday, 1954).

Wilkerson, Marcus M., *Public Opinion and the Spanish-American War: A Study in Propaganda* (Baton Rouge: Louisiana State University Press, 1932).

Williams, E. W., *Life of S. Wells Williams* (New York: G. P. Putnam's Sons, 1899).

Williams, Frederick Wells, *Anson Burlingame and the First Chinese Mission to Foreign Powers* (New York: Charles Scribner's Sons, 1912).

Williams, S. Wells, *Journal of the Japan Expedition*, printed in "Transactions of the Asiatic Society of Japan" (Tokyo: Asiatic Society of Japan, 1910), Volume 37, Part 2.

Williams, William T., *Destruction of the Whaling Fleet in the Arctic Ocean in 1877* (New Bedford, 1902).

Wu, Chao-Kwang, *The International Aspect of the Missionary Movement in China* (Baltimore: Johns Hopkins Press, 1930).

Index

Abeel, David, 31
Adams, Commodore, 69
Adams, John Quincy: 54; on Russian expansion in North America, 78; 155
Aguinaldo, Emilio, 200, 207-208
Alaska: Russian activity in, 73-76; early American interest in, 76-80; Russian decision to sell, 80-82; negotiations for sale to U.S., 82-87; as a U.S. territory, 87-88
Alcock, Sir Rutherford, 121
Alexander I, 74, 78
Allyn, Dr. H. N., 189
Alta California: quoted on Alaska acquisition, 85; quoted on Chinese immigration, 103
Amelia, 17
Amundsen, Roald, 75
Angell, James B., 107, 178
Anglo-French wars against China, 45-48, 50-60
Anglo-Japanese Alliance, 212
Apia, 141, 142, 143
Appleton, Assistant Secretary of State, 82
Archer, 27
Armstrong, Commodore James, 47
Arrow, 46-47
Arrow War, 45-48
Arthur, Chester A., 108, 180

Astor, John Jacob, 10, 77
Astoria, 10
Aulick, Commodore John H., 60, 61
Austin, Elijah, 10
Ave Maria, 198

Baffin, William, 75
Bailey, Thomas A., quoted on Denis Kearney followers, 105
Baker's Island, 135
Bakufu, 53
Balaena, 13, 148
Bancroft, Hubert Howe, quoted on imperialism, 73-74
Banks, N. P., 86
Baranov, Alexander A., 75, 76, 154
Bartlett, E. L., 88
Batavia, 8
Bayard, Thomas F., 141-142, 159
"Bayonet Constitution," 160
Beaver, 13
bêche-de-mer, 9, 11
Bering, Vitus, 74
Berlin Conference (1889), 143
Beveridge, Senator Albert J.: speech urging expansionism, 192-193; 194; defends annexation of Philippines, 206; on importance of Pacific, 209
Biddle, Commodore James, 58
Bingham, Hiram, 149-150

Kalakaua, 160, 161
Kamehameha, 149
Katsura, Kogorō, 210
Kearney, Commodore Lawrence, 37-38
Kelly, Commander, 172
Kendrick, Capt. John, 9
Kianghwa, Treaty of, 177-178
King, C. W. 56
Kiying (see Ch'i-ying)
Kodiak Island: establishment of Russian settlement in, 74
Korea: 174-186; background, 174; troubles with U.S., 175-176; opened to commercial intercourse, 176-180; Sino-Japanese dispute and war over, 182-185; Russo-Japanese rivalry in, 186-189; U.S. actions in, 188-189; U.S. recognizes Japanese sovereignty over, 210
Kowloon: ceded to Britain, 51
Kuang Hsu, 100
Kublai Khan, 22
Kung, Prince: 51, 92; on missionaries and opium, 98
Kuo Sung-tao, 93
Kurile Islands, 171, 172
Kuroda, General, 177
Kussaie, 205

La Mamea, 140
Ladrone Islands, 199
Lady Washington, 9, 55
Lagoda, 59
Ledyard, John, 5, 9
Lee, Fitzhugh, 193
Li Hung-chang: on opium trade, 107; and Korea, 178, 179, 182
Liaotung peninsula, 185, 187, 189
Liholiho, 149, 152
Liliuokalani, Queen: ascends throne, 161; attempts restore royal power, 162; overthrown, 163; counter-revolution supporting her fails, 165; protests U.S. annexation of Hawaii, 167
Lin Tse-hsü, 32, 34, 35
Lincoln, Abraham, 94

Lobanov-Yamagata Agreement, 188 n.
Lodge, Henry Cabot: 191, 192, 193, 194, 195, 202; views on secret discussions of treaty with Spain, 205; defends annexation of Philippines, 206-207; on demise of Spanish power, 207
London Times: quoted on despoiling of Samoans, 145
Long, Secretary of the Navy, 200
Low, Frederick F., 100, 176

Macao, 22, 23
Mahan, Alfred Thayer, 134, 194, 202
Maine incident, 193-194
Malakhov, 74
Malietoa Laupepa, 140, 141, 142, 143
Manchuria, 189
Manhattan, 56
Manila, 8
Marcy, William L.: 47, 80n., 137; instructions regarding Hawaii, 157
Maro, 13
Marshall, Humphrey: 46; on Taiping Rebellion, 90-91
Maryland Journal and Baltimore Advertiser: quoted on initial U.S. voyage to China, 25-26
Masafuera, 11
Mason, Senator William E., 206
Matsusaki, 68
McDonald, 59
McKinley, William: action on Samoans, 145; supports annexation of Hawaii, 166, 167, 178; and Cuba, 192-193; moves toward war with Spain, 194, 195, 196, 201, 202; swings to annexation of Philippines, 203-204; discloses how he arrived at decision to annex Philippines, 204
McLane, Robert: 46, 47; on the Taipings, 91
Meade, Captain, 139-140
Meiji, 186, 124, 124n., 177
Merrit, General Wesley, 200

Shaw, Major Samuel, 25, 26
Sheffield, Capt. James P., 11
Shelikhov, Grigory, 75
Shelikhov-Golikov Co., 75
Shenandoah, 14
Shimoda: opened as treaty port, 68
Shimonoseki: incident, 123; indemnity, 123-124
Shimonoseki, Treaty of, 185
Shōgun, 53
Shufeldt, Commodore R. W.: concludes treaty with Korea, 178-180; 179n.
Siam (Thailand): 8; treaty with, 39; 56, 111
Sill, Minister, 188-189
Sino-Japanese War, 182-185
Sitka, 76, 85
Smith, T. H., 27
Society of Friends (memorial), 198
Soejima, Taneomi, 177
South Georgia, 10
South Seas: early American trade, 11-12
South Shetland Islands, 10-11
Spain: troubles with U.S. over Cuba, 191-195; war with U.S., 196-207
Spanish-American War: origins in Cuba, 191-195; journalistic support for war in U.S., 196-198; attitude of U.S. business, 198; attitudes of Germany and Great Britain, 198-199; the war, 199-200; peace negotiations, 201-205; U.S. Senate discussions on peace treaty, 205-207
Spooner, Senator John C., 206
St. Louis, 40
Stanton, E. P., 86
Steinberger, Col. A. B., 140
Sterling, Admiral James, 69
Stevens, John L.: recommendations on Hawaii, 162; recognizes revolutionary government in Hawaii, 163
Stevens, Thaddeus, 86
Stevenson, Robert Louis, 142-143
Stewart, Captain, 55

Stoeckl, Baron Edouard de, 80n., 81, 83, 84, 86
Stonington (as sealing center), 10-11
Strong, Josiah, 133-134
Sulzer, Senator William: on commercial importance of Pacific, 209
Sumatra, 8
Summer Palace: looted and burned, 50-51
Sumner, Charles: explains reasons for Alaska purchase, 84; 85
Superior, 14
Susquehanna, 60, 62, 63
Sutter, John A., 76n.
Swift, John F., 106
Syren, 13

tael, 49n.
Taft, William Howard: heads civil administration in Philippines, 208; concludes agreement with Katsura, 210-211
Taft-Katsura Agreement, 210-211
Taiping Rebellion, 89-91
Taiwan (see Formosa)
Taku forts, 48, 50
Tamasese, 142
Tani, Viscount, 170-171
Tattnall, Josiah, 50
Tea trade, 16
Ten Eyck, Anthony, 153-154
Terranova, Francis, 30
Thaddeus, 150
Thomas, Admiral Richard, 156
T'ien Wang, 89
Tientsin Massacre, 98-100
Toeywan, 50
Tokaidō, 113
Tokugawa (government), 52-54
Tong Hak rebellion, 183-184
Treaties (in chronological order): Paris (1783), 3; Anglo-American, or Jay (1794), 7; Ghent (1814), 10; Russian-American (1824), 78-79; Hawaiian-American, or Jones (1826), 152-153; Nanking (1842), 35-36; the Bogue (1843), 36; Chinese-American, or Waghia

240

(1844), 41-42; Hawaiian-American (1849), 154; Japanese-American, or Kanagawa (1854), 68-69; Japanese-American, or Shimoda (1857), 112, 113; Japanese-American, or Edo (1858), 117-118; Tientsin (1858), 48-49; Shanghai commercial regulations (1858), 49-50; Peking Convention (1860), 51; Convention with Bakufu (1864), 123; Tariff Convention with Japan (1866), 125; Russian-American, or Alaska Purchase (1867), 83-86; Chinese-American, or Burlingame (1868), 95-96; Hawaiian-American (1875), 159; Chinese-American (1880), 107; Korean-American, or Shufeldt (1882), 179-180; Hawaiian-American (1884), 159; Japanese-American Extradition Convention (1886), 127; Anglo-Japanese (1894), 128; Japanese-American (1894), 128; Shimonoseki (1895), 185; Hawaiian-American, or Hawaiian Annexation (1897), 166-167; Paris (1898), 202-205; German-American on division Samoan Islands (1899), 144

Trescott, William H., 107

Trident, 59

Tripartite Agreement (on Samoan Islands), 143

Tripower Intervention (against Japan), 187

Tristan da Cunha, 10

Tsungli Yamen, 92-93, 100

Tsushima Incident (1861), 171

T'ung Chih, 100

Tutuila, 144-145

Tuyll, Baron, 78

Tyler, John: 39; letter to Chinese Emperor, 40-41; doctrine on Hawaii (1842), 155

Ukaz of 1821, 78

Uraga, 62

Van Buren, Martin, 152

Vancouver, George, 75, 154

Victoria, Queen, 199

Vincennes, 58

Vladivostok (founded), 81, 170

Von Diederichs, Admiral, 200

Wade, Thomas, 173

Waeber-Komura Agreement, 188n.

Wake Island, 201

Walker, R. J., 79, 86

Wanghia, Treaty of, 41-42

Wang-hsia, 41n.

Ward, Frederick, 90

Webb, William H., 139

Webster, Daniel: 40, 60, 155; on Hawaiian policy, 155

West Indies, 4

Whaling: 12-15; opening of new whaling grounds by Americans, 12; Bering Strait disaster (1871), 15; utilization of Hawaii, 148-149

Whampoa, 25

White, Henry, 193

Wickersham, James, 88

Wilhelm II, 141

Wilkes, Lt. Charles, 11n., 139

Williams, S. Wells: 31, 62, 93; eulogy of Burlingame, 97

Willis, Albert S., 164

Wilson-Gorman Tariff (1894), 161, 191

Woodford, Stewart L., 194

Wyoming, 121

Yap, 205

Yeh Ming-ch'en, 32, 45, 46, 47

"Yellow Journalism," 196

Yüan Shih-K'ai, 182

Zagoshin, 74

Zanzibar, 8